26 in 26
Neighborhood Resource Centers
26 Neighborhood Strategies in a 26 month time frame
A Grant Funded by the LSTA
(Library Services & Technology Act)

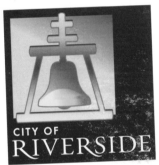

CITY OF
RIVERSIDE

Riverside Public Library

Relationship Fundraising

Relationship Fundraising

A Donor-Based Approach to the Business of Raising Money

Second Edition

Ken Burnett
The White Lion Press Limited

Foreword by
Jennie Thompson
The Resource Alliance

JOSSEY-BASS
A Wiley Company
www.josseybass.com

Published by Jossey-Bass
A Wiley Imprint
989 Market Street, San Francisco, CA 94103-1741   www.josseybass.com

Jossey-Bass books and products are available through most bookstores. To contact Jossey-Bass directly call our Customer Care Department within the U.S. at 800-956-7739, outside the U.S. at 317-572-3986, or fax 317-572-4002.

Jossey-Bass also publishes its books in a variety of electronic formats. Some content that appears in print may not be available in electronic books.

Library of Congress Cataloging-in-Publication Data

Burnett, Ken, date–
   Relationship fundraising: a donor-based approach to the business of raising money / Ken Burnett; foreword Jennie Thompson.—2nd ed.
        p. cm.—(The Jossey-Bass nonprofit and public management series)
Includes bibliographical references and index.
   ISBN 0-7879-6089-6 (hardcover: alk. paper)
   1. Fund raising.   I. Title.   II. Series.
   HG177.B874   2002
   658.15'224—dc21

                                   2002008577

Printed in the United States of America
SECOND EDITION
HB Printing   10

The Jossey-Bass
Nonprofit and Public Management Series

Contents

Foreword, *Jennie Thompson* xiii

Preface to the Second Edition xvii

Acknowledgments xxix

The Author xxxiii

1 Much More Than Raising Money 1

A Unique Business Area • What Is a Donor?
• Fundraising Is Important • Action Points

Donor Profile: Mary Tewson

2 Proud to Be a Fundraiser 13

Limited Public Image • Pride in Our
Profession • Nonprofit Doesn't Mean Not
Profitable • Essential Overheads • Any Need, on
Any Scale • Value for Money • Double Agents
• The Initiation • Action Points

Donor Profile: Molly and Don Patterson

3 The Essence of Good Fundraising 27

Why Do People Give? • Giving Is Good • What
Makes a Successful Fundraiser? • Action Points

Donor Profile: Rose Lister

4 The Vital Ingredients for Success 37

What Is Relationship Fundraising? • The Benefits of
a New Approach • A Total Philosophy • What
Relationship Fundraising Can Do for You • The
Nine Keys to Building a Relationship • Variations

of Donor Geometry • Setting Up and Maintaining a
Relationship Database • Action Points

Donor Profile: Richard West

5   Understanding Your Donors   **61**

Basic Research • How to Do Research • The
Hidden Flaw and Other Perils • Implementing Your
Findings • Donors of the Future • Action Points

Donor Profile: Mrs. Chester

6   Learning from Recent Research   **83**

Where Do I Start? • Some Really Important New
Insights • Action Points

Donor Profile: Rachel Shapiro

7   Avoiding Common Errors and Pitfalls   **95**

In the Heart of the Machine • The Way We Talk to
People • The Mail Mountain • Low Organizational
Self-Image • The Importance of Nonresponse
• The Power and Perils of Emotion • Boring, Boring,
Boring . . . • Personal Dislikes • The Benefits and
Risks of Marketing • Following the Crowd • Action
Points

Donor Profile: John Collins

8   Building Better Friendships Through Marketing   **127**

What Is Marketing? • The Marketing Mix: Creating
an Effective Marketing Strategy • Ten Marketing
Questions • Search for the URG! • Personality
Problems • Fundraising by Phone • Relationships
with Companies and Foundations • Publicity and
Public Relations • Action Points

Donor Profile: Marsha Robbins

9   Making and Keeping Friends   **155**

What Is a Donor Worth? • Recognition and
Rewards • Reciprocal Mailings • Cold Direct

Mail • Different from the Herd • Off-the-Page
Advertising • Inserts • Recruiting Face to Face
• The Internet and E-Mail • Gathering Names
• Membership • The Information Line • The
Video Party • The President's Task Force • Action
Points

Donor Profile: Kevin Tuckwell

10   Keeping in Touch with Your Donors   185
General Awareness Advertising • Selling Like
Soap • Disaster Advertising • Communicating by
Letter • The Ideal Thank You Letter • Newsletters
and Magazines • The Annual Report • The Ideal
Reply Form • Creative Use of the Phone • Even
Closer Encounters • Television • Radio • Video
• Getting It All Together • Action Points

Donor Profile: Ian Dunlop

11   Creative Approaches to Relationship Building   223
The Non-Event • Getting the Best Out of
People • Provide Involvement • Major Gifts
• Pricing and Propositions • Creative Targeting
• Sponsorship of Publications • Commercial
Partnerships • Employee Fundraising • Volunteers
• Inform Your Ambassadors • The RFM Route to
Upgrading Donors • Thank You, Thank You, and
Welcome • New Products and New Product
Development • Planned Giving • Central
Promotion • What's in a Name? • Change
Brings Opportunities • Action Points

Donor Profile: Eric Levine

**12   Bequest Marketing: The Last Great Fundraising
     Opportunity   247**
Different Strokes for Different Folks • What Bequest
Marketing Means in Practice • More Rigorous
Strategy • Some New Approaches • Creativity in
Bequest Marketing • Action Points

Donor Profile: Alice Jenks

13   Keeping Up with Change   275

Changing Ideas About Boards and Governance
•   Mergers and Acquisitions   •   Entrepreneurial
Donors and the New Rich   •   Venture Philanthropy
•   What's New in Customer Relationship Management
•   Disenchantment with Relationship Marketing
•   Face-to-Face Fundraising   •   The Revolution on
Our Desktops   •   How Ethical Are We?   •   Some
Thoughts on Future Change   •   Action Points

Donor Profile: Sophie Cairncross

14   Fundraising for the Twenty-First Century   311

But How High Is Up?   •   A Happy Ending?
•   Changing Fundraisers' Behavior   •   SAVE THE
DONOR—An Urgent Appeal   •   Action Points

Donor Profile: Mr. and Mrs. Christisen

Glossary   335
Bibliography   339
Index   343

Foreword

How do you have a relationship with a number? It'd be rather difficult, I would think—not easy to get your arms around. But every day
that's how many so-called service professionals relate to us: credit
card companies, insurance agents, brokers and banks, stores and air-
lines, and even a few nonprofits, if we're honest about it.

At some unremembered moment, it seems we lost our names
and became records on databases and codes on envelopes. And
since that dreadful day when our Social Security number, Zip code,
and customer I.D. came to define us, something real has been lost.
But it's not too late to get it back.

It's time for us to look beyond the profiled categories, the
focus-group assumptions, the characterizations of baby boomers
and busters, and look at what is essential in our transactions: the
courtesy of receiving information we value, respect for loyalty, and
recognition and appreciation for a shared commitment.

Relationship Fundraising drills into the core of our value system
to remind us that fundraising is not, most definitely, the science of
predictable responses to predictable actions based on hard-and-fast
rules of experts. No indeed. In this age of "professionalism"—the
era of the marketing guru—it's all too easy to forget that fundraising is more art than science. It is people giving to people . . . the
hope of a shared dream . . . the success of a worthy cause. And it
will not be effective if we continue to treat our donors simply as
computer records within gift categories.

Ken Burnett's book, first published in 1992, set the fundraising world on its ear. Now, with this brand new, updated and expanded edition, he once again challenges the bromides that stand
in for experience and the techniques that too often replace substance. And Ken puts his ideas into the context of today's (and tomorrow's) world.

Everyone talks about how the world is changing, and how quickly trends and techniques come into vogue and then fall out of favor. It's the opening sentence in the opening paragraph of most books and most speeches. But it seems to me that too many people in our profession just don't get what this means. My Dad often says, "Not everyone who talks about heaven is going there." Well, I think not everybody who talks about change is really doing it.

In the last decade, since the first edition of *Relationship Fundraising* was published, there has been a growing restlessness about traditional approaches—mostly because the old ways haven't been working like they used to. But we need to look beyond the statistics and realize it's the donors who have changed. They are different now. The techniques and the level of service that worked yesterday may not be effective in attracting and holding onto *today's* donors, who expect consideration—and are determined to get it.

We need to be out there trying new things and taking some risks. Maybe we'll find that it's not so much about *replacing* traditional methods as it is about trying to *supplement* those methods. Whichever it is, it's going to take much more than the color of an envelope, a string of stamps, and a catchy phrase to keep today's and tomorrow's donors involved, satisfied, and committed.

I think what makes this new edition of Ken's landmark book so important is that he challenges our priorities; he asks us to forgo our obsession with techniques and formulas and to rethink how best to connect donors with causes. He asks us to consider the acts of mutual consideration, thoughtfulness, and appreciation—the hallmarks of our better relationships—and then determine how to bring those attributes into our world at work. He reminds us that we are indeed a service industry and all that it implies. And he helps us understand how we can accommodate ourselves to a changed marketplace populated by a discriminating citizenry.

As you examine his very big Point of View (as titled in the first edition by our mutual friend, George Smith), you may find some ideas you already knew but had forgotten; others, you might have put away and never tried, and still others will be totally new. But all these ideas, when examined within the context of our rapidly changing world, can be thought provoking and action inspiring. And they may oblige you to take a second look at what you have been taking for granted.

I am fortunate that my career in fundraising has coincided with the years that Ken launched and built his agency in London. He is, without a doubt, one of the most respected figures in the international fundraising community. Through the years, I have borrowed shamelessly from his writings and his wisdom. And if the direct mail packages from his wide range of clients could have been delivered to my door in Washington, D.C., I would have borrowed even more!

George Romney, U.S. politician and industrialist, once remarked, "There is nothing more vulnerable than entrenched success. You become a prisoner to what you've done in the past." Fortunately, Ken Burnett's *Relationship Fundraising* has thrown us a key. Just in time.

JENNIE THOMPSON
Chair, The Resource Alliance, 1998–2001

Preface to the Second Edition

I remember clearly the precise moment that I decided to write the first edition of this book. It was on a train coming back from Bristol to London in November 1990 after the Institute of Fundraising's Wales and West Region's annual conference. (The Institute of Fundraising is the professional association that provides training and standards for fundraisers in the United Kingdom, similar to North America's Association of Fundraising Professionals, the Fundraising Institute of Australia, and others.) I was with the institute's director at the time, Stephen Lee, and we were discussing the absence of any good British books on the subject of fundraising. We both agreed there was a gap that needed filling, but I felt what was wanted was a simple, factual guide to how to do fundraising, while Stephen believed any new work should have more attitude, take a ballsier, more confrontational stance, particularly as there was so much going wrong in fundraising at the time, which needed putting right.

I remember this conversation well not just because of its unusual setting, nor because it probably set me on the path to becoming an author (of a sort), but because at intervals during the course of this discussion we were trying to listen to the crackly radio on Stephen's personal stereo, which he held against the train's window to improve reception as we rumbled across the West Country. This was not normal commuter practice. Our interest in the radio that day was the promised announcement of the results in the ballot electing a leader for Britain's Conservative Party, which led ultimately to the ousting of Britain's first woman Prime Minister, Margaret Thatcher. In between bouts of broken reception and occasional excitement from Westminster, Stephen and I would return to debating the need for a good, up-to-the-minute British book on fundraising, and what shape it should take. So the germ of the idea for what became *Relationship Fundraising* was planted on that train journey, and grew from there. Within about a year the first edition was written. Its almost immediate success on publication rather surprised me and, I suspect, a few others too. Copies were sold in around forty countries and instead of having remaindered copies on my hands the book had to be reprinted twice.

Since then, of course, quite a few other books have appeared from British authors on the subject of fundraising, which reflects the growth of interest and professionalism in fundraising over the last decade and the health and vigor of the fundraising profession. However, the growth of Britain's fundraising book publishing industry has been nothing to match the explosion in fundraising publications on the other side of the Atlantic. Not just general texts, either. You can now get books, and good ones too, on almost any aspect of fundraising, from ethics to the Internet and from major gifts to managing change. Such a wealth of knowledge just didn't exist in the early 1990s.

I suppose my book's claim to special recognition, however, is not just that it was one of the first in the United Kingdom but that it addresses a subject that struck a chord then and still continues to do so. My summary of fundraising practice revolves around a particular point of view, that technology and aggressive marketing may be getting in the way of what really matters to fundraisers, our relationships with our donors, and could even be undermining the basis of trust and confidence that are so crucial to effective fundraising.

So in that first edition I set out not just to review current procedures and practices but also to point toward a better, more sustainable way for the future. Much has moved on since that first edition, and much has stayed the same. But my objectives now in revising and expanding this text are unchanged.

Relationship Fundraising 2: The Donor Strikes Back!

In 1996 a sequel to *Relationship Fundraising* appeared. After five years of sustained and healthy debate generated by its predecessor I wrote *Friends for Life: Relationship Fundraising in Practice* partly as a practical guide to show through real examples how organizations are tackling the challenges and opportunities that relationship fundraising provides, and partly to show its many doubters that, correctly applied, the original theory can actually enable fundraisers to raise substantially more money than its application will cost. *Friends for Life* features sixteen detailed case histories from fundraising organizations from the United Kingdom, the United States, and Canada. As well as illustrating the problems and the pitfalls, these stories show how relationship fundraising can be made to work and the substantial benefits it can bring. Extracting the lessons from these cases was an instructive yet sobering experience, because although I was undoubtedly able to report success and to show that relationship fundraising does work, much of that success was also partial, half-hearted, and transient, the result of a flaw not in the concept but in its application. And I was presenting the stories of the best. What about the rest? I came to realize that initiatives to develop a donor-based approach were stalling and ultimately failing because the organizations behind them were not fully committed to the concept and so were failing to invest the time, people, and resources necessary to ensure success.

The Choice

In the spring of 2001 I had to make a choice. Copies of *Relationship Fundraising* were running low again, so I had to decide either to print the book as it was for a fourth time or allow it to die a natural death. There was another option. I could update and reissue my book to ensure it stayed as relevant as possible to a new generation of fundraisers in a new millennium. That's what I chose to do, mainly because even after ten years I still get correspondence on the book, still get invited around the world to give seminars based on its theories, and still have people telling me that despite its age most of the original text remains as relevant as it was when written, if not more so.

For this new edition I have adopted a policy of not changing anything unless I've had to. So the only changes I have made have been to update or add knowledge that wasn't around at the time, to correct a few instances where time has proved me wrong (and to comment on some where the original has been proved right), and to add pieces of new information that now feel right for this book. But it has not been a simple text revision. So much has changed in the fundraising world over the past decade that I found the original book needed quite extensive surgery. The result is two completely new chapters and substantial revision and addition.

I've also added a new ending, and should explain why. In a quotation reproduced on the sleeve of the first edition, Giles Pegram (appeals director at Britain's National Society for the Prevention of Cruelty to Children) prophesied that "the ideas contained in this book will revolutionise fundraising in the next decade."

I'm sorry to say his prophecy was only partly fulfilled. Certainly the last decade of the twentieth century did see concepts of relationship building very much in vogue among fundraisers around the world, and I'm sure my book played a part in this. The mantras of being "donor-led" and "customer-focused" became fashionable and commonplace, as did ritual denial of mass marketing and denouncing of the blunderbuss approach to communication. Concepts such as donor care and customer service were enthusiastically embraced by fundraisers in conference halls and workshops, if not in their daily fundraising practice. Nevertheless throughout this period the volume of fundraising communications still mushroomed while their diversity remained fairly static and their relevance frequently questionable. Donors have become much more exposed to and more concerned about their role as targets for inappropriate, indistinguishable requests from fundraisers.

Please Note

This is not intended to be an expert work. I am not an expert, and I am rather anxious not to become one—ever since I realized that Noah's Ark was designed by an amateur and the *Titanic* was designed by an expert.

Fundraising is delightfully free of experts. Most people in fundraising, even those who are very long in the tooth, are only too ready to admit they haven't seen it all. I am lucky enough to have been involved in the business of fundraising for a comparatively long time. I am further fortunate to have worked alongside many of the world's best and most experienced fundraisers on a wide range of promotional projects for virtually every type and shade of fundraising organization. I have had at least as many dismal failures as spectacular successes and the majority of the rest have been somewhere in between—quiet, unspectacular little money-earners. So this book is also not a scholarly work. It is a practitioner's observations. Parts of it may be controversial. You may disagree with some of what I say. If so, please let me know.

It is also not complete. My fundraising experience does not include much that's worth saying about several specialist areas of fundraising—special events, corporate fundraising, local activities, volunteers. That's why you won't find much about these areas in this book—it's not because I don't think they are important. I wish I did know more about volunteers, because that seems to me to be an area of enormous potential for the organizations we work for and for the good work they support. People who give their time are in every way as important as people who give their money. Their gift of time can achieve every bit as much as a financial donation. I have been a volunteer myself and I find it a richly rewarding experience. So I know that here again there is a two-way relationship where both volunteer and cause can benefit. I hope that some of what I say in this book will also apply to volunteers and that those people whose job it is to encourage and coordinate the efforts of volunteers will find at least some parts of it useful.

Inevitably there is a large amount of overlap between chapters, although I have tried my best to limit it. The subjects I am writing about—donors, research, marketing, communications, dangers, opportunities, and so on—are not isolated compartments and each in some way or other inextricably involves most of the other subjects. Consequently, editing out duplication is not only difficult but often impossible. I have tried to remove the more obvious areas, save those where a bit of repetition is justified by the importance of the subject.

Also, of necessity, I have assumed that you, the reader, have a reasonable knowledge of the major areas of fundraising. As a result, I haven't sought to describe the basics of fundraising marketing such as direct mail or press advertising, in absolute detail.

One Word or Two?

One of the great fundraising mysteries, still unsolved, is to do with the very word *fundraising* itself. How should it be spelled? Is it *fundraising* or *fund raising*? Or is it hyphenated?

I think it is one word to describe one area of activity and that is the style I shall use in this book. Many others hold an alternative view. There is no obvious solution so not surprisingly a further group, no doubt confused, uses all three forms with seeming abandon. The *Oxford English Dictionary,* source of arbitration in such matters, is not much help. Until recently it didn't even mention us. Now it does, but as two words, hyphenated. I'm pleased that *fundraising* as one word now seems to be winning, as the style most widely used.

Outline of the Book

If I have missed anything important while preparing this book, I apologize—and trust you will let me know so I can put it right in the future. For further information on a wide range of fundraising and marketing subjects, please refer to the Glossary and the Bibliography at the end. Although as I write I have pictured my audience beginning at the beginning and reading eagerly and transfixed through to the end, you may well find specific topics of such interest that you wish to go directly to them. If you paid for this copy of my book, then that's surely your prerogative. Here then is a brief summary of what each chapter has to offer:

Chapter One is essentially an introduction to the field of fundraising as I see it, to lay the groundwork for a shared understanding of the topics discussed in subsequent chapters. It concludes—as do all the chapters—with a list of action points, which I hope you will find useful as convenient *aides-mémoire* to enable you more easily to put relationship fundraising into practice.

Chapter Two considers the public's attitude to fundraisers and fundraisers' attitudes to themselves. It shows how important fundraising can be and reviews the range and scale of opportunities that confront today's fundraisers.

Chapter Three sets out in detail the essential foundations of fundraising. It describes why people give and what makes a successful fundraiser.

Chapter Four offers a definition of relationship fundraising as a philosophy and illustrates what it can do for you. It describes the nine keys to building a relationship and considers one fundraising essential that is the cornerstone of relationship fundraising.

Chapter Five reviews what donors want. It looks at the positive and negative aspects of research, introduces "the golden generation" and the donor of the future, and considers the importance of trust, faith, and pride.

Chapter Six looks at the body of general and academic research that has grown up over recent years and considers the significance of donors' trust and confidence, as well as why it is important that you should strive to stay ahead of your competitors.

Chapter Seven is about making—and avoiding—mistakes. It begins with the recognition that fundraisers are no less fallible than the rest of the population, and it works through the major pitfalls and the ways to bridge or avoid them.

Chapter Eight takes us from mass marketing to individual relationships, describes the marketing plan, targeting, segmentation, the five marketing P's, how to create the right image, and how to use the telephone creatively. Through these it shows how the culture of fundraising can positively influence, direct, and control the culture of marketing.

Chapter Nine is all about keeping your friends and making donors feel special. It shows how much more cost-effective it is to develop relationships with existing friends than it is to have to find new ones, and it gives practical advice on how to retain, recognize, and reward your existing donors.

Chapter Ten outlines the myriad ways in which we now choose to communicate with our donors. It offers lots of practical advice on ways to be much better at it.

Chapter Eleven is all about recognizing opportunities and getting the best out of people. It outlines a variety of ways of offering donors real involvement in your organization's work and mission and describes a range of practical opportunities you might introduce to boost your fundraising performance and strengthen your relationships with donors.

Chapter Twelve looks in detail at the fundraiser's Aladdin's cave, bequest marketing, an area of vast potential where those brave enough, creative enough, and early enough might discover the keys to the last great opportunity to help a donor influence the world.

Chapter Thirteen is all about change. It reviews a wide range of recent developments in fundraising including a few controversial new challenges, and offers some thoughts on future change.

xxiv Preface to the Second Edition

Chapter Fourteen concludes the book with a little crystal-ball gazing, and comes up with some serious threats to our future which you can consider alongside a raft of genuinely exciting opportunities. It also shows why preparing suitable strategies for both will be time well spent.

Fundraising—and especially relationship fundraising—is all about individuals rather than groups. To bring this concept to life, after each chapter I pause to introduce and profile a specific donor—one composite but readily identifiable individual who demonstrates a part of the spectrum of possibilities that every donor presents. Their purpose is to remind you that donors are all different and that each represents an opportunity. Make of them what you will. As you prepare your fundraising appeals, picture how these people, and others you have met, will react to them; you may well form a clearer idea of the persuasiveness of your work than you can by reading it from the fundraiser's point of view.

Some Closing Remarks

For many years the closing remarks at the International Fund Raising Congress (the gathering of professional fundraisers from around the world that takes place each year outside Amsterdam, in the Netherlands) were delivered by Guy Stringer, formerly director of Oxfam, one-time senior executive with a major manufacturing company, and now one of fundraising's most eminent and respected gentlemen. He has more experience of and insight into the power and potential of fundraising than most of us are likely to achieve in a lifetime.

As Guy addressed the several hundred delegates, who had just survived three intensive days learning at the frontiers of the art and science of their profession, he sought to remind them of the larger purpose of being there. Techniques and skills are limited without a clear purpose, he told them. To remind fundraisers of what it's really all about Guy used to recount some stories from his own long experience designed to send the delegates off with their spirits soaring and sights set high. He invariably succeeded, because he knows what makes good fundraisers tick.

With Guy's permission I'll relate two of his stories here.

Who Am I?

Surat is a town in western India and the last time that I was there I arrived by train. You come out of the station and walk across a square, up a long hill and down a lane, where at the top, on the left-hand side, there is a leprosarium. It is run by sturdy Catholic sisters, some Indian and some Spanish. I arrived late at night and was quite tired and would have preferred to have thrown a bucket of water over myself and lain down. But Sister Mary insisted that I walk round the leprosarium with her and I have found it a mistake to disagree with Catholic sisters.

So round we went and to my astonishment there were little collections of people sitting round hurricane lamps on the ground, and I said to the sister, "What are they doing?" She said that the young patients were teaching the old people to read and write. And so they were—with the children saying, "No granny, you don't do it that way but like this." The only things that Oxfam had provided were the slates, the chalk and the little hurricane lamps.

When we got to the gates of the leprosarium I saw they were closed, but in the gloom you could see on the far side a little gang of people and the sister said to me, "Guy, open the gates." I did so and a family carried in a man. The sister led the way and they put the man on a table in the clinic. If they had put him on the ground he would have fallen down because his legs stopped at his knees. The sister knelt down and looked at the patient and she said to me, "There are worms in his wounds," and I looked and there were. Then a strange thing happened and it was rather like a camera going click, click. I could see who the sister was, she was somebody who could bring effective help to the patient. And I could see who the patient was, he needed help and badly. But who was the third person in the frame, in a Marks and Spencer sweater, size 40, do not boil. How did he fit?

The deduction from this of course is that if you are to be concerned in trying to help the poor, the handicapped, and the deprived you must be totally involved. You must try to project in what you write and say in your advertisements and public addresses the courage of the people, their determination to advance the lives of their families, their responsibility one to another, and you must never at any time undervalue them.

Flying a Kite

El Salvador has probably the worst record for human rights in the world. It is a tiny country the size of Wales, but people are murdered at night and if you wish to see your friends again you visit the city rubbish dump and there you will find their bodies. That's where they are battered to death. As a result a large number of families are in church refuges where they live under the care and defense of the church, because if they left these places they would end up, as so many others do, outside the city.

I visited one with about two hundred families and hundreds of tiny children. It was a classic demonstration of the ability of women because the place was immaculate. I would have got it in a muddle in five minutes flat. There was only one small piece of land open to the sky, which was surrounded by a very high wire fence. The children congregated in masses on this tiny piece of playground— the only bit of open air to be found. And they were making paper kites with newspaper, little bits of stick, and some string. But of course if you fly a kite you need wind and you need some space and the children found it extremely difficult to get their kites off the ground. The result was that the big wire fence was simply covered with battered kites.

Eventually I left to go, walked out into the road, looked up and down—it is always wise in El Salvador to see who is about—and walked down the road to turn right at a corner at the bottom. Before I did I turned round and looked up and two little kites had cleared the fence and were lifting up jerking bit by bit into the dark blue sky. Some people would say that this is just some string, a bit of newspaper, some little sticks, and two little boys, but in fact it is more than that. It is a triumph of the human spirit over the grim environment in which so many dwell.

You came here to learn about fundraising and will have learned much about new techniques and skills in your time here. I hope you have enjoyed it, but do not forget that techniques and skills themselves are limited. What you must do is to stand up and encourage and develop a vision of a new society in which all of us may dwell in peace and harmony.

In quoting Guy's words I can't invoke the sincerity and passion of his delivery or recreate the emotional charge in his voice that ensured there wasn't a dry eye in the house. Guy's stories were magic. They gave fundraisers a lift and reminded us that our profession is more special than most other trades or businesses. For me, that made Guy's closing address perhaps the most important part of each year's International Fund Raising Congress.

Fundraising is more than a job. In the right hands, it is a powerful force for change and while that change is under way it should be an inspirational beacon of hope. Fundraisers have good reason to be proud of their profession.

In producing this new edition I aim to do more than just amplify and reinforce the wisdom of a relationship fundraising approach and so strengthen the position of those who believe it right for their organization. I hope to show that both for the prosperity of our organizations and for the long-term health and viability of the nonprofit sector, fundraisers have to start taking relationship fundraising more seriously. The investment of time, people, and money in building mutually rewarding and beneficial relationships with donors is not just prudent, it is essential. Our futures depend upon it.

Kermarquer, France   KEN BURNETT
May 2002

Acknowledgments

The ideas and efforts of a large number of people have helped in the preparation of this book and I owe them all a considerable debt. Lack of space prevents me from listing everyone.

I am grateful particularly to the International Fund Raising Group (now known as The Resource Alliance) for having faith in my original idea back in the early 1990s and for providing the encouragement that enabled it to see the light of day.

I am indebted to all my colleagues at Burnett Associates who made it possible for me to disappear for weeks on end to work on this book. I am grateful also to all clients, past and present, who have allowed me to work on so many interesting projects over the years and at whose hands I have learned more lessons than I care to remember. Through them I have been able to meet a large number of donors, members, and supporters, those endlessly fascinating people who are the lifeblood of all the organizations for which I work, and who appear as composites in the donor profiles that appear at the end of each chapter.

I would also like to thank a number of authors, many of whom I have never met, whose published works have played an important part in my research for this book. It amazes me how many people I meet in fundraising and direct marketing who have never read any of the many great textbooks that have been published recently in our business area, both in the United Kingdom and abroad. I have been in the marketing business for more than thirty years and I still couldn't exist without them. In preparing this publication on relationship fundraising I have been inspired and guided by several works and I owe their authors a tremendous debt of gratitude. I have always advocated plagiarism and consider it the most sincere form of flattery, so I hope they will be flattered if they find some of their ideas (always properly acknowledged, of course) reproduced in my pages. True creativity is borrowing someone else's idea and adding to it, rather like the sparrow who climbed on the eagle's back to fly just a little higher. In such ways is knowledge advanced. I would like to pay tribute here to the following eagles: Stan Rapp and Tom Collins for *MaxiMarketing,* Drayton Bird for *Commonsense Direct Marketing,* Robert Leiderman for *The Telephone Book,* Judith E. Nichols for *Changing Demographics: Fund Raising in the 1990s,* Graeme McCorkell for *Advertising That Pulls Response,* James Gregory Lord for *The Raising of Money,* Penelope Burk for *Thanks! A Guide to Donor-Centred Fundraising,* Albert Anderson for *Ethics for Fundraisers,* and Peter F. Drucker for *Managing the Non-Profit Organization.* I also owe a lot to *Professional Fundraising* magazine (from the United Kingdom) and *Fund Raising Management* and *The Chronicle of Philanthropy* (from the United States), three indispensable journals on fundraising. A fuller list of relevant publications can be found in the Bibliography.

My gratitude also to John Durham, Lawrence Stroud, and all involved in fundraising at Botton Village in Yorkshire, where any reader inspired by relationship fundraising will find what I believe is the world's most remarkable fundraising success story. Much of what I know about developing donor relationships I learned working with the fundraisers of Botton Village.

Specific chapters have been read and commented on at manuscript stage by several acknowledged experts and I am grateful to them for their time and commitment. Thanks to Anne Wrangham of Crossbow Research, telemarketing specialist Rich Fox of Rich Fox Associates, and David Ford, Richard Radcliffe, and Tom Smith of Smee and Ford Limited, the world's leading authorities on wills and legacies.

Others whose ideas also shaped my thoughts include Guy Stringer, John Groman, John Hambley, Roger Millington, Susan Kay, Ian Ventham, Redmond Mullin, Michael Downes, Gavin Grant, Giles Pegram, George Smith, and the late Harold Sumption. You each might recognize a little bit of what I learned from you in this book.

For the first edition Cary Goode and Sanchi Heesom both cast their professional eyes over the final manuscript and made valuable suggestions. Theresa Lloyd and Annie Moreton also provided help in the final stages. I must also credit contributions from my colleagues Ernst Goetschi, Derek Humphries, Celia Cole, and Jackie Fowler. Marie Burnett supervised research, production, and the editing of the text.

For the revised edition I am very grateful particularly to Jennie Thompson for her warm and generous foreword and for her unfailing support and encouragement throughout this project. Also to Stephen Lee and professor Adrian Sargeant of the Henley Management College, David Carrington, Annie Moreton, Jan Chisholm, Harvey McKinnon, Tom Smith, Neil Sloggie, Daryl Upsall, Nick Allen, Rich Fox, George Smith, Jason Potts, Simon Turner, Jackie Fowler and her colleagues at Burnett Works, John Rodd, Terry Hunt, Chris Barraclough, Guy Mallabone, Tony Myers, Mike Simpson at ActionAid, Peter Sweatman, Kitty Hilton, and John Clark.

And of course sincere thanks to my editors for this edition, Johanna Vondeling and Mary Zook of Jossey-Bass in San Francisco, and to Carolyn Uno of Tigris Productions and Beverly Miller.

Whatever value this book has, it wouldn't have been as good without any of you. Thanks.

K.B.

The Author

Ken Burnett has worked with more than two hundred fundraising organizations during the past twenty-five years, from large national and international charities to small local and specialized appeals, from universities and medical schools to arts organizations and charitable trusts. He has written and produced fundraising promotional material for many of the most effective voluntary and campaigning organizations in Britain and around the world.

After eight years in magazine and book publishing, Ken Burnett joined ActionAid, the international development nonprofit, as U.K. director in 1977.

In 1983 he founded Burnett Associates Limited, an advertising and communications company that grew to become a leading supplier of promotional and marketing resources for fundraising organizations all over the world. Burnett Associates won numerous awards for its work, particularly in the design and production of printed and electronic communications and for innovation in direct marketing for fundraising. Ken Burnett continues to work closely with the London-based communications agency Burnett Works Limited.

In 1995 Ken was appointed as a member of the board of Action-Aid, his former employer and Britain's third-largest international development agency. In 1998 he was elected chairman of Action-Aid's board.

Ken Burnett is a regular speaker at seminars and workshops throughout the world and has written and cowritten three other books on fundraising communications and marketing, including the sequel to the first edition of this book, *Friends for Life: Relationship Fundraising in Practice*, which was published in 1996. He is an Honorary Fellow of the United Kingdom's Institute of Direct Marketing, a Fellow of the Institute of Fundraising, and a founding patron of the Charity Technology Trust.

Ken Burnett can be reached at http://www.kenburnett.com and at http://www.whitelionpress.com.

Chapter One

Much More Than Raising Money

One thing has remained constant in fundraising for two thousand years, that is that the more personalized approach works the best. For the future of fundraising, no matter what happens, it will come back to the levels of personalization and interaction that can be provided.
NEIL SLOGGIE, AUTHOR OF *THE TINY ESSENTIALS OF FUNDRAISING*, WHEN ASKED TO COMMENT ON THE FUTURE OF OUR PROFESSION

The night-time adventure on the Bristol-to-London train that I described in the Preface was the trigger, but it has little to do with *why* I decided to write *Relationship Fundraising* in the first place. My real reasons have more to do with lessons learned from the wide variety and large number of fundraising organizations I have worked with during my years as a fundraiser. They were also to do with a growing unease I felt and still feel about some aspects of the direct marketing explosion in fundraising and the way that the onset of "professionalism" is leaving a sour taste in the mouths of many of the donors I meet. The scale of advance in training and technique in fundraising has been spectacular. But, not surprisingly, amid all the excitement some of the fundamentals of fundraising have been neglected, if not overlooked entirely, in the rush to professionalize.

A Unique Business Area

In recent years, fundraisers have seen some remarkable changes. Although very many of the old ways and prejudices still exist, the

1

new fundraiser coming in for professional training now will see a very different career area from the one I joined. I keep telling myself that twenty-five years is not really a very long time, but twenty-five years ago even some of the biggest nonprofits had barely heard of marketing, or training, or even professionalism.

Looking back, I'm astonished at how rapidly and, in some cases, how completely the naive and often counterproductive amateurism of the past has given way to professionalism in strategy, materials, and approach from nonprofit organizations. Nonprofits are now better managed, more clearly focused, and stronger as a result. In general, increased professionalism has been a great blessing for both organization and donor, but there has been a downside because most donors don't understand professionalism in nonprofits. Many are suspicious of it and don't like it.

Nowhere has the increase in professionalism been more evident than in nonprofit marketing, particularly in the growth of direct mail and other printed communication. The last two decades of the twentieth century were a boom time for nonprofit marketing in Britain. It wasn't a time of much new invention. It was rather a time for learning the lessons already understood by our brothers and sisters on the for-profit side, taking what has been proved to work for them and applying it to the business of raising money.

But raising money for a cause is a unique business area. It benefits from many of the highest human emotions and is lucky enough not to be burdened by some of the basest. One thing is certain—a fundraising transaction is fundamentally different from a commercial business transaction. Although fundraisers have much to learn from commercial practice they will commit a fatal, suicidal error if they embrace commercial practices too enthusiastically.

Nonprofit marketing professionals have certainly appeared in numbers in recent years, but I suspect that their short and unglamorous career is coming to an end. A new breed of professional will have to emerge to take their place. I hope that this new breed will be what I call "relationship fundraisers."

These relationship fundraisers will have learned all the lessons of commercial marketing that old-style charity marketers had learned. But they will have something else—a deep commitment to their chosen profession of fundraising and a clear understanding of all the important aspects that mark fundraising out from other commercial applications.

They will, of course, be supremely skilled and well-trained professionals in every aspect of their trade. But they will realize that to succeed in fundraising marketing they must *adapt* commercial marketing methods, not simply *adopt* them. Above all they will understand their donors—their version of customers.

They will study and appreciate the unique bond, the relationship, that exists between donors and the cause that they support. And preserving, developing, and extending that relationship will be the relationship fundraisers' primary goal.

What Is a Donor?

Notions of what constitutes a donor are probably very varied. The following story impresses me and seems a good example of what an inspirational and effective thing it can be to be a donor. And that just about anyone can be one.

At the time of the war between India and Pakistan that gave birth to the nation of Bangladesh, monsoon floods had devastated what was then known as East Bengal. The combination of conflict and natural disaster killed millions and created perhaps the largest exodus of refugees the world has ever known. Cast adrift into a ravaged countryside these refugees had nothing but the prospect of starvation and disease. In the path of many of them was the sprawling, congested metropolis of Calcutta, which had troubles enough of its own.

Socially the lowest of Calcutta life were the beggars, and they were having a particularly hard time. The region's troubles had seen off the tourists upon whom the beggars depended for their livelihood. In the district of Calcutta known as Chowringhee the one dependable thing in the lives of these beggars was a soup kitchen run by the Salvation Army, which each day provided a single square meal to each of the beggars, for most the only sustenance they had.

But word reached these beggars of the terrible troubles of the refugees who had recently arrived in their neighborhood. They could readily imagine their suffering. Then the leader of the beggars' community approached the organizers of the soup kitchen with an extraordinary request.

The beggars, he said, wanted to help. They requested that the soup kitchen cut their daily ration in half from now on, so the other half could be sent to the refugee camp. These people, who were so poor themselves, were prepared to sacrifice half of the little they had to help people they didn't even know.

Being a donor means giving up something from your personal, individual surplus to help others. Most donors will make a lesser sacrifice than that of the beggars of Calcutta, but will be inspirational just the same. It's a good thing to be a donor, and should be encouraged. It should certainly be a mandatory requirement for anyone wishing to be a fundraiser.

For the purpose of this book, however, donors are people who actively support the work of nonprofit organizations through their sustained financial contributions. Nonprofit organizations don't depend by any means on donors for all their income, but donors do provide a large and vitally important part. They also have many other valuable uses.

Your donors are your organization's friends. With friends you can share good news and bad, keeping in touch and developing a long-term relationship that brings benefits to both sides. Your donors benefit from their role in the work you do, from sharing in your successes and achievements and from the satisfaction of knowing their contribution has been effective. You benefit, of course, from the level and frequency of their donations, but also because they will often be the most enthusiastic ambassadors of your cause. They will recruit their friends, they will enable you to undertake reciprocal mailings with other nonprofits, they will purchase your mail order products and will respond to your crises and your emergency and special appeals. They will tell you what your organization is doing right and what they don't believe in. They'll help you lobby for change. They will involve their families, will support your events, will help you build a network of local activity, will raise funds for you, will volunteer for all sorts of unpaid work, will provide free public relations, will introduce you to valuable business contacts, and much more besides. They will also, in the fullness of time, make their largest contribution to your cause by leaving you a bequest in their will.

Two quite different anecdotes illustrate the value of committed donors. Several years ago a major British children's organization became involved in a scandal. A social worker employed by the charity falsified records to show that a child at risk had received supervisory visits when no such visits had been made. Later the child died at the hands of its own parent. The news was carried in the press and caused a national uproar. The organization involved wisely made no attempt to disguise its responsibility. Instead it wrote a detailed account to all donors, explaining what had happened and outlining the action it proposed taking to ensure nothing similar could happen in the future. Donors applauded this admission of failure and responded accordingly. They were asked to renew their support at this difficult time and money came flooding in spontaneously, for these people really cared.

During the Ethiopian famine of 1984 Oxfam learned that already weakened children were dying of cold. Its staff wrote to volunteers and donors, asking them to knit woolen sweaters that could be airlifted out. The response was overwhelming. Donors were placed in the front line of disaster relief and willingly did what they could. Oxfam flew literally millions of knitted garments into Ethiopia to meet that need immediately.

In *Managing the Non-Profit Organization* management guru Peter Drucker says, "We can no longer hope to get more money from the donor, they have to become contributors."

I suspect his definition of a donor may be narrower than mine, but I believe that really to thrive in the future we have to *involve* donors even more: to make them more than donors and more than contributors. We have to be genuinely accountable to them.

We also have to share disappointments as well as achievements. Some years ago one of Oxfam's small overseas programs failed because the responsible individual on the spot was ill. As a result, Oxfam's investment was a complete flop. One particular donor, a bank, had put up a sizable part of the money. Oxfam went to see the bank and explained exactly what had happened. That bank still supports Oxfam in many ways.

In developing donor relationships we are seeking ways to enable our donors to participate actively in the work we do through their giving. We have to see donors as co-owners of the organization, partners in a common aim. And we have to enable them to feel that sense of co-ownership too.

In return for all this contribution and commitment from donors the fundraiser has to ensure that the donors' money is well spent and their trust is not misplaced. Every fundraiser has a responsibility to the donors, to find out for certain that the organization's programs are sound and to report back to the donors that they are. This often means the fundraiser has to ask awkward questions of the program managers and to insist on full answers. That's the fundraiser's job.

Fundraising Is Important

The fundraising role is crucial. Each one of the service organizations for which fundraisers work can only succeed if it receives the voluntary financial support that pays for the work it does. It is up to fundraisers to make this happen. They have to work on many fronts, across an enormous range of commercial marketing disciplines—from managing a local and regional network to national press advertising, from retailing and catalogue trading to publications design and production, from press and public relations to organizing large-scale public events and including every aspect of direct marketing, television and radio appeals, managing volunteers, corporate campaigns, and a host of other promotional specialties to boot.

Few professions offer such variety as fundraising. In addition, of course, the overstretched fundraiser also has to ensure that the needed funds are raised ultra-efficiently and cost-effectively. If you think selling a product is difficult, try getting someone to give you money for nothing.

Also, because there is no tangible product or service in most fundraising transactions, the fundraiser has to meet and satisfy a range of complex emotions and conditions in the donor. To do this over a sustained period of time—the donor's life cycle—requires consummate skill and understanding at the highest professional level.

I start from the conviction that the relationship fundraiser must be one of the most skillful, most proficient, and most versatile marketing and communications professionals to be found anywhere in the world. Anyone who has any doubts about the high commercial standards of fundraisers should look closely at the thousand-plus entries submitted each year for the United Kingdom's annual Direct Marketing Awards, about fifty of which are in the fundraising category. Some years ago I was asked to be one of the judges for these prestigious awards, which are the highest accolades awarded by a thriving direct marketing industry. I not only learned a lot through looking at the best submissions in twenty-two categories of direct marketing activity, I was also immensely impressed by the high standard of the fundraising entries. I was proud beyond measure to hear my fellow judges overwhelmingly agree that the most outstanding category of all, the category with the highest overall quality in creativity, strategy, and performance, was—fundraising.

This will come as a surprise to many, but it shouldn't. In fact, anything else would be something of a failure. Fundraising should be the best area of marketing. We should set the standard others follow. Why? Because we have the best stories, the best case histories, and the best reasons why people should buy our product. And the best incentive to present our case distinctively.

Confusion with a commercial marketing career should swiftly be put to rest. Fundraisers are not selling products such as baked beans or razor blades and there is little similarity in the underlying motivations fundraisers invoke. We simply share a few of the processes. What fundraisers do is *make caring service possible* by enabling donors to realize their capacity and potential to support good works. The techniques, approaches, and systems that will achieve this have similarities with other areas of marketing endeavor but, essentially, they are unique to fundraising.

That is relationship fundraising.

Fundraisers are members of a profession that is one of the world's most powerful catalysts for change. After all, without the money raised by fundraisers there are no good works. Deprived of the funds that fuel their every activity the aims and objectives of the organizations that employ us would simply fail. But when fundraisers are successful and increase the resources that enable these organizations to go on to do *new work,* then there is literally no limit to what we can achieve and to the good we can do.

Voluntary agencies lead the way in the welfare sector. It is fundraisers who provide the means that let them do it.

Spot the Difference

What difference will it make if fundraisers become more donor-oriented? Will nonprofits, in time, present a different image and identity to their audiences from the image and identity they present today?

I think they will. Imagine if television advertising, for example, were to be consumer-oriented rather than sales-oriented. It's a radical thought.

I'm not suggesting that anyone take relationship fundraising to that extreme, or at least not immediately and without fully considering all the consequences. But, despite its risks and its costs, consumerism has done a lot to improve the public acceptability of a range of industries and, along with the rest of society, those industries themselves have ultimately benefited. Our society and our employers can similarly benefit from relationship fundraising.

Something Special

If this book can convey something of why fundraising is such a special field of work then it will have achieved one of its objectives. If it can encourage fundraisers to active concern for their donors and their donors' feelings and thereby avoid shooting themselves in the foot through inappropriate promotion then it will have achieved another objective.

And if it can find its way into the hands of nonprofit directors and senior management and help them to appreciate some of the complexities and importance of the donor/fundraiser relationship then I'll be satisfied. The most common problem voiced at fundraising seminars I attend is, "That's a great idea, but how on earth can I get it past my board?" This is a dreadful indictment of the state of our profession, but in far too many of our organizations, it's true. Although the governance of nonprofit organizations is one area where there has been substantial improvement in the last decade, still too many nonprofits have boards that, because they have not addressed basic issues of structure and governance, are functioning *despite* rather than *thanks to* their boards. (See Chapter Thirteen for more on governance.)

I have one other important aim for this book. It is to encourage fundraising organizations to invest for the future, not in stocks and shares, but in building a body of committed supporters and in developing and extending the commitment of these donors through relationship fundraising. This is the most important investment any fundraising organization can make. In fact, it seems to me to be entirely ridiculous for any charity to have large investments in real estate or in stocks and shares if it hasn't invested in the development of its donor list.

Action Points

▲ Prepare to change your approach to fundraising to become a "relationship fundraiser."

▲ Learn from commercial practice, but adapt the methods used rather than adopt them.

▲ Be aware of the variety of ways in which donors help your organization. Make sure others are aware of it too.

▲ Never attempt to disguise a mistake.

▲ See your donors as partners in a common aim. Enable them to feel a sense of co-ownership.

▲ Make sure that donors' money is well spent and that their trust is not misplaced.

▲ Don't forget that people who give their time can be as valuable as those who give money.

Donor Profile: Mary Tewson

Mary Tewson lives in a well-to-do modern housing development on the outskirts of a large town. She is fifty-four years old, unmarried, and lives with Agnes, who is eight years older and her only surviving sister. They share Mary's detached three-bedroom house, which Mary bought on a mortgage nearly twenty years ago and has now almost paid off. The house is just two miles from where Mary works as receptionist for a veterinary surgeon. She is popular with her colleagues and highly regarded by her employer. Mary earns a reasonable salary and her living expenses are low. The house is comfortable and well furnished.

Mary is of medium height, in very good health, and is particularly proud that her long black hair has so far avoided any signs of gray. Always smartly dressed, she drives a small family sedan that rather surprisingly houses a sporty engine, which she likes because it gives her that extra bit of acceleration.

Both Mary and her sister are regular churchgoers. Most of their social life revolves around a variety of church-related clubs and committees. These activities keep both sisters very busy, and of course they see a lot of each other. But from time to time, Mary likes to go out on her own, to the movies or shopping in town. Last year she also went on holiday alone, to Europe, breaking the habit of a lifetime of holidays spent at home with her sister.

Mary is actively involved with her local hospice and in fundraising for the local group of friends of the nearby general hospital. Although she's not interested in politics she is much concerned about world affairs, particularly injustice. She shows her love of children and her concern for their problems by supporting several children's charities both at home and abroad. She sponsors two children, one in India and one in Africa, and gains great comfort from providing this practical and tangible help. She eagerly awaits news from either of the sponsored children, or their projects.

Mary receives a lot of mail from nonprofits, some of which she supports and some of which she doesn't. She welcomes opportunities to be useful, particularly if it helps children. She recently accepted nomination for the committee of the local branch of a national child care organization, and was delighted to be elected. In due course she hopes to be able to use her secretarial skills as branch secretary.

Mary hasn't made a will, but plans to in the near future. She no longer thinks that one day she might get married. Her priority now is to be as useful as she can be to as many people as possible.

Chapter Two

Proud to Be a Fundraiser

*I am still looking for the modern-day equivalent of those
Quakers who ran successful businesses, made money
because they offered honest products and treated their
people decently, worked hard, spent honestly, saved
honestly, gave honest value for money, put back more
than they took out and told no lies. This business creed,
sadly, seems long forgotten.*
ANITA RODDICK, *BODY AND SOUL*

I don't know of anyone who, from an early age, was telling their
parents that what they really wanted to be in life was a fundraiser.
Most of us have only drifted into it by accident and some may feel
they just ended up in fundraising. Part of the reason for this is
that fundraising in most countries has not hitherto been seen as
a legitimate career area and most of us had never even heard of it
until we found ourselves doing it.

Fundraising is a relatively new career. Most people still don't
know what it means or what it involves. Surprisingly it has a fairly
low public image relative to its importance, although a few years
ago fundraising's image was, if anything, even worse. I know this
because it was brought home to me dramatically at parties and
other social gatherings when I started in fundraising. I used to respond confidently to the customary question, "And what do you
do?" with, "I am a fundraiser. I raise money for charity." In my
naïveté I expected to be met by enthusiastic acclaim, admiration,
and expressions of interest. But instead people reacted as if I'd just
announced myself to be a badger gasser or apprentice on a North

Sea sludge dumper. I was left in no doubt that asking people for money was not considered a suitable occupation for a grown man. Thereafter—for a short while at least—I took to saying I was in "overseas development" or "with a Third World agency" or something equally vague so people felt too embarrassed to ask any further. It's rather like the insurance salesman who terms himself "investment counselor" because it sounds better when he tells his mum what he does for a living.

Always negative, these reactions to my being a fundraiser were sometimes openly antagonistic or overtly critical. At times, I suspect, they came from people who did not give much to nonprofits and appeared to feel rather bad about the fact. I am sure most fundraisers have experienced this chilling reception. It takes courage to come out as a fundraiser, to acknowledge your chosen career in front of friends, acquaintances, and those you might wish to impress.

Limited Public Image

Yet this negative view of fundraising is a strange reversal of reality. It's not just a question of job satisfaction. Few career areas present as many opportunities for real responsibility as quickly as fundraising. At the age of twenty-six I was appointed U.K. director of an international charity with more than a hundred staff members in Britain. I had responsibility for a multimillion-pound business with a team of regional fundraisers, a chain of shops, a catalogue marketing operation, a substantial advertising budget, a press and public relations program, a publications unit, a headquarters administration staff, and a new computer system. I wasn't particularly qualified for all this responsibility, so like many other fundraisers I learned the hard way. Nevertheless I managed to cope reasonably successfully with everything except the computer. I doubt I could have found comparable career development opportunities anywhere else. Even now, many years later, I find fundraising still offers some of the best opportunities for real responsibility and challenge as well as, of course, unparalleled job satisfaction. But the downside is that the public rarely, if ever, appreciates this. You have to learn to live with it, but you can also fight to change it. Many of the reasons for the public's poor perception lie at our own door, for we have promoted what we do rather badly.

And it's not only the general public that has a low opinion of fundraising. Many organizations that depend on fundraising still undervalue the process and the individuals that carry it out. One of the saddest and most limiting aspects of our profession is the refusal of some board members and senior nonprofit managers to acknowledge the economic realities of their position and accord to fundraisers proper resources, consideration, and encouragement. Too many fundraisers still see their boards as an obstacle rather than an asset. This may be changing, but there's still a long way to go.

There have been some changes in fundraising's status in recent years, both good and bad. My off-putting impressions of public lack of esteem for fundraisers were formed before the great fundraising boom of the 1980s, when, in the United Kingdom at least, careers in fundraising started to blossom along with the growth of nonprofit direct marketing, the use of professional external agencies, and the proliferation of the fundraising consultancy. But still I find fundraisers themselves are often strangely shy of admitting what they really do for a living. They prefer to say they're in marketing, or advertising, or public relations, or whatever. The truth is the fundraiser is *all* these things and more. If we don't believe in ourselves, why should anyone else believe in us?

Our generally low public image is getting worse in some ways. We see ourselves as nobly applying professional techniques and understanding to improving the lot of our fellows. They still see us as benevolent busybodies, gracious ladies (and sometimes gents) whose quaint and condescending hobby is more designed to push us up the social ladder than kick off the shackles of injustice. It may just be that, from being entirely ignorant of our existence a few years ago, some of the public now see us as "those people who send that awful junk mail."

Pride in Our Profession

The voluntary sector is no longer marginal, it is central to our society. Voluntary giving has always been important, but government policies in recent years have increasingly deemphasized the role of the state in social provision, resulting in an inevitable increase in society's reliance on a strong and diverse voluntary sector. The voluntary sector is increasingly being called on to complement and substitute for government action in areas where the state has withdrawn and commercial enterprise has proved to be inappropriate, inadequate, or inefficient. This trend is unlikely to reverse and can be seen in several countries. Voluntary action is likely to become even more important in the future.

But the extent and diversity of the voluntary sector in developed countries throughout the world is not widely appreciated. In Britain the total annual income of all charities is reckoned to be £24 billion (using the U.S. version of that number, a thousand million), or roughly $34 billion at the exchange rate prevalent in early 2002. Charitable donations from the British public are estimated to be around £5.75 billion per annum. That's somewhere around 1 percent of Britain's gross national product and bigger than several of its other major industries, including agriculture and the combined value of U.K. domestic consumption of coal, gas, oil, and electricity.

Clearly this is a big business by anyone's standards. It is also a growing business. Although growth may have slowed lately, most industries would envy the real expansion of the voluntary sector over the past two decades. In the United States, after accounting for inflation, growth from 1981 to 1990 was 78 percent. It was equally impressive in the United Kingdom, and although growth slowed and may even have declined in the mid-nineties voluntary giving is growing again. However, according to Britain's National Council for Voluntary Organizations, the recovery is almost entirely due to current donors giving more, as the percentage of the population giving to charity has barely increased.

Individuals in Britain give around 80 percent of the total and around 70 percent of adults give something during the course of the year—a fairly creditable market penetration. (That figure is broadly consistent in other countries such as the United States, Canada, and Australia.) However, the vast majority of people give tiny, virtually negligible amounts, and according to some research the percentage of British people giving to charity has fallen from over 80 percent in 1993 to the current 70 percent.

In America the voluntary sector is reported to be the largest employer (1990 figures), and its value represents 2.24 percent of the country's gross national product. By contrast some 19 percent of the French population over the age of eighteen volunteer, giving an average of eighteen hours per month, the equivalent of 650,000 full-time employees at work. But by comparison with the British and Americans, the French do not yet donate generously to their nonprofit sector. Other European countries lag even further behind, but the statistics available are poor so comparison is difficult. There are signs of some catching up in the last decade.

There are over 185,000 registered nonprofits in Britain and their number is increasing every year. Only a fraction of these are fundraising in the public arena, but of course this small part includes all the largest ones and, while not recorded, the number of causes raising money from the public is almost certainly growing faster now than ever before. Approximately 7 percent receive over 77 percent of the total annual income. It's a sector dominated by a few big guys.

In Britain the voluntary sector employs 485,000 people, about 2 percent of the workforce. Fifty percent of these are employed full time and an estimated 3 million people work voluntarily. Of paid staff in the sector, 75 percent are female.

The average gift in the United Kingdom is low (and may even have fallen), but this simply shows the considerable potential there is for growth in improving the public's perceptions about giving, encouraging planned giving, encouraging more people to leave bequests to nonprofits in their will, and targeting specific groups and individuals known to respond to fundraising appeals. (Much is made in the media about fluctuations in this average figure. In practice, a universal average is irrelevant to fundraisers as most of our effort is rightly geared toward a smaller market segment that comprises our real customers—the donors.)

This already large industry sector still has significant opportunity for further financial growth. It also has considerably increased competition for funds. It's not hard to see why these are such interesting times for fundraisers.

So fundraisers have scale, growth, and opportunity in their profession. What else should motivate the new recruit? It's unlikely to be high pay, good benefits, and job security because as yet these aren't often found in fundraising. But there are more positives than negatives. In the first chapter I outlined the importance of fundraising to society. The work fundraisers do is interesting and challenging. It frequently takes them to exciting places and enables them to meet interesting people. Many fundraisers travel the world, gaining vital firsthand experience of often highly dramatic situations. They also seem constantly to be meeting celebrities, important political figures, the media, and even royalty. Fundraisers get access to the people of the moment.

Fundraisers can also gain great satisfaction in knowing that what they are doing is really worthwhile. Not only can they bring about change, they can influence people's thinking and extend their interest and involvement in a range of worthwhile activities. Fundraising is the perfect occupation for the wishful thinker, as success in fundraising means the direct ability to turn those wishes into reality.

Fundraising organizations have other benefits. They encourage compassion and provide millions of people with a practical means of direct involvement in solving the problems and serving the needs of others. They provide opportunities for volunteers (see what pleasure and companionship some men and women get from working with their local thrift shop—which also recycles clothes and other goods), they campaign for social and even political change. Unlike commercial organizations, charities don't produce dividends. The fruits of their labors are something more special— changed lives.

Fundraising also is, or soon will be, a true equal opportunity profession. There are at least as many effective women fundraisers as men, and although men may still dominate in senior positions, that won't last. Ethnic background and physical abilities or disabilities are also largely irrelevant to effectiveness as a fundraiser, so there really is no valid reason why the fundraising profession should not be a model of equal opportunities.

Nonprofit Doesn't Mean Not Profitable

Charitable works often come in for criticism, and nonprofit organizations are frequently accused of inefficiency and bad management. Although all organizations have some shortcomings and some nonprofits have more than their share, my experience of working with commercial clients indicates that by and large the public is quite harsh in its views of nonprofit management. Perhaps that is a good thing, as it keeps the sector on its toes, but I think nonprofits could certainly do much to improve their collective image.

After all, most nonprofits in the United Kingdom at least are obliged to apply at least 80 percent of their total income directly toward their charitable objectives. This factor, known as the expense ratio (80 percent charitable, 20 percent expenses), is in fact a remarkable achievement in commercial terms, for that 80 percent represents what most companies would call net profit (the residue after all direct costs, administrative costs, overheads and cost of sales, and the like have been deducted). How many commercial organizations do you know that can claim anything like 80 percent profit on turnover? That represents, usually, quite staggering efficiency on behalf of nonprofits and the public should be very proud of this.

Of course, this is an unfair comparison. Voluntary organizations don't have raw material costs or manufacturing costs and can include their costs of service provision in their overall distribution figures. So direct comparison with commercial enterprises is difficult. Nevertheless the gap between the average company's profit ambition (around 10 percent keeps most companies happy) and the nonprofit's need to distribute 80 percent of its funds is huge, more than enough to cover all costs of sales.

And raising funds for a cause is a much more complicated and difficult process than selling.

Fundraisers are not professional beggars—beggars are almost invariably asking for themselves and give little or nothing in return. We ask on behalf of others and we have to be prepared to give a lot. Nor is asking for money on behalf of a third party anything to be even remotely ashamed about—quite the reverse. We promote a unique product. It is something people *want* to buy.

Essential Overheads

I am fond of responding to the traditional accusation that nonprofits spend too much on administration by explaining that I wouldn't be prepared to give any of my money to a nonprofit that *didn't* spend a sizable part of its income on administration. Because, if it didn't, how could I have any faith that my donation wouldn't be completely wasted? If the proper administrative machinery wasn't in place, how could the organization get anything done? I have never yet found a donor who couldn't follow that logic.

The general public, unfortunately, is often considerably less well informed than donors and few subjects are more calculated to raise the public's ire than visions of a nonprofit overspending on administration. Sadly this paranoia often rubs off on donors who should know better. In some ways the concern has become an idée fixe in our publics' collective consciousness.

Fundraisers, therefore, need to recognize this concern, to treat it seriously and tackle it comprehensively. Like most serious issues, it won't go away if we ignore it.

Different organizations need widely differing administrative machineries and the reasons for this are not difficult to explain. A grant-making nonprofit inevitably requires less administration than one that manages its own programs. An overseas aid organization may have to spend far more on transport and distribution than it does on service delivery, purely because of a project's location. Most donors can be persuaded to accept that this does not mean a project near a port is any more worthy of support than one that is deep inland. For a nonprofit such as The Samaritans the major cost is in administration—telephone bills, premises, and the like—because that organization is so effective at recruiting volunteers to provide its round-the-clock life-saving service.

The *Report of the Charity Commissioners for England and Wales 1989* is worth quoting on this subject.

> The cost of administering charities is a matter which arouses strong feelings and varied opinions. It is sometimes assumed that people who work for charity should do it for nothing, or, at most, for a pittance. Donors often express a wish that their money should go exclusively to the objects and beneficiaries, and not towards the cost of administration. Charities have on occasion colluded with such attitudes, advertising that no part of any contribution from the public will be spent on administration, and some claiming ever lower administrative costs in a competitive downward spiral. Such attitudes, however, imply that administration is a bad thing, and that the ideal administrative cost is nil. If carried into actual practice, such an attitude can only lead to badly administered charities and to inefficiency and abuse.
>
> Effective and efficient administration cannot be bought on the cheap. . . . The critical task is, therefore, not simply to reduce

administrative costs as an end in itself . . . it is to identify what level of administration is necessary in each case and to ensure that the strength of a lean and efficient administration is wholly devoted to the objects of the charity in question.

I'd go along with that. If that's what Britain's major government agency for the voluntary sector is saying on the subject, fundraisers have little excuse for failing individually to publicize their necessary costs of administration and doing so with pride.

Any Need, on Any Scale

Fundraising is remarkably diverse. Appeals range from campaigning to save the whales to caring for the terminally ill, from medical and scientific research to anti-vivisection and opposing exploitation of animals, from wheelchair access for disabled people to sports facilities for disadvantaged youth, from preservation of our heritage to the protection of abused children.

If there is any kind of need on any scale, however urgent, emotive or unlikely, it concerns fundraisers. Without doubt the products of our sector, both in inspiration and in actual good works, are infinitely more useful and valuable to the human condition than those of virtually any other business area.

I've seen enough of fundraising organizations to realize that whatever their shortcomings they are an indispensable force for good in our world. They provide a unique avenue through which the ordinary individual can take action to help put the world's troubles right.

Public preferences in giving are remarkably consistent. In the United States, charitable contributions are divided into eight subsectors: public and society; arts; culture and humanities; education; human services; environment and wildlife; international; and religion. According to *Giving USA 2001,* in 2000, giving to religion substantially exceeded the other subsectors, receiving $74.31 billion. International affairs, which received an estimated $2.71 billion in charitable giving in 2000, remains the subsector receiving the smallest amount in contributions.

When it comes to leaving legacies (bequests) public preferences are generally equally consistent. Money is given in the same areas as other charitable contributions.

Value for Money

Despite the important work nonprofit executives do, many members of the public seem to feel that this group (and that includes a lot of fundraisers) should not be well paid nor should they be seen to be well paid. This may be a consequence of the low esteem in which charity workers and fundraisers are held, and may also derive from the poor job we fundraisers have done of explaining ourselves, selling ourselves, and generally of encouraging the climate of respect we seem to think we deserve.

This penchant for holding back on salaries in the voluntary sector may be a spectacular false economy. (False economy is something to which nonprofits are remarkably prone.) It is not just a question of peanuts and monkeys. The overwhelming tragedy that limits the potential of the voluntary sector more, perhaps, than any other single thing today is the alarmingly high turnover of good-quality, well-motivated staff who join this sector for a few short years and then leave it, often to secure a better salary and living conditions the only way they can, by joining a commercial organization.

Fundraisers' salaries have improved in recent years but by common consent they still lag behind other commercial equivalents by as much as one-third or even a half. So more is spent in recruitment and training of staff, only to see people move on just as they become most effective. Is that the best way to help the poor and needy? It doesn't seem likely to me.

The director of appeals for one of Britain's largest charities recently visited the headquarters of one of America's most successful fundraising campaigns. He was greatly impressed by the high morale, the quality, and the dedication of the staff he met. The organization radiated an atmosphere of commitment and success.

"Do you pay your people market rate, or below?" he asked. "Oh no, neither." was the reply, "Our policy is to pay 10 percent *above* market rate because we need to employ the best. We work them hard, we make tough demands, but we get value for money." Not surprisingly, that organization raises more than $4 billion each year.

Nonprofits are often complex businesses with many levels of customers, many operational restrictions, some peculiar advantages, and a moral as well as a legal imperative to be properly run.

They need to attract the best, because second best will simply not do for this kind of work. Somehow we have failed the public if we have allowed them to think that cheeseparing will suffice when it comes to finding our management material.

Nonprofits shouldn't compromise just because of some vague notion that they can't afford the best. It's more likely that they can't afford *not* to have the best. But if they can get the best, whatever it may be, for free or at a reduced rate, then the nonprofit should pursue that gift with vigor, without any fear or inhibition. Nonprofits shouldn't be afraid of asking, but equally they shouldn't be afraid of paying.

Double Agents

Perhaps the public's attitude to and view of fundraisers would be improved if we had a clearer vision of ourselves and what we do. According to an article by David Boaz in *Fund Raising Management,* a monthly journal for fundraisers in America, there are three basic roles we might adopt as fundraisers, depending on the way we see ourselves. These are the chess player, the modern Robin Hood, and the double agent.

Chess players see themselves as part of a great game, shifting money from one part of the chessboard to the other, every move efficiently and meticulously calculated, each step one move closer to the goal—completion of the target—checkmate.

Robin Hood types, on the other hand, have a much more noble and righteous view of their calling. Their mission is to take money from the haves and redistribute it to the have-nots. They are keenly aware of the injustice that has made this task necessary. If they see that the nonprofit they serve has enough money to be considered a have itself, rather than a have-not, this usually causes them something of a dilemma.

The double agents serve two different groups equally faithfully, the donor and the cause. Their role as fundraiser makes them the perfect agent of both with no compromise involved. They serve as the enabler in between, bringing satisfaction to both sides when the job is well done. I prefer this analogy. It's quite important to have a vision of what we are doing—and I always wanted to be a double agent.

The Initiation

If I were in charge of training new fundraising recruits I'd make sure that each and every one of them spent at least their first two days working in the mail room, opening and answering the incoming mail. It's one of the best ways I know of finding out what—and who—an organization is for.

It is also certain to be two days of fascinating experience for the new trainees, during which the hopeful apprentices will see at first-hand the generosity, the interests, the concerns, and the criticisms of the people that power the cause—the donors. They will also learn a lot about the other contacts of the business—suppliers, other agencies, government, volunteers, and so on. Such an introduction should be mandatory in all fundraising organizations. And just like a driving test, it should be revisited every few years for a refresher course.

One of Guy Stringer's favorite management techniques is similar to my "two days in the mail room" exercise. It is equally easy to put into practice and also very effective. Guy calls it "management by walking about." Each day Guy would stroll around the departments of Oxfam, talking to people, seeing what was going on, being seen, accessible. Equally important is the concept of "management by walking outside"—visiting all points of public contact and meeting people outside the organization. No fundraiser should hide behind a desk. It's a simple point, but well worth remembering.

Action Points

▲ Take pride in your profession.

▲ Explain fundraising's purpose and peculiarities whenever you can and be prepared to defend it if you have to.

▲ Help promote fundraising as a worthwhile profession and a quality career area.

▲ Campaign vigorously for competitive salaries and better conditions for fundraisers.

▲ Don't feel inhibited about asking for donations for your cause or about paying for what you need.

▲ Think of your fundraising role as that of a double agent, providing a service to two different markets—the donor and the cause.

▲ Spend at least two days in the mail room. Go back there, every now and then, just to keep in touch.

▲ Practice "management by walking about" and "management by walking outside."

Donor Profile: Molly and Don Patterson

There are six different nonprofit stickers on the back window of Molly Patterson's car. Her husband, Don, hates them and would throw them all away, but he doesn't say anything because it is easier that way. In their family Don makes the big decisions, like whether globalization is preferable to trade regulation or what will happen when world demand for oil slumps, and Molly makes all the small decisions, like which programs to watch on television and what to do with their money.

Molly and Don are not rich but they do support several well-known nonprofits. Molly does all her Christmas shopping from about a dozen colorful charity gift catalogues she receives each June. She even acts as an agent on behalf of her bridge circle, rounding up all their orders and sending in one large payment, often with a donation thrown in for good measure. She doesn't need any more fridge purifiers or plastic potato racks but will probably buy some again this year, just to make up the order. Most of the nonprofits Molly deals with have earmarked her as a substantial donor and buyer and she's beginning to notice they're starting to treat her rather more personally, which she likes. When their weekly lottery ticket came up with a modest win last March, Molly sent more than half of it to an animal welfare charity that had recently sent her a harrowing letter about cruelty to cats. Don sulked over this for a week.

Although she treats him severely, Molly is really quite dependent on Don, particularly as her health isn't good. In her will she has named Don as her sole beneficiary, but if he should go first then she wants all her assets to be divided equally between her six favorite nonprofits. Unfortunately for her chosen charities, Don is in excellent health and he hates nonprofits.

Chapter Three

The Essence of Good Fundraising

*The object of a business is not to make money. The object is
to serve its customers. The result is to make money.*
JOHN FRASER-ROBINSON, *TOTAL QUALITY MARKETING*

In my early years as a fundraiser I had the good fortune to be
guided and advised by Harold Sumption, who was on the board of
the nonprofit I worked for. If all directors were as practically useful and encouraging as Harold was to me fundraisers' lives would
be much easier and probably there would be little need for this
book. Twenty years ago Harold Sumption co-founded the International Fund Raising Group (now The Resource Alliance). Many
years before that, his wise counsel was benefiting numerous good
causes including some of the largest and most effective nonprofits
in Britain. Harold was instinctively a relationship fundraiser and
from him I learned most of the fundamentals of fundraising.
There are no absolute rules in fundraising and slavish adherence
to formulas will win no donors, but I have found some basic principles both consistent and helpful in virtually every fundraising endeavor. In the year Harold died I was asked by the organization he
founded, The Resource Alliance, to prepare a training seminar for
new fundraisers outlining the main foundations. I collected and
expanded on the truisms Harold had taught me and called the resulting seminar "The Essence of Great Fundraising."

Here, in summary, are its key points. They are the basics of
fundraising that no amount of technology or development will
change:

The Essential Foundations of Fundraising

- *People give to people.* Not to organizations, mission statements, or strategies.
- *Fundraising is not about money.* It's about necessary work that urgently needs doing. Money is the means to an end.
- *Fundraisers need to be able to see things through their donors' eyes.* Or to put themselves in their donors' shoes.
- *Fundraisers need to really understand their donors.* If they are to understand you, you must first understand them.
- *It helps if you are a donor yourself.* No one should be a fundraiser without first being a donor.
- *Friend making comes before fundraising.* Fundraising is not selling. Fundraisers and donors are on the same side.
- *Fundraising is about needs as well as achievements.* People applaud achievement, but will give to meet a need.
- *Fundraisers need to learn how to harness the simple power of emotion.* Fundraising has to appeal first to the emotions. Logic can then reinforce the appeal.
- *Offer a clear, direct proposition people can relate to.* For example: "Make a blind man see. £10."
- *First open their hearts and minds.* Then you can open their wallets.
- *Don't just ask people to give.* Inspire them to give. Fundraising is the inspiration business.
- *Share your problems as well as your successes with your donors.* Honesty and openness are usually prized more highly than expert opinion and apparent infallibility.
- *You don't get if you don't ask.* Know whom to ask, how much to ask for, and when.
- *Present your organization's "brand" image clearly and consistently.* It'll pay you if your donors can readily distinguish your cause from all the others.
- *Successful fundraising involves storytelling.* Fundraisers have great stories to tell and need to tell them with pace and passion so as to inspire action.
- *Great fundraising is sharing.* Share your goals and encourage full involvement. When donors become truly involved in your campaign, great things happen.
- *Always try to turn complaints into support.* The most loyal donor

is the donor who has complained and received a satisfactory response.

- *The trustworthiness of fundraisers and their organization is a reason both to start and to continue support.* Trust appears to increase in importance as people get older.
- *Great fundraising requires imagination.* Too much fundraising looks like everything else.
- *Great fundraising is getting great results.* If your results are mediocre, your fundraising probably is too.
- *Always be honest, open, and truthful with your donors.* Donors will not forgive you if you are less than straight with them.
- *Avoid waste.* Donors hate waste.
- *Technique must never be allowed to obscure sincerity.* As all actors know, you can't fake sincerity.
- *Fundraisers have to learn to talk to their donors where they are.* That's not necessarily where the fundraiser might want them to be.
- *Fundraisers and donors have a relationship of shared conviction.* This is much more important than their shared commercial interest.
- *Great fundraising means being "fifteen minutes ahead."* To keep just a little bit ahead you have to learn to spot opportunities and take (careful) risks.
- *Fundraisers should learn the lessons of history and experience.* Anyone who wants to be an effective fundraiser needs first to do some homework.
- *Always say "thank you" properly and often.* It's also a good idea to be brilliant at welcoming new donors when they first contact your organization.

I could go on. Great fundraising also involves being appropriate, innovating, using your imagination, using new technology creatively, patience, and, of course, being modest and unassuming!

This list is universal but it is almost certainly not comprehensive and may exclude some important principles that relate particularly to your organization. Whatever your principles I advise you to capture them: write them down, communicate them to colleagues, board members, donors, and suppliers. And when you prepare a fundraising or marketing plan (see Chapter Eight) check how it measures up to your principles of fundraising.

Why Do People Give?

Ask a North American fundraiser this question and you'll get the instant answer that a donor's greatest desire is for recognition. The approval and respect of one's friends and colleagues would certainly figure high on many donors' unwritten list of motivations for giving. The following list sketches some other reasons—and you can probably think of quite a few more.

- Tax planning to escape, say, inheritance tax
- Ego, self-esteem (that's the kind of person I am!)
- The quest for immortality
- Emotional response
- Self-preservation (for things like cancer and heart research)
- Vested interest (in a school or sports facility)
- In memoriam
- Giving something back
- Identifying with the cause
- Religious heritage
- Social ambition
- Guilt
- Altruism
- Compassion
- Authority
- Value for money
- Because they were asked
- Because it feels good

Giving Is Good

Much has been written about the psychology of giving, and it certainly pays fundraisers to study their donors closely and find out where to place their emphasis so as to encourage and maximize giving. But in my experience people have widely varying reasons for supporting nonprofits. Few have a single motivation for making a donation; donors are generally impelled by a combination of feelings. Donors respond emotionally to the plight of starving people in Africa. Their religious beliefs tell them they should help, they feel some guilt because by comparison they have so much, they feel their gift is good value for money and will be well used, they feel good that they can make a gift and sometimes will tell others that they have done so. They may even feel that giving grants them an authority to be involved, some kind of ownership of the problem or need. They may feel all these things simultaneously and yet still not give until they are asked. People are like that.

I suspect that the underlying reasons for giving have changed little over the years and won't change much in the future. I'm just glad that people will keep on giving. Despite criticisms of paternalism and dependence, tendencies we must certainly guard against, I believe this would be a sorry world indeed if people were not to be encouraged to give when they can, and as much as they can, to help others in great need.

What Makes a Successful Fundraiser?

In the opening pages of *Born to Raise,* Jerold Panas details a seemingly endless list of qualities indispensable to a good fundraiser. These include boundless energy, zest for hard work, single-mindedness, intuition, patience, dogged determination, the ability to be unrelenting, unwavering, optimistic, good at listening, creative, aggressive, consistent, lucky, courageous, willing to take a risk. . . .

It all seems a little tiring. These attributes all apply and I am sure you could add to the list—but claiming all that runs the risk of seeming a little sanctimonious. I suspect other professions could create similar lists and I don't want to encourage a host of "what makes a good airline pilot" or "what makes a good bricklayer" copies. Perhaps there are equivalent handbooks out there, such as *Born to Be an Actuary* or *Born to Collect Taxes.*

Fundraisers also need to be salespeople. If the idea of selling is unappealing then perhaps fundraising is not for you—but it should be a very soft sell indeed. Certainly intuition and the ability to listen would come toward the top of my list of essential qualities for a relationship fundraiser. Intuition is vital: who is the right person to ask, who should head a particular campaign or event, when is the right time to ask, the right time to wait? I would also include persuasiveness, being a good talker, a good writer, well organized, and so on through a whole catalogue of skills and virtues. This is a demanding job. The list could go on and on. But the key word missing from the list, the word that describes the most important attribute of any fundraiser, is . . .

This is a cue for one of the few fundraising jokes I know. I might as well tell it now and get it over with.

A young apprentice fundraiser is being shown the ropes by an older and wiser hand. Eventually, his head spinning with new information, the young tyro asks the sage the $64,000 question, "What is the most important quality of a good fundraiser?" Without hesitation the sage replies, "The most important quality of a good fundraiser is commitment. Mere involvement is not enough. You must be committed."

This response puzzles the youth, who can't see that there is any difference between commitment and involvement. "The difference between commitment and involvement," explains the sage, "is the difference between bacon and eggs. In bacon and eggs the hen is involved, but the pig is committed."

I think this is very true. A capacity for commitment is our most important qualification. While we may need to have all those other admirable attributes, we must above all be genuinely committed to the work that we do. If not, donors will see through it instantly and nothing will more swiftly and more surely deter them from giving any further support. But when they see the fundraiser's commitment come shining through in every word and every action, that will do more to reinforce their faith and commitment to the cause than anything else. This potential for commitment is just one of the differences between fundraising and other marketing activities that makes fundraising so special.

It is a difference fundraisers ignore at their peril.

Action Points

▲ Remember there are no rules in fundraising. Very few things work for absolutely everybody. Use your judgment to decide what is best for you, then test before you proceed.

▲ Make a list of your principles of fundraising. Share that list with others if you can and keep it handy, for you never know when you'll need it.

▲ Study your donors carefully. Find out what they give, who they give to, and—most important—why they give to your organization.

▲ Consider the qualities that make a successful fundraiser and see if you can match up to them.

▲ Be proud of your commitment to your work. Let it show.

Donor Profile: Rose Lister

Every morning Rose Lister turns up at the door of the thrift shop just as the manager, Liz Medley, is turning the key. Rose is never late. She does nine to twelve, the morning shift, every Monday to Friday. She is never off sick, has never tried to change her time, and is so regular you could set your clock by her. Liz puts it all down to the fact that Rose enjoys her job so much.

Along with Rose, Liz usually finds a few other things on her doorstep. Several black plastic bags of old clothes, sometimes some carrier bags, occasionally some loose bundles, and, of course, always a bottle of milk for the tea. From time to time there is also a customer or two waiting in the morning cold to have first crack at the bargains.

Liz hardly has time to close the door behind her before Rose sets to work sorting out the new material. Anything that looks in nearly new condition is displayed and the rest goes to the dry cleaners or a less selective used clothing distributor, depending on what it is worth. Any books or bric-a-brac are separated and carefully put to one side. They are like gold dust. Then Rose goes round all the rails and dump bins, sorting, rehanging, tidying, making the place look presentable and appealing.

The display of the nonprofit's work is Rose's particular achievement. Most of the other volunteers are not all that interested but Rose has a flair for display. You can see it when she does the shop windows and her montage of posters has turned a dull pile of leaflets into an exhibition.

Rose is a model volunteer and Liz is proud of her. She is also a little puzzled. Most of the others come in to fill their time but Rose seems to enjoy an active life outside the shop. There's a mystery in Rose's life too.

When there was an emergency appeal in the shop recently Liz couldn't help but notice that rather than putting a few coins in the collecting box or saying she gave time and not money, as many of the others had, Rose had quietly filled out a donation form. Liz hadn't been nosy, of course, but she couldn't fail to see that Rose was writing in the number of her credit card on the form and her donation had been for no less than $200.

And then Rose just quietly sealed her envelope and went on with her work.

Chapter Four

The Vital Ingredients for Success

The future will be a future of more and more intensified relationships.
THEODORE LEVITT, *THE MARKETING IMAGINATION*

Relationship fundraising—a donor-based approach to the business of raising money—is a simple concept, and it's not new. Although relationship marketing is a currently fashionable term, it is something fundraisers have been practicing almost instinctively for years. Many fundraisers are already undertaking relationship fundraising and are well aware of what they are doing and why. But as fundraisers adopt ever more sophisticated marketing techniques—and as donors, the inevitable victims of unregulated growth, become more and more resistant to these techniques—relationship fundraising becomes increasingly important and increasingly likely to prove more profitable and sustaining in the long term.

What Is Relationship Fundraising?

Relationship fundraising is fundraising where people matter most, a sort of Fritz Schumacher approach to fundraising. (Schumacher invented the concept "small is beautiful" and through his book of that name started the appropriate technology movement, which concentrates on using only low-cost, available materials rather than expensive imported technology.) Small *is* beautiful. Relationship fundraising advocates a return to the intimacy of the one-to-one relationship between donor and cause but, thanks to the miracle of modern technology, it makes that intimacy possible on a national scale for thousands, even millions, of people at the same time.

Above all, relationship fundraising is not just about raising funds. In case you feel a definition would be useful, here is mine. The concept is too complex for one succinct sentence, but a brief paragraph can catch the essence.

> Relationship fundraising is an approach to the marketing of a cause that centers on the unique and special relationship between a nonprofit and each supporter. Its overriding consideration is to care for and develop that bond and to do nothing that might damage or jeopardize it. Every activity is therefore geared toward making sure donors know they are important, valued, and considered, which has the effect of maximizing funds per donor in the long term.

I'm not, incidentally, advocating conversion to relationship fundraising because I'm sentimental about fundraising. I'm advocating it because I speak to a lot of nonprofit supporters and this is the kind of thing they're telling me more and more. Donors generally are distressed to see blatant commercialism from the nonprofits they support. They often resent the repeated process of being asked for money with precious little offered in return. They dislike being written to by a marketing machine and regard the transparent techniques of direct mail and telephone appeals as little short of deliberate deception.

I hasten to say that what I am opposed to are the transparent techniques, not direct mail or even telephone fundraising per se. They are potentially efficient means to a very important end. Donors repeatedly reaffirm their willingness to hear from their chosen nonprofits but they express great concern about *how* that contact will be carried out.

Professional fundraisers of the current generation have been vigorously extending and upgrading their transactions with donors—their "customers." They should have been moving away from a transaction orientation and moving toward a relationship orientation.

People coming into the fundraising profession now are more likely to be trained in an appropriate professional discipline such as marketing or finance, but may perhaps be less well versed in some of the thinking behind the fundraiser's art. This new blood might prove to be of great value to our profession, but if it is unable to appreciate and adopt the theory and practice of relationship fundraising then it is more likely to do lasting damage instead. There are some signs that this has already happened in some communities where, rather like the used-car sales rep, the well-rehearsed and trained professional fundraiser is not always held in great esteem. For fundraisers, increased professionalism doesn't automatically equate to increased status. Unless it is carefully managed, the effect of increased professionalism can be quite the reverse.

The Benefits of a New Approach

I saw a wonderful example of relationship fundraising in my first few months with ActionAid—the first nonprofit I worked with—when we came to evaluate our fundraising efforts in schools. ActionAid is now one of the United Kingdom's top twenty nonprofits, an international movement fighting poverty and the denial of basic rights in more than thirty countries around the world, and is arguably the most successful at producing innovative development education materials for schools. Back when I joined it was much smaller, a relatively unknown and new organization and a very minor player among the many national nonprofits that had targeted schools—particularly primary schools—as a lucrative source of funds. We found considerable resistance from teachers to yet another fundraising effort. They were busy people who couldn't support every cause, and so, not surprisingly, little ActionAid lost out most of the time to the bigger boys.

So we changed our approach. Instead of directly asking schools to raise money, we became very indirect indeed. The ActionAid Education Service was started and our offer to schools was not that we would organize a sponsored walk or swim for them to raise funds, but that we would provide schools with a detailed illustrated lesson on Third World development that they could slot conveniently into their timetable. We had a model African hut children could build themselves in the classroom, and lots of tangible, tactile examples of how different life is for children of a similar age in Africa. There was no fundraising sales pitch at all.

The schoolchildren loved it. So did the teachers. It gave them time off—they could leave the lesson to the woman from ActionAid. We even provided hand-out notes. Soon the word spread and ActionAid didn't have as much difficulty getting into schools after that.

But then came the extraordinary motivation to give. Children who had learned so much about the lives of others of their age overseas began to ask how they could help ease some of the difficulties these other children faced. Teachers began to request details of ActionAid projects for which they and their pupils would be keen to raise funds. In a short while ActionAid was raising more money from schools than ever before.

This is a good illustration of a nonprofit thinking about its donors, putting itself in their shoes and allowing its donors' enthusiasm for the cause to be the driving force that will increase the fundraiser's "market share." It's also a good example of the "double agent" at work.

A Total Philosophy

Although I could cite many such examples to illustrate the point, relationship fundraising is not a series of isolated incidents, it is a total philosophy. It deals with every aspect of donor contact, channeling that contact toward building a specific lifelong relationship and ensuring that the relationship is as fruitful as possible for both parties. It involves notions that may seem unnecessary or even uneconomic, such as quickly and effectively answering every letter and acknowledging by return of post every donation, however small, sending a personal letter that any donor might wish to receive. The commercial logic in this is simply that small donors leave large bequests. Not all of them, of course. But the relationship fundraiser assumes they all will or at least treats them as if they will.

The relationship fundraiser also notes the warnings in negative, critical letters and responds appropriately and positively. People, even complainers, write because they care. American fundraiser Richard Felton calls it "criticism with love." If they didn't care they wouldn't bother. Worse by far is that they ignore you.

Lawrence Stroud, fundraiser at Botton Village in Yorkshire, the largest of the Camphill Village Trust communities for mentally handicapped adults, was surprised to see how many donations he received from people who had initially written to him to complain, most often because they had received unsolicited mailings from Botton. Lawrence's policy has always been to write a warm and friendly letter honestly explaining how the village had acquired their name and address and describing in some detail Botton's direct mail program and how it is benefiting the village. He also includes details of the U.K. Mailing Preference Service (which enables members of the public to "opt out" of receiving certain types of direct mail) and helpful advice on how to avoid receiving unwanted mail in future.

It doesn't surprise me that this approach has brought in donations. I am also not surprised that it has prompted many congratulations and comments such as "I wish other nonprofits reacted as you did." So a lot of useful relationships for Botton Village got off to a very good start—thanks to an efficient and effective complaints procedure oriented not to justifying the nonprofit but to serving the donor.

What Relationship Fundraising Can Do for You

In this noisy world, with so many competing promotional voices clamoring for our customers' attention, we all know that our communications have just seconds in which to make an impression. When our carefully prepared and costly appeal package is finally delivered to Mr. and Mrs. Donor, we know the odds are stacked against its even getting opened before it is consigned to the trash. Our attempts to inject compulsion to open and to make reading irresistible are, by and large, rather futile and pathetic. If our promotion is read, it is as often an indulgence as an inevitability. Our donors, always drawn from the more intelligent and rational sectors of society, are now among the most sophisticated and aware people on earth—most of them.

They know when they're being sold to and they may tolerate it but they don't like it. They know when they're being written to by a marketing machine and they don't like that either. They may respond to our most recent mailing just as they did the time before because of their commitment to the cause, but that doesn't mean they like the way they've been asked. And while we are congratulating ourselves on achieving a 20 percent response to our latest warm mailing, what about the 80 percent who didn't respond? What do they think of our aggressive fundraising approach and what, ultimately, will they do about it?

But consider what a difference there is when Mr. and Mrs. Donor receive a letter from a friend. We all know the apathy with which most people greet junk mail, but don't forget that millions of people still rush to the mailbox to see what the day's mail has brought. When they see it is from someone they like, they eagerly open that letter first to see what news and information their friend has sent.

Imagine how nice it would be if donors were to telephone you to inquire, rather worriedly, as to why they hadn't received the last issue of your newsletter and to say how much they looked forward to hearing from you. I know of one nonprofit whose donors are so involved and interested that it does get such calls and letters (although less so now that their publication schedules are a little more regular and reliable).

Fundraisers are most often writing to people who have already shown that they believe in the cause. And they are writing about subjects that are almost invariably interesting, dramatic, newsworthy, touching, exciting, and positive. So there is no excuse whatever for fundraisers to produce junk mail or junk anything.

There is every reason for fundraisers to strive to produce interesting, exciting, and relevant information which they can send to friends who share their interest and commitment. But that's just a start. Relationship fundraising can help you to find out all you need to know about your donors, it can help you to locate and recruit others like them, it can encourage your donors to introduce their friends, it can help you to write appropriately and personally to your donors as individuals, it can help you identify the right offer to make them. Relationship fundraising can show you how to avoid making mistakes in dealing with donors, how to avoid wasting money and how to make your promotion pay, how to increase your donors' annual giving and extend their "life" as donors, how to manage your staff and present your organization, how to approach your marketing strategy, how to make your donor your friend, how to increase the value of your donors and how to en-sure a gigantic leap in your income from bequests (also known as legacies).

It can also be very satisfying and rewarding.

Welcome as a Letter from a Friend

Relationship fundraisers gear their offers to what their donors want to buy, not what they (the fundraisers, that is) want to sell. They recognize that people are different from each other, and also vary in their own response to different appeals over time. As we all know, donors frequently don't give to some appeals, which seems to me to provide an interesting answer to the apparently endless question of how many letters to send. If you listen to your donors, some would receive just one appeal each year, some as many as ten or twelve, and most of the others would receive some number in between.

It depends on the donor. Of course, if you give donors the choice they may choose to receive your appeals less often than you would wish them to. This is where the relationship fundraiser has to get clever; see Chapter Ten, which describes in detail how to communicate with your donors. Fundraisers tend to think auto-matically of their communications with donors as "appeals." We talk of "mailings" and "packs." I'm as guilty as the next person, but really we should think in terms of *letters* instead—and we shouldn't always expect or ask for a response.

Because each donor is different the relationship fundraiser is also aware that it makes little sense to send the same mailing pack-age with the same offer, letter, or leaflet to every donor. While the practical difficulties are obvious, technological change is provid-ing fundraisers with the means to do something about this. Maga-zines are now being published where you can choose the editorial mix that most interests you. Who knows? We may yet be able to choose our own personal daily newspaper with the foreign cover-age of the *Observer,* the sport section of the *Guardian,* the arts re-views of the *New York Times,* the financial analysis of the *Wall Street Journal,* the *Times* (of London) crossword, and a few juicy sections from a favorite tabloid, if we feel so inclined. It would make for happier readers and many more newspaper sales.

As my experience has grown I have become increasingly convinced that developing a relationship with donors is the key to success in fundraising. Our business is donor development and that is only possible through the formation of a tangible relationship. As donors, by and large, are honest and intelligent people it is a process that can only be done with honesty and intelligence. You may be able to pull the wool over the eyes of some of your donors for a while, but you can't do it in the long term—and successful relationships are based on trust and confidence, both long-term concepts.

Neglecting the relationship can be expensive too. I once worked with a national nonprofit that, as policy, didn't send any acknowledgment to donors giving less than £5 and sent a preprinted receipt to those giving between £5 and £10. The purpose was to discourage small donors, who probably went to other nonprofits and left their bequests to them.

Getting Through Hard Times

As I write this, most of the world's economies appear to be heading toward a rather deep recession. Nonprofits are not immune from recession's harrowing effects. Like every other business, nonprofits don't need sympathy in difficult times, they need ingenuity and imagination to market their way out of difficulties. But they also need the underlying strength of a sound business base, and that strength in times of recession can only come from a wide spread of well-established and well-maintained relationships. When times are hard, relationship fundraising is even more important than usual.

Avoiding the Pitfalls of Success

However, it makes sense to proceed with care. It might prove unwise for some organizations to attempt to rush the theory of relationship fundraising into practice overnight. There is a cost, even if it is an initial cost that is later repaid several times over, that is inevitably associated with the introduction of relationship fundraising.

Relationship fundraising may be particularly prone to a rather common dilemma in fundraising, where the organization literally becomes a victim of its own success. Better materials, better communications, more care and attention all result in more satisfied customers—which leads to greater take-up of services and increased costs in all service functions. So it is important to plan and to introduce these costs in a manageable way. And it is equally important to relate these costs to benefits.

The Nine Keys to Building a Relationship

The process of building and sustaining lasting and mutually beneficial relationships with hundreds, even thousands, of individual donors has a number of cornerstones. Inevitably, when written down, these seem trite and obvious—but they are worth listing here. Any fundraiser who can put hand on heart and say "I do all this" is not doing too badly.

• *Be honest.* If any business area should be honest, it is fundraising. The public expects fundraisers to be honest. Those that don't view fundraisers as inherently honest and trustworthy certainly don't give, so it pays to be seen to be honest.

It also pays to *be* honest. A former colleague of mine once ran the trading arm of Britain's biggest child care nonprofit. While there he offered his customers a product: a machine that plays chess with you. It sold well, but after a while, my colleague began to get a large number of returns—25 percent as opposed to the usual 5 percent. Puzzled, he conducted some basic telephone research. He found that the machines worked all right; they just weren't sufficiently advanced.

So he wrote back to all the customers who had complained, offering them a full refund. Then he went on to ask if they might want to buy a machine that was much more advanced but cost three times as much. Twenty-five percent bought the new machine. A relationship was established because the nonprofit behaved honorably. As a result it made more money. It pays to be honest.

• *Be sincere and let your commitment show.* Donors are donors because they care enough to take action and support your cause. Let them see that you care too and that that is why you're there as well. When this happens, immediately you and they are on the same side, with a common concern and aim. Your commitment will then encourage them to go even further for the cause.

• *Be prompt.* Reply quickly and efficiently to any request. Answer letters the next day, or sooner if possible. If the issue is important, telephone the donor and explain what action you are going to take. If it will take time to provide a full answer, write or telephone the donor quickly to say that an answer is being prepared and let them know when to expect it. Prompt response shows you take your donor's concerns seriously.

• *Be regular.* Regular planned communication keeps donors in touch, informed, and involved. If you are irregular in your communications be aware that other fundraisers are not so lax. They also have access to your donors, so they'll be in touch when you are not.

• *Be interesting and memorable.* By their very nature nonprofits have access to compelling material. Use it to the full; present it well. Fundraising is all about telling stories. Make all your material stand out for its interesting content, style, and presentation. And its unforgettable visuals.

• *Be involving.* Don't allow donors to take a passive role. Ask for their opinions, contributions, and even complaints. Encourage feedback in any way you can. Invite them to events, offer visits to projects. Make the dialogue as two-way as you possibly can.

• *Be cheerful and helpful.* Advertise your helpfulness. Never let donors feel that asking is a trouble. That's what you are there for— to help them. Teach customer care to all your colleagues. I have never forgotten a simple piece of advice from the days when I sold advertising space over the telephone—smile and dial. When you smile on the phone, what you are saying sounds much better at the other end. It really works. Try it. (Tell your colleagues first, otherwise they'll think you've gone mad.)

• *Be faithful.* Always stick to your promises. Let donors see that you are honorable and trustworthy. Stand by your organization's mission and don't compromise what it stands for.

• *Be cost-effective.* Donors expect and appreciate good stewardship of their gifts but are generally well aware of the potential for false economies, which they dislike as much as conspicuous waste. Be open and informative, explain your reasons for financial decisions and show your donors that their money is in good hands.

Of course, this list is not exhaustive. But if you can inject these key elements into your relationship with donors they will not only be encouraged enough to continue their support, they will derive increased satisfaction from their giving and will even go out and tell their friends, encouraging them to do the same. And that, I believe, is what fundraising is all about.

Variations of Donor Geometry

Three variations of donor geometry—the donor pyramid, the donor trapezoid, and the donor wedge—classify donors in different ways.

The Donor Pyramid

This familiar old triangle, the donor pyramid shown in Figure 4.1, crops up again and again wherever fundraisers congregate. It is useful as a simple way of illustrating the traditional idea of the donor life cycle, the not-quite-universal fact that a donor's involvement starts with a general query and then moves or is led through various stages of ever-increasing involvement to the ultimate gift—a bequest. This paradigm is inevitably limited, as all simplifications are, but it is also potentially misleading.

The pyramid represents the approximate numerical values of a nonprofit's supporters at their different stages and levels of involvement. So immediately outside the pyramid is what might be considered the untouched potential, or the entirely indifferent: the general public. The lowest rung of the pyramid, not that pyramids have rungs, is the general inquirer, the person who has been in contact but not yet given. Above this level is the first-time giver or responder, next is the casual giver, then comes the committed donor or regular giver, followed by the big gift donor and, ultimately, those rare few who leave a bequest. These are broad divisions, of course, and the assumption is that as fundraisers do their job and upgrade supporters through each stage then the numbers involved will become sharply fewer until from the initial broad base we are ultimately talking to very few people indeed.

This, I think, is at best a negative view. Why should fundraisers accept that so many supporters will be lost along the way? Would it not be better if this pyramid were considered as a ladder, a ladder of involvement? You can move people more easily up a ladder than up a pyramid—and a ladder *has* got rungs.

Figure 4.1. Donor Pyramid.

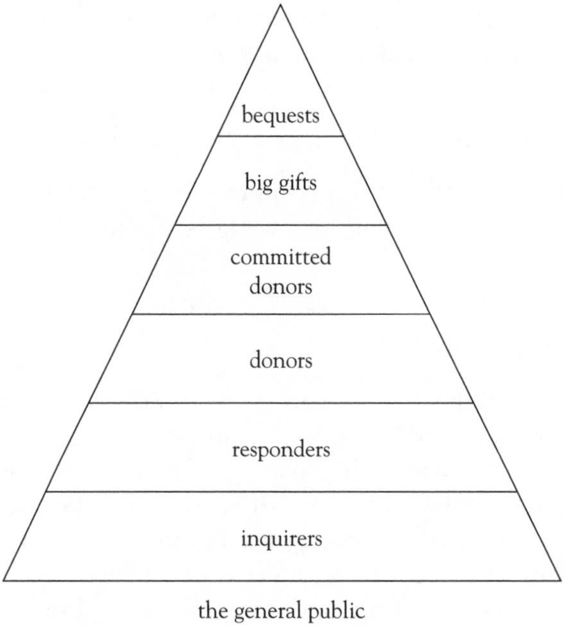

the general public

Of course, it would be foolish to delude ourselves that we won't lose people along the way as we attempt to gently upgrade our supporters, and often we will lose them for quite good reasons. Nevertheless I feel that the donor pyramid is not quite complete as a model and we should add to it two more shapes, a trapezoid and a wedge.

The Donor Trapezoid

The donor trapezoid (Figure 4.2) has the same bands and levels as the donor pyramid but is steeper at the sides and flat at the top. Looked at another way it might be seen as a roadway, disappearing in the distance toward the horizon. However, it assumes that far fewer people will drop out and—the ultimate reward for the relationship fundraiser—a lot more people will make it to the top band and leave a bequest.

These figures are mere scribbles, of course, just a convenient way of illustrating an abstract theory. But think of the implications

Figure 4.2. Donor Trapezoid.

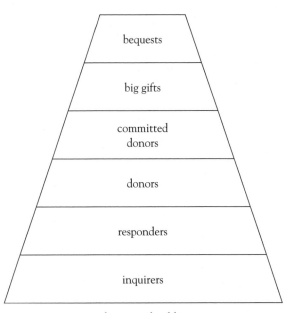

the general public

for your fundraising income if you were to work a donor trapezoid rather than a donor pyramid. The financial difference in the long term is immense, so the donor trapezoid is a simplified way of illustrating what relationship fundraising is all about.

The Donor Wedge

This intriguing shape, simply the donor pyramid turned upside down, results from looking at supporters not in terms of numbers but in terms of their combined financial value (Figure 4.3). The bands are the same and in the same vertical order. So we see that the rewards of donor development are that each individual gives vastly more in the course of moving to higher levels of support. There may be numerically many fewer people who leave bequests, but they still tend to give the largest amount of money. If the donor trapezoid is approached in the same way the top line would be very long indeed and the inverted triangle, or wedge, would have rather a flat point. (Put another way, it is a small but significant point.)

Figure 4.3. Donor Wedge.

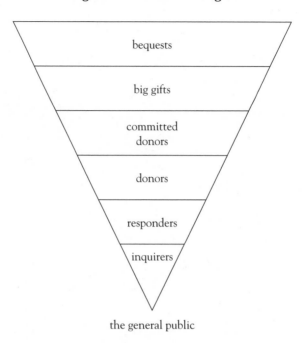

the general public

We would be foolish to imagine that donors will readily and consistently conform to such simplifications of their behavior, however convenient it would be for us if they did. Irritating though it may be, some donors will persist in moving straight to leaving us a bequest after their initial donation without first having served their time as regular, committed, and major donors. (I can hear legions of fundraisers exclaiming, "How dare they!" as I write.)

Setting Up and Maintaining a Relationship Database

In practice, the one essential key to effective relationship fundraising is not an abstract principle, it is a tangible piece of technology—and it is vital to the success of any strategy for relationship fundraising. It's what I refer to as a *relationship database*. This is the core of relationship fundraising, and without it true individual marketing is impossible. With a relationship database fundraisers can return to the intimacy and individuality of the corner shop. A database is simply a list of individuals. It can be very small and contained in a card index file. More likely it will be computerized and quite sophisticated, if not horrendously complex.

But computerized customer lists have come a long, long way in recent years and the technology now exists to make our retention, selection, and application of customer information very sophisticated indeed. The miracle of the modern database is that it enables the fundraiser to talk individually to thousands, even tens of thousands of donors, sending unique messages to every one, all at the same time.

For the non-computer specialist, the difficulty is in finding an affordable system that is easy to operate and does exactly what you want. There is a bewildering choice. To keep proper records of your donors you need to do six things:

- Choose an adequate system with multiple fields of information.
- Input data carefully.
- Undertake continual, thorough cleaning.
- Update your records continuously with all donor transactions.
- Add all new information gleaned from correspondence, mailing returns, research, the telephone, or any other source.
- Use your data conscientiously and responsibly, abiding by whatever rules and standards might apply in your country for data protection.

The fundamental core of relationship fundraising is the creative use of your database. It is the keystone. With an effective relationship database and a commitment to the theory of relationship fundraising, everything else will fall into place.

The fact that it is a list or is computerized is almost irrelevant. What matters is what it enables you to do—keep an individual track of *all* your communications with *all* your donors. But your data, in itself, will always be the most costly part of your database and should always be treated as the valuable asset that it is.

Making Sense of the Modern Database

I'm one of those people (there are lots of us) who can drive a car reasonably well but have no idea of nor interest in what goes on under the hood. I find this mechanical and technical illiteracy shows up in an increasing number of areas of life, but it's not necessarily a problem, for, when in need, I tend to turn to others who are not so handicapped. But it is a restriction that has to be recognized. So at this point when describing donor databases my lack of technical aptitude and limited attention span causes me to turn to an expert. Someone who does understand fundraising and how database systems work and should work is computer expert John Rodd, who commutes between London and Toronto, working for a wide range of fundraising organizations. His help in preparing the following paragraphs is gratefully acknowledged. (In North America John works with Stephen Thomas Associates in Toronto. He can be reached via that organization's Web site, http://www.stephenthomas.ca/.)

A donor database is a required asset for any nonprofit organization that wants to make long-term profitable revenue. It is only a flow of repeat gifts, leading, we hope, to many years of consistent giving, that provides profitable nonprofit revenue. Unfortunately, there is no such thing as a "relationship database"—in the first edition of this book I simply made that term up! What we have to do is to infer or deduce the relationship we have with donors from data held in the database—particularly gift data. Then we use the database as the vehicle from which to launch communications to donors that are based on our relationship with them and their stage in the donor life cycle.

There is one exception to this and that is where "who knows whom" relationships can be enshrined in the database. In major gift fundraising and capital appeals it is best practice to set up linked groups of wealthy or influential people and to plot their relationship one to another. Some systems actually allow you to join donor or prospect records and show the nature of the relationship onscreen and in a printed report.

Although "relationship databases" don't exist, you'll often hear of *relational databases*—which are standard fare in computerized data management. You need to refer to technology specialists like John to get the full picture, but essentially data in complex donor systems is created in two-dimensional tables, a bit like a spreadsheet, linked by the donor's ID and constituent numbers. Thus a name table is linked to an address table, to a gifts table, to a communications table and so on, and this is how relational database management systems (called RDBMSs for short) are built. Why? I hear you ask. Because it allows the ever-changing complexity of business needs to be accommodated inside this linked-table structure, and allows for change and growth in a system.

What we are seeking is true one-to-one marketing, where no matter how many thousands of donors we have, we can create at least the illusion of intimacy and individuality that characterized the best marketing of the corner shop from pretechnology days, the "How are you today, Mrs. Brown—as it's Wednesday I'm guessing that it's time for your weekly order of soy, ginseng, and dog treats."

In practice true one-to-one marketing is unlikely to be feasible, and what we will do instead is engage in segmented communications, that is, to groups of donors who all share common characteristics— called *cohorts* in the United States or Canada. For example, they may be at the beginning of their donor relationship, and so will receive induction and welcoming materials that are personalized only to the extent of being individualized at the name, address, and salutation level. Very loyal donors may get a "special" to acknowledge their contributions. Conspicuous volunteers may receive a "recognition" piece.

However, true one-to-one marketing can take place at the high end, where donors either have given large gifts or have the potential so to do. Here it makes good business sense to individualize the whole process, especially where six- or seven-figure sums are involved. Paradoxically, for high-value donors communications generally take place outside the donor database, as interchanges become more detailed and pass beyond letters to face-to-face meetings and negotiations, although the best databases can record all these too.

Database Systems

Donor databases have to be computerized and the technology can seem at first overwhelmingly complex. In truth it is not, as long as you remember some principles that are common to all systems worldwide:

- The basic, absolute minimum data structure will always consist of the donor's name and address linked to gifts and communications; this will be replicated for the hundreds or thousands of donors on the database.

- The database presents controlled "views" of the data to screens, which the software lays out in an easy-to-understand format.
- These views will be different according to the work you do in your nonprofit: a data entry person will need different screens from the ones management people use, for example.

Database Costs

Donor databases are a software market of their own, what is called a *vertical market* because nonprofits alone use the systems that are now sold all over the world as fundraising packages. The cost of packages varies widely but generally the capital cost to acquire one is not cheap. It is important to look at the cost of a package versus the benefits that it brings, because the system, in fact, does a great deal of work and nonprofit systems are among the most complex in the world, strange as that may seem.

When looking at system costs remember that a fundraising system has to handle the following chores:

- Maintain the donor's history across donations, tax-efficient giving schemes (most countries have them), gift receipts, and allocation of income to projects, funds, or accounts
- Provide a watertight audit trail of gifts
- Maintain data on the increasing number of monthly giving schemes that provide thousands of transactions that have to be reconciled with donors' promises or pledges
- Keep biographical and personal information (legitimately obtained) on donors
- Provide personalization and individualization functions for letters and correspondence
- Provide specialist functions for trust and foundation work, corporate fundraising, volunteering, payroll giving, bequests, other forms of planned giving, and support for regional and local fundraisers across your territory
- Do the segmentation and marketing, reporting on campaigns, ad hoc analysis, and so on

- And, as we advance into the Internet age, support e-mail fundraising and provide a Web "face" to the outside world for donors to access as they want

This requires a lot of careful software building and the investment by software companies is considerable. As a result the systems sold as fundraising packages also do most of your fund processing—and most of the marketing, too. They are complex and require considerable training and support. This is why they are often costly.

However, it is possible (but not within the scope of this book) to calculate costs and benefits for your fundraising database system and show unequivocally that the database is the engine that drives long-term donor revenues. Whatever you do, don't shortchange the donor database. Always strive for effective database functions and apportion budgets fairly against print, postage, creative fees, fulfillment, staff, and infrastructure costs.

Renting Software

Note also that buying the package is not the only way to get software. You can rent software using the traditional bureau (or, to give it its modern appellation, outsourcing firm). And the bureau has a new lease of life due to the explosive growth of the Internet: the ASP or Application Service Provider. The ASP is old wine in new bottles. As with a traditional bureau, you access the software via a phone line—digital for best results—using all the facilities for cheap communal working that the Internet supports. This way of getting software is new to the sector at the time of writing but is predicted to grow. There is no time or space to go further into this but you can find debates and discussions on ASPs in the nonprofit magazines and the on-line forums for technology that have sprung up in most countries.

A final word of warning. *Do not* try to build your own donor database system. History records that those nonprofits that do try to build and maintain software, often in the mistaken belief that they can, and quite easily—usually come to grief and are left looking at failed projects, black holes that suck in money and divert the focus from fundraising.

Data Management

Databases have to be managed carefully if they are to work, and it is essential that data quality is maintained by applying the following principles of good practice:

- Data quality controlled from outside the software: this means a data supervisor either within the nonprofit or in any fulfillment house that you might use. These people are the gatekeepers of the database and are crucial to quality control.
- Careful data entry, quality controlled from within the software by the use of validation tables (so that only valid entries of, say, personal titles or appeal source codes can be entered) and for the automatic recognition of duplicates.
- Background data cleaning, particularly on addresses. Post offices in most countries now supply address and postal or Zip code software that can be integrated with the database, where it sits in the background making sure that addresses are consistent.

If you believe in relationship fundraising you will carefully read what donors write to you, about their changes of address, preferences for communication ("Only mail to me at Christmas!"—"I am retired and can't afford to give as much"), and other matters that show that you are listening and that you care about and respect their needs. You can enshrine their preferences using fields or codes in the database, which most vendors provide for the purpose. And of course, you must abide by your country's data protection or data privacy legislation at all times.

Action Points

▲ Practice relationship fundraising as a total philosophy, not as a series of isolated actions.

▲ Take care when putting the theory into practice not to try to do too much too soon. Remember the initial and ongoing cost of relationship fundraising.

▲ Devise a policy for responding to complaints. Include an explanation of what you are doing and why. Offer practical help where possible.

▲ Acknowledge every gift, however small.

▲ Carefully assess *every* communication with your donors. Make sure it is interesting, relevant, and timely. Erase any possibility of junk mail from your organization.

▲ Set up a donor-oriented customer service function.

▲ Give your donors the choice—let them tell you how they want to be communicated with.

▲ Smile and dial.

▲ Follow the nine key steps to relationship building: be honest, sincere, prompt, regular, interesting, involving, helpful, faithful, and cost-effective—and show you are!

▲ Handle data with care because your ability to communicate accurately depends on it. Treat it as one of your organization's most valuable assets.

▲ Invest wisely and sufficiently in database hardware and software, but first seek the advice of a database specialist who knows and understands fundraising.

Donor Profile: Richard West

Richard West runs a high-class restaurant in a small country town. He lives well in a large house with extensive grounds, dresses very sharply, and drives a big, expensive car. By anybody's standards, Richard West appears to be a success. In part the wherewithal for his expensive lifestyle comes from the profits of his restaurant, and that's what he likes people to believe. But the truth is that the business is not going as well as it originally did, and for most of the past ten years, Richard has, out of necessity, had to fall back on his own resources. Luckily for him he has a substantial capital reserve, inherited from his mother. The interest on this alone is more than enough to provide for all his and his family's needs.

Richard West's wife, Lisa, also likes the high life and doesn't mind spending to keep up appearances. Their children are not yet grown and so haven't developed their own expensive tastes; however, their schooling more than makes up for that. One way and another, large amounts of money leave the West household on an almost daily basis, but it was ever thus, and Richard keeps fairly close track of each individual's expenditure. He doesn't take his wealth for granted, but he has grown up with it and accepts it.

The restaurant keeps Richard busy. With that, the family, and his passion for sailing, he has little time for much else. He doesn't join clubs or serve on committees. He does have a social conscience, however. If you asked him, he could list five or six nonprofits that he currently supports, but if you asked those nonprofits, only one could find him anywhere on its database. He is an enthusiastic member of at least one leading animal welfare organization, whose annual membership fee of $15 he never has to think about because his bank pays it automatically by standing order.

Last year, a close friend approached him on behalf of a building appeal for a new hospice organized by one of the local churches. Richard has no connections with any church, but the appeal sounded urgent and worthwhile. Richard's friend was asking for a large amount of money, so Richard gave him $20,000. He could easily have given more.

Chapter Five

Understanding Your Donors

*While the individual man is an absolute puzzle, in
aggregate he becomes a mathematical certainty.*
SHERLOCK HOLMES, IN *THE SIGN OF FOUR* BY
SIR ARTHUR CONAN DOYLE

Relationship fundraising starts with finding out what your donors
want and need and then supplying it to them as completely as possible, in the most cost-effective way. So detailed research into who
your donors are and what they think and feel is essential.

Basic Research

Research is one of fundraising's most underused tools. Those nonprofits who have done it have usually struggled to afford it and
have often underinvested. Yet some basic research can cost little or
nothing to carry out. When fundraisers find out what research can
do for them and how it can help increase their income, then they
quickly reassess its importance. Many nonprofits now are setting
aside sufficient resources to carry out research properly and continuously.

It's obvious good sense, of course. With good research information you can confirm your hunches, track shifts in your important markets, find out which offers and styles of presentation have
most appeal, what people think of your publications, whether your
priorities are out of step with your donors', and a whole range of
other vital things. The more you know about your supporters, the
more accurately you can structure your relationship fundraising.
Here are some of the things you need to know:

- Why have people become your supporters?
- What do they like about what you do and what do they dislike?
- Are your instincts and gut feelings borne out?
- What should you be doing to improve your relationships and thereby encourage donors to support you more?
- What is their basic lifestyle and demographic information (their individual characteristics)?
- Is there a geographical difference, age difference, or any other relevant split?
- Who else do they support and why?
- How do they compare what you do with those other nonprofits?
- Do longer-established supporters view you in the same way as new recruits?
- What is your supporters' attitude to bequests?
- Why do some inquirers never become donors?
- What (in detail) do your current supporters and potential supporters think of your magazine, or your press ads, or your mailings?
- What does the general public think of you, or your press ads, or your mailings?

And so on. You could, of course, do some of the most basic research in-house among your existing records.

Here's another question you need to answer: what percentage of your warm list actually *gives* each year? The answer to this and similar questions can only be found from your own information. Very few nonprofits know the answer. It can vary from 5 percent to 75 percent. This also highlights another possible area of confusion. Never assume that database means the same thing as donor base. They can be quite different.

How to Do Research

Research is a continuous process. It should be planned and budgeted for on an annual basis so you can not only find out about your donors but can track changes in attitudes and perceptions over the years. The characteristics of your supporters may not shift, but if your relationship fundraising materials (see Chapter Ten) are doing their job you should be able to see changes in how they view your organization and its work.

For the purposes of this book, most of what follows is concerned with market research among individual private donors. (Academic and generic research are covered in the next chapter.) Fundraisers are also becoming increasingly sophisticated at researching other groups such as company directors, shareholders, and various types of larger donors. An increasingly important aspect of this work is the tracing of networks. Specialist firms in prospect research can now be employed who will tell you all you need to know about a given donor—club or institution memberships, circles of friends, co-directors, or other associates, even fellow alumni.

There are six common methods of research on individual donors:

1. *Postal questionnaires:* A printed questionnaire is sent to a random, numerically valid segment of the list you want to research.
2. *Telephone research:* A random selection of your target group is talked through a questionnaire over the phone.
3. *Personal interviews:* You or your representatives hold formal meetings with donors, one to one.
4. *Focus groups:* A gathering of donors and potential donors is invited to discuss your organization, usually on neutral territory or in the donor's home and moderated by a trained researcher.
5. *Omnibus surveys:* Your question is included with a whole range of unconnected issues in a questionnaire addressed to a standard sample of society.
6. *Meeting supporters:* You simply go out and talk to people face to face, for free.

These research methods are listed in Table 5.1, with my views of their advantages and disadvantages. The last method is the least expensive and most obvious—yet many fundraisers don't take advantage of its splendid simplicity and so lose out. They forget that continually meeting supporters, individually and in groups, is an indispensable fundraising aid. (It should be compulsory for chief executives and board members.)

Table 5.1. Donor Research Methods.

Method	Advantages	Disadvantages
Postal questionnaire	Low cost	Needs professional analysis
	You can do it yourself (very simple questionnaires only)	Questions might be leading if not professionally prepared
	Specific questions	Only most active supporters respond
	Quantitative	
	Not obtrusive	Low response levels compared to some other methods
Telephone research	Accurate cross-section	Needs professionals
	Immediate response	Costly to find phone numbers
	Very few refusals	
	Qualitative and quantitative	Danger of deviation
	A chance to listen	Intrusive
Personal interview	Qualitative and quantitative	Requires careful preparation
	Very detailed	High cost
	Reliability can be immediately assessed	Needs professional interviewers
	No leading questions	Attracts activists
Focus groups (group interviews)	Honesty	High cost
	You can join in and listen	Needs professional interviewers
	Qualitative	Attracts activists
	Reliability can be immediately assessed	Strong may intimidate the weak
Omnibus surveys	Inexpensive	Interviewer may not have any experience of nonprofit matters
	Representative of population	
	Quick	Lacks in-depth advantage
	General public only	
Regularly meeting supporters	Cheap	None
	Rewarding	

Postal Questionnaires

Of the others, my favorite is the oft-maligned postal questionnaire. It may not be 100 percent reliable in the mathematical sense, but if you accept its shortcomings it will always tell you a lot and has the advantages of being relatively inexpensive and easy to organize. Open-ended questions are of most value—but don't include too many as response will be reduced if the questionnaire is too long or arduous to complete. If you can sit down one evening with a pile of around a hundred completed questionnaires and just flip through, I guarantee that you will have a fascinating evening, at the end of which you'll know what interests and concerns your supporters. You'll have created a mental picture of them and it will be of great value to you.

It is worth writing down this mental picture. If you have segmented your list or if the age range of returned questionnaires is noticeable you may be able to create more than one picture of different parts of your list.

The covering letter that introduces and explains the questionnaire is vital, as is properly thanking participants and if possible reassuring them that in due course they will learn the results of the survey. Don't keep research results to yourself. Share them with donors and invite comment. It will almost always do you good.

Nonprofits can expect much higher returns from postal questionnaires than companies experience when researching customers by mail. Nevertheless, you want to get as high a percentage of completed questionnaires as possible, so it is often worth sending a reminder three or four weeks later. In my experience this can increase response by up to 50 percent.

Once you have your picture of your typical donor, don't file it away with last year's questionnaires. Circulate it within your organization and get everyone to agree to it. Refer to it when defining the objectives of a new publication. Use it when you are briefing writers and designers when you prepare any new promotion. Use it for list and media selection. Segment your list so you can write to the different groupings (see Chapter Eight). But don't forget you are communicating with individuals—although this picture will help you focus your message it is still a composite and may not exactly correspond to anyone on your list.

Confidentiality

Research surveys usually promise absolute confidentiality and of course this encourages a larger response. However, you have to be careful that the promise of confidentiality does not unnecessarily restrict your subsequent use of valuable data. It is worth explaining in the covering letter as many of the potential uses of this data as possible and making clear that, for example, the information in certain sections of the questionnaire will be used to help you update your records. If you intend to add any of the information gathered via research to your donor's individual file on your database then you must say so clearly on the questionnaire and the accompanying letter.

Focus Groups

Focus groups, also known as group discussions, are worth special consideration because they give you qualitative analysis—a chance to dig below the figures to find out in detail what people really think. Focus groups have to be drawn from a representative sample or a specific segment of your list and the research sessions must be conducted by an independent and professional researcher. They can be quite expensive, but they are also great fun and can be very instructive.

Be sure to participate in at least one of the groups. Go as part of the research team so that there is no possibility of inhibiting donors from talking honestly in front of someone from the nonprofit they support, and be careful not to influence responses, however strongly you feel about what you are hearing. The possible benefits from this exercise are enormous and I do urge you to try it. It gives you the chance to find out what turns your donors on and what switches them off.

With both group and telephone interviews it is recommended, if possible, that you send an advance letter alerting potential responders to the research and the reasons for it. This is particularly important for elderly donors who may be less familiar with research and may not like answering the phone or may be nervous about opening the door. It may also make sense to check your findings from a small number of focus groups with wider quantitative research, such as a questionnaire.

Telephone Research

I think research is one of the best and most inoffensive uses of the telephone, but some people do find it intrusive. Everybody hates telemarketing, of course (except those fundraisers who have tried it—see Chapter Eight).

The fact is, more people by far respond to the telephone than to mailed communications. It is the most economical form of direct personal contact, with all the obvious benefits that brings. Fundraisers should use the telephone far more than they do (it's also invaluable for lobbying—see Chapter Nine) and also, perhaps, far better than they do.

As with telefundraising, a simple script has to be prepared to introduce the call and explain the questionnaire and its purpose. This is a crucial opportunity to strengthen donor relationships but of course is just as easily an opportunity to offend. The questions must be prepared professionally so as not to lead or encourage an unrepresentative response, and the interviewer should be professionally trained, entirely competent and relaxed. Telephone research is costly and must be carried out efficiently within time restraints, but a good relationship fundraiser will take this opportunity to listen, to let donors talk about the subjects that interest them, and will never exert pressure to move on or close the conversation.

The Hidden Flaw and Other Perils

For fundraisers any kind of research has one important drawback—the process of giving research information is entirely different from the process involved in giving money to a cause. Answers to research questions are guided by logical thought, reasoned responses to a series of reasonable questions. This is what people think they will feel or think they will do in given situations. But as we all know, the true motivation of a charitable gift is very often not logical at all. Responses are often emotional, spontaneous, and sometimes even irrational. No amount of research will pick that up. This is one reason why I place great emphasis on a fundraiser's gut feelings—instincts often overruled by marketers in favor of more concrete, but sometimes suspect, research data.

This hidden flaw is unfortunate, but it doesn't invalidate research for fundraisers—far from it. It simply has to be borne in mind, and research findings have to be viewed against this background. Major misunderstandings have occurred when people who should have known better have misled the public and nonprofits themselves by quoting research figures as absolute fact while ignoring the hidden flaw. Research is a useful guide, not a rigid path.

Beware of Nice People

In addition to the hidden flaw, you also have to bear in mind that donors tend to tell their favorite nonprofit what they think that nonprofit wants to hear. They are often reluctant to be critical (although some can be vitriolic). If you know your donors, you'll be aware of how likely or not that is and can weight your results accordingly.

This is not a unique problem for fundraisers. Market researchers found a similar situation when conducting product research in Japan. The Japanese, of course, are such well-meaning, polite people, they can't bring themselves to say anything nasty or unpleasant about any product—odious or not. So beware of nice people. Researchers want objectivity.

The Hazards of Faulty Research

Some things are particularly difficult to find out even through the most stringent and demanding research methods. Most notorious of these is the virtual impossibility of assessing whether a particular television, press, or poster advertisement (here I am referring particularly to indirect rather than direct response advertising) has any immediately recordable impact on product sales.

It is also virtually impossible to pre-test advertisements accurately by research methods. A famous example of this is Maureen Lipman's splendid "Beattie" advertisements for British Telecom in the 1980s. When these were pre-tested as draft scripts to focus groups they were pronounced an obvious flop. However, BT had faith in the concept (a rare client) and agreed to pay to have an actual commercial made. This expensive test was then duly given the thumbs down by a random sample of British averageness. But British Telecom had spent so much that its managers felt they had to go ahead, whatever the public might think. As a result, one of television's most popular characters was launched on the British public, an event that did British Telecom no harm at all.

These ads, incidentally, were intended to do more than just project the image of British Telecom. Their other purpose was to improve the culture of the telephone, to let people see it as a useful, friendly, easy-to-use, everyday tool, not as the black thing in the hall that only rings when there's bad news. This culture of the telephone is an important consideration for telefundraisers (see Chapter Nine).

Another campaign that failed twice in pre-tests was Heineken Lager's wonderful series of ads that claimed that Heineken "refreshes the parts that other beers cannot reach." Watch out for this when you test your advertisement visuals on focus groups. Sometimes they have little better than a random chance of getting it right.

Of course I'm being a little unfair to the market research fraternity by selecting two spectacular failures without mentioning any successes. Pre-testing often does get it right and is almost always useful for establishing consumers' interests and areas of concern as well as what turns them on and off. But faulty research can be expensive and damaging to your relationship with donors, so all results should be analyzed and viewed with care.

The final protection against faulty research or the natural flaws in any research is, as I said earlier, not to neglect the dictates of your own gut feelings. While this in no way invalidates the need for research, most experienced and competent fundraisers will find their instincts are pretty near the mark—but it helps to have this confirmed by research!

Implementing Your Findings

A major key to your fundraising success will be knowing how to use your data. But one of the most common faults with commissioned research is the "filing cabinet" syndrome. Research, expensively commissioned, is summarily scanned and then filed away without further action because what it uncovered has implications that would be, at best, inconvenient to put into practice.

This of course is a wasted opportunity. Research will not repay your investment nor reveal its potential unless you are prepared to act on its findings. It has to be agreed at the highest level necessary that results will be acted upon, before you undertake any research project.

Categorizing Your Donors

We all know that not everybody gives, or is likely to give, to support nonprofits. Our universe is not universal. To find new donors, therefore, we need to identify those subsections of society that have a proven track record of giving to our cause or similar causes or, because of characteristics shared with existing donors, seem likely to be prospects for our kind of appeal.

Wouldn't it be nice if we could divide society up into convenient little groups that correspond to the different behavior patterns we want or expect? Clearly this is dangerous ground, because we are trying to classify the unclassifiable. People, thankfully, are individuals and constantly refuse to conform to the labels we put on them, with almost total disregard for the fact that our lives would be much easier if they did.

But imperfect and limited in use as they may be, most systems of classification are still likely to be more helpful than sticking to the idea that donors are all little old ladies living in Tunbridge Wells, Kent, or Key Biscayne, Florida. Two areas seem worthy of further attention from fundraisers:

- Can we usefully categorize the population to help us identify those people most likely to become donors?
- Can we predict any changes in society that might influence who will be our donors in the future?

To look at these we need to understand two common pieces of research jargon: demographics and psychographics.

Demographics are sets of characteristics that relate to people's behavior as consumers. This includes age, gender, race, marital status, education. We are all aware that people who have certain demographic characteristics are more likely to support us than those who do not.

Psychographics are, according to American sociologist Arnold Mitchell, "the collective essence of an individual's attitudes, beliefs, opinions, prejudices, hopes, fears, needs, desires and aspirations that, taken together, govern how he or she behaves and that, as a whole, expresses itself in a 'lifestyle.'" It can also be clearly seen that psychographic features, too, will have a distinct influence on whether or not someone might become our donor.

Numerous other pieces of classification jargon have entered our language, such as geodemographics, behaviorgraphics, Target Group Index, profiling, targeting, market segmentation. . . . I won't go into these here, although the last two at least are discussed in Chapter Eight.

Is it possible to categorize people psychographically? And is it possible to overlay demographic factors onto psychographic categories and locate our ideal prospective donors?

The answer to both questions is yes. Or rather yes, but. . . . Yes, but don't blame me if you are rather confused by the outcome. As I've said, people have a habit of irrational behavior that confounds most classifications. But, that accepted, some attempts at classification can be of value and certainly some of the "lifestyle" lists and attempts at donor profiling are producing impressive results for fundraising nonprofits in the United Kingdom and other countries just now.

In the 1960s Arnold Mitchell invented a system for categorizing the population called VALS (values and lifestyles), which studied social values. This original VALS system was adopted by marketers because it was perhaps the best-known marketing model covering these. VALS is described as a comprehensive framework for characterizing the lifestyles of Americans. However, the original VALS system's ability to predict consumer behavior began to weaken as social values changed. In the late 1980s a new VALS system based on psychographics was developed. Although based on people in the United States, VALS, or something similar, may have some value for fundraisers in other countries, because when it comes to giving, people are essentially the same everywhere. It also has some major limitations. But it's a start.

VALS divides U.S. adult consumers into eight categories based on primary motivations and resources. Very briefly, here is an introduction to the categories:

- *Innovators* are successful, active, "take charge" people with high self-esteem and abundant resources. They are interested in growth and seek to develop, explore, and express themselves in a variety of ways, sometimes guided by principle and sometimes by a desire to have an effect, to make a change.

• *Thinkers* are mature, satisfied, comfortable, reflective people who value order, knowledge, and responsibility. Most are well educated and in (or recently retired from) professional occupations. They are well-informed about world and national events and are alert to opportunities to broaden their knowledge. Content with their career, family, and station in life, their leisure activities tend to center on the home.

• *Achievers* are successful career- and work-oriented people who like to, and generally do, feel in control of their lives. They value consensus, predictability, and stability over risk and are deeply committed to work and family. Work provides them with a sense of duty, material rewards, and prestige. Their social lives reflect this focus and are structured around family, church, and career.

• *Experiencers* are young, vital, enthusiastic, impulsive, and rebellious. They seek variety and excitement, savoring the new, the offbeat, and the risky. Still in the process of formulating life values and patterns of behavior, they quickly become enthusiastic about new possibilities but are equally quick to cool. At this stage in their lives, they are politically uncommitted, uninformed, and highly ambivalent about what they believe.

• *Believers* are conservative, conventional people with concrete beliefs based on traditional, established codes: family, church, community, and the nation. Many Believers express moral codes that are deeply rooted and literally interpreted. They follow established routines, organized in large part around home, family, and social or religious organizations to which they belong.

• *Strivers* seek motivation, self-definition, and approval from the world around them. They are striving to find a secure place in life. Unsure of themselves and low on economic, social, and psychological resources, Strivers are concerned about the opinions and approval of others.

• *Makers* are practical people who have constructive skills and value self-sufficiency. They live within a traditional context of family, practical work, and physical recreation and have little interest in what lies outside that context. Makers experience the world by working on it—building a house, raising children, fixing a car, or canning vegetables—and have enough skill, income, and energy to carry out their projects successfully.

- *Struggler* lives are constricted. Chronically poor, with little education or skills, without strong social bonds, and often elderly and concerned about their health, they are often resigned and passive. Because they are limited by the necessity of meeting the urgent needs of the present moment, they do not show a strong self-orientation. Their chief concerns are for security and safety.

VALS claims to put a face on different donor segments. Whether or not you believe in a system such as VALS, it is inescapable that values and personal beliefs are crucial to the decision to support nonprofits. Until somebody comes along with a better model this may be the best way we have of finding out who might be tomorrow's donors. Further information on VALS and on demographic and social change in general can be obtained at http://www.sric-bi.com/VALS and by reading Judith Nichols's excellent book *Changing Demographics: Fund Raising in the 1990s.*

The Golden Generation and Their Elders

People are not only living longer, they are also retiring earlier (or they were until recently) and they're reaping the benefits of increased prosperity and better financial planning for things like pensions and that "rainy day" insurance. They generally have more spare time and they're more affluent. Older people fall into four basic groups:

- The older, age fifty to sixty-four: the golden generation. The children have grown up and left home, and the mortgage is paid off. They can revel in the knowledge that they have the highest disposable income of any age group and they've got time to enjoy it. They're also our prime targets.
- The elderly, age sixty-five to seventy-four: these are unsettling years. The number of female-headed households begins to climb.
- The aged, age seventy-five to eighty-four: by now the majority is female. At eighty-plus it's two-thirds. Life now is more insular.
- The very old, age eighty-five-plus: not surprisingly, this group has higher than average assets.

As they get older, people tend to stick together in clear geographical clusters. England's best-known "retirement area" is along the south coast from Hastings to Worthing, but there are many other clearly identifiable enclaves of elderly people. In America and Australia, retirement "villages" are common.

These are vitally important groups for fundraisers. Recognizing their needs, interests, and concerns—and then providing appropriate communications to address them—will ensure success for any fundraiser. But, of course, this is an area fraught with ethical dangers and the need for strict adherence to a clear code of practice is obvious.

Jeff Ostroff, author of *Successful Marketing to the 50+ Consumer,* identifies seven areas of need for the aging population: the home, health care, leisure time, personal and business counseling, education service, financial products and services, and products that combat aging. Fundraisers, says Ostroff, should position themselves as providing solutions to these needs.

It will help if fundraisers can combine to create a positive image of older people and to banish myths and stereotypes such as those that equate old age with inactivity, poor health, and decline.

There are some special tips for writing to older people, such as saying "fifty years old or over" rather than "older," writing long, explanatory copy giving reasons in detail (older people have the time, like to read, and like to make up their own minds), and, of course, setting the type in 10-point at least, with adequate spacing between the lines, so older people can read what you have to say in comfort. (How one nonprofit turned this information to advantage is briefly described in Chapter Thirteen.)

Donors of the Future

Who will be the donors of the future? What will they be like and how will they feel? How will we find them? How will they differ from today's donors? These are crucial questions for fundraisers. Competition is increasing. We all want the committed donor. We all want "relationship" donors.

One might be forgiven for assuming that, if the best way to find a new donor is to find someone exactly like our current donor, then the donors of the future will be exactly like our current donors.

Such an assumption may well be horribly wrong because society is changing radically for a whole variety of reasons. Each passing year sees an increase in both the numbers and the affluence of older people—at least it did until recently. We are all living longer and planning better and this, with the baby boom of the postwar years, will ensure a growing and probably increasingly affluent elderly population for many years to come. Also the explosion in the numbers of working women since the end of the Second World War, described as the single most significant social trend of the twentieth century, means that a different kind of woman is now coming up to retirement (prime donor) age with, perhaps, a significantly different set of interests and motivations. And, finally, the hippie generation of the 1960s, with its revolutionary standards of morals and outlook, is now middle-aged. These are the baby boomers whose numbers should swell the ranks of prospective donors, but will their different values and attitudes mean they are more, or less, likely to support our cause?

The traditional donor pyramid may well be changing (see Chapter Four). According to Judith Nichols it already has in America. Instead of the good old 80:20 rule the ratio now is more likely to be 95:5. For example, Britain's Royal National Lifeboat Institution, which at some time or other touches everyone in the land, gets more than 80 percent of its annual income in bequests from less than two thousand people. This rule, known as the Pareto principle, asserts the almost universal truth that whatever area of business you are in—retailing, licensed trade, bookmaking, fundraising, or whatever—around 80 percent of your sales will come from around 20 percent of your customers. Examine your business and if this is true it is a fair clue as to where you should be concentrating your resources.

Also the "age of prospecting," the last ten to twenty years during which so many nonprofits expanded their supporter lists in quantum leaps, has created a bulging middle section in the pyramid with all those newly recruited donors waiting to be moved up. The bottom of the pyramid, unfortunately, has apparently remained the same except, perhaps, that many of the prime targets for recruitment have been creamed off.

Baby boomers are the first generation raised on television. Will this make a difference for fundraisers? If so, what?

Unsettling though they may be, most of these social changes at least seem likely to be positive for fundraisers. In *Changing Demographics,* Nichols details how during the 1990s U.S. baby boomers moved into their prime earning years, causing the number of affluent households to skyrocket. During the last decade of the twentieth century the number of house owners was predicted to increase by 40 percent and those with income of $75,000 and above to multiply by an incredible 300 percent.

According to American demographers, fundraisers in America are segregating their baby boomers by VALS type to see where their donors are going to come from. These not-so-young-now people have quite different attitudes from the preceding generation and these may have substantial implications for the future of fundraising. (After the baby boomers, apparently, come the baby busters and the baby boomlet—but that's another matter.) According to Cheryl Russell, author of *100 Predictions for the Baby Boom,* baby boomers differ from their parents in that they

- Are more likely to be university educated
- Are two-income couples
- Believe men and women should be equally responsible for cleaning the house
- Own VCRs and microwaves; may have home computers and telephone answering machines
- Frequently go to movies, plays, concerts, and museums
- Think divorce is acceptable and abortion should be legal
- Are more suspicious of authority
- Stress fun and enjoyment rather than duty and obligation
- Focus on opportunity rather than security
- Are likely to be candid rather than tactful
- Are self-concerned rather than loyal to organizations
- Stress individuality and differences rather than groups and sameness
- Prefer experience to possessions

Can it be that a generation that is so different from its predecessor will behave in the same way when it comes to making donations?

I think it is unlikely. Of course, we all change as we get older—but we don't all become the same. So if basic values are different, how should fundraisers market to the new middle-aged?

It's an urgent question for many nonprofits, who are seeing their current list atrophy as donors grow old and die. While this may bode well for immediate bequest income, it's not very encouraging for the future if these donors are not being satisfactorily replaced.

Fundraisers also need to find an appropriate language for appeal materials to make sure that they do indeed appeal to this new audience. Older donors don't like slickness or padding. They appreciate straight talking and are quite prepared to accept honest emotion in appeals.

Transparent accountability—the active reporting of detailed accounts of what nonprofits have done and are doing with donors' funds—will also be important. So will flexibility in devising ways of helping and in planning special schemes, such as planned gifts and even bequests. Schemes that clearly recognize a donor's contribution will also pay off. Tomorrow's donors, raised on increasingly sophisticated media, will also expect quality communication (no more bleak, gray, badly designed publications) and will expect to be communicated with via the most modern media, such as fax, video, e-mail, the Internet, and their mobile phones.

Of course, it may be some time before the baby boomers become tomorrow's donors in appreciable numbers, but it'll pay to bring them in now, if you can find appropriate ways. Concern as to how this new breed will behave can be balanced against the undeniable fact that as people's disposable income grows they become more generous. This will happen to baby boomers too.

Consumer Attitudes Are Changing

There's no doubt that fundraisers are living in times of rapid change and consumer attitudes are changing too. Consider how your donors view direct mail now compared to their understanding of it just ten or fifteen years ago (an important consideration when you contemplate the future of fundraising direct mail).

The only way to keep up with people's feelings and how they affect you is through a carefully planned and consistent program of properly conducted research. If you can't afford to do it on your own, join in with other similar nonprofits and share the cost. Concentrate first on the basics—a questionnaire and maybe some focus groups among your own supporters. But again the most simple, yet most essential and best, research is just to go out and meet your supporters and talk to them—regularly.

You can take psychographics a long way. For example, you may wish to direct your fundraising particularly toward women. But what kind of women? A woman with a career is very different from one who views work just as a job and different again from someone who has never worked in any job outside the home. Age, education, and social background also subdivide your target group. Women are individuals.

It is worth reading Judith Nichols's book, even if you are not living in North America (it is particularly focused on people in America). Most of what she says has universal application.

What Donors Will Allow

One of the surprises that research (and meeting people) has shown me is just how tolerant, understanding, and encouraging donors can be. The general public seems to be constantly moaning about nonprofits, trying to undermine everything they do through destructive criticism that is usually misinformed or imagined. I suspect this quite often only thinly conceals a cynical attempt to disguise guilt feelings brought on by not giving enough.

Donors don't share this lack of confidence. They have greater respect for and faith in the organizations they support, which is perhaps not surprising. In supporting your cause they have made a commitment and don't want to be proved wrong. The degree to which most donors have faith in their favorite causes and trust them to do the right thing is something fundraisers should never underestimate or take for granted. This trust is one of the motivating rewards that comes to the fundraiser and helps to compensate for the lack of more tangible benefits of the job. (This trust is in fact the essential foundation of fundraising. Worryingly, marketing and other communications may be putting it at risk—see Chapter Fourteen).

Donors like to be asked their opinions and like to feel those opinions are listened to, but most will turn the question around and tell you that they'll be happy to go along with whatever the fundraising organization thinks is the right thing to do. So don't always expect your research among donors to reveal staggering truths and insights into where you should be going. Most of the responses will, in fact, be telling you precisely what the donor thinks you want to hear, because the donor likes you, believes in you, wants to help you and certainly doesn't want to create offense. (There are, of course, some who revel in the chance to be as critical as they can be!)

Donors are wonderful people. In my experience they are generally prepared to endorse brave decisions, to accept that nonprofits like all organizations have to take calculated risks. They will understand that, at times, mistakes will be made. If they are fully informed of a situation and the decision that needs to be made, I have found they will not seek to make it themselves but will back the organization 100 percent, whatever the consequences, providing they can believe the decision was honestly based on what the organization believed was right.

Donors are not fools. They know that nonprofits have to meet costs and can readily understand that they have to spend money properly to be effective and efficient. I find they are likely to despise false economies as much as they dislike conspicuous extravagance. When the arguments are explained to them, without exception, they seem to understand the need for achieving value for money. That includes the value of investing in a sound administration—see Chapter Two.

Fundraisers should realize that, just as they are committed to their cause, so too are the donors. In a remarkable demonstration of their belief, they've all put their hands in their pockets and freely given of their own money to meet a need, help realize an ideal, or achieve a dream. In doing so, the donors all invest a part of themselves. Their personal commitment has been demonstrated. It is a tangible thing. And it's a precious resource for the fundraiser.

Fundraising is perhaps the ultimate "people" business. To fundraise effectively you need the people's understanding. How can you expect them to understand you if you don't understand them? The way to understand your donors, and to avoid making mistakes, is through research.

Action Points

▲ Research helps make fundraising relevant, so ensure you understand your donors as completely as possible.

▲ Meet your donors as often as you can. Ask their opinions on the things you need to know.

▲ Plan a questionnaire or some focus groups. If you have to, share the cost with another nonprofit. Then spend an evening with a pile of completed questionnaires.

▲ Create a written picture of your typical donor. Circulate it. Get your organization to adopt it as part of your fundraising plan.

▲ Clearly explain to donors how you will use the data they will provide and why it will be useful to you.

▲ If you intend to add any research information to your database, spell this out fully on your survey materials.

▲ Thank donors for taking part in your research.

▲ Don't assume that *database* means the same thing as *donor base.* They can be quite different.

▲ Keep reminding yourself of the dangers of faulty research, and see research results as a useful guide rather than a rigid mandate.

▲ Make sure your findings are fully used and implemented, not filed away.

▲ Publish a summary of your findings in your supporter newsletter or provide feedback to donors in other ways. Invite comments. But take care to present your findings in a way that donors will understand and accept.

▲ Concentrate the bulk of your attentions and your resources on the small group of individuals who provide most of your income.

▲ Plan for changes in society. Try to identify and track down the donor of the future.

▲ Make your research part of an ongoing annual program.

Donor Profile: Mrs. Chester

Mrs. Chester doesn't like to come to the capital city, but she does love her annual meetings. They are definitely a high spot of the year—and have been for the past eighteen years. "In those days they were held in a church hall some miles from the city center. I doubt if there were more than fifty of us then, including the staff," she explains. "Now, well, there are thousands of us, aren't there?" she exclaims, looking around. She obviously feels considerable pride in what the organization had become and the small part she has played in it.

"You see, I *am* the charity in my home town, you know," she explains in a very modest way. "I am the secretary and the treasurer combined for our branch and I make sure to organize one major event each year and several small things too. I get lots of help but it takes quite a lot of organization. It's been a big commitment but I wouldn't have missed it for the world."

There's no complaint in what she says, just enthusiasm, so it comes as quite a surprise to her new-found companion to discover that this nonprofit isn't the only cause Mrs. Chester supports.

"Oh no," Mrs. Chester says, as she realizes her friend's assumption. "This is only Mondays, Tuesdays, and Wednesdays. Thursdays, Fridays, and Saturdays I'm local organizer for—" and she mentions another national nonprofit, operating in a similar field of concern. In the latter half of each week she does just as much for them and has been doing so for just as long.

Then the conversation heats up. Mrs. Chester loves both organizations and wouldn't hear a word said against either, but her eighteen years with both have given her plenty of opportunity to compare and contrast. Nothing either of them could do would put Mrs. Chester off, for really she doesn't support these *organizations,* she supports the *cause*—the needy children both organizations exist to help.

But one of her two nonprofits has upset her quite a lot—the one that keeps writing alarming letters and that always seems in need of more money than she is able to give. She's told them before that she'd rather give her time than her money, yet they still keep writing. Mrs. Chester wishes "they" would listen but doesn't believe they will. Really, she doesn't feel she knows who "they" are.

She also wishes they were a bit more like her other nonprofit. But it doesn't bother her too much—not yet.

Chapter Six

Learning from Recent Research

*He urged us to work for their freedom, not to despise even
the small help that each of us can give. He told us where
their courage comes from. It comes from you.*
AMNESTY INTERNATIONAL, REPORTING THE WORDS OF
RELEASED BEIRUT HOSTAGE TERRY WAITE

Much has changed since the first edition of this book in terms of
what fundraisers know about their donors and prospects. Over the
last decade a valuable and substantial body of research has grown
up on both sides of the Atlantic and elsewhere. We can now call on
experience, techniques, and tools designed to measure donor loyalty, to predict giving levels, to understand the roles of trust and
confidence in public giving, and to predict how donors will behave,
how they will react to different types and styles of fundraising efforts, and much, much more. In a recent research study called
Charitable Giving—Towards a Model of Donor Behaviour professor
Adrian Sargeant of the Centre for Voluntary Sector Management
at Henley Management College in the United Kingdom drew on
literature from the fields of marketing, economics, clinical psychology, social psychology, anthropology, and sociology, and listed
reference sources from 167 different expert academic studies in
areas of interest to fundraisers.

To find out more of what's available now to fundraisers I decided to visit Adrian and his colleague Stephen Lee (my companion on the fateful train ride described in the Preface) in their

splendid academic retreat overlooking the river Thames. Henley College is a vast, pristine white Victorian mansion set in an equally impressive acreage of prime English landscape that rolls gently down to one of the finest stretches of that lovely river. I couldn't have imagined a better setting to seek the views of such an illustrious pair of academics on what's significant and what's not in recent donor research. But no sooner had I strode through the portals of their imposing pile than they each unloaded an enormous, equally imposing pile of research documents into my arms and invited me to go through them to see for myself. Their relief at passing on this burden was equaled only by my dismay. As I staggered down the corridor to find somewhere to unload my burden, I couldn't but be struck by how things have changed. A decade ago there wasn't enough of this stuff. Now there's too much.

Hardly any of this research existed ten years ago, particularly in Europe. Fundraisers now have access to some really startling and useful insights that might prove priceless to their fundraising efforts, in fields as varied as giving behavior, donor types, what donors will read, what turns them on and off, preferences for methods of fundraising, demographics, timing, and so on. The trouble is, only about 5 percent of all this mountain of new information is really valuable. The rest is at best vaguely interesting but not useful and at worst padding or twaddle. So how does the fundraiser of today know where to look for what?

Donors, of course, are largely unaware of all this academic analysis of their actions, and still seem determined to confound us wherever possible. Don't expect all the answers from research, or even from the halls of academe, where some researchers wouldn't recognize a donor if they met one in their soup. But it would be foolish to ignore the valuable resources that now exist.

Where Do I Start?

This emerging body of empirical knowledge is both fascinating and frightening for a grizzled old fundraising hand like me. Think about it. . . . For the past however many years, we've been able to pose as experts by banging out the same old lists of well-worn shibboleths that we ourselves inherited from some predecessor or other, and have perhaps embroidered a bit along the way. And there's been no one to challenge us. So if I said, "People give to people; not to organizations, mission statements, or strategies," who was there to disagree with me? Now all that's changed. These days people can point to soundly based research studies in all the areas of past cliché and say, "Let's weigh up the evidence."

I have nothing but enthusiasm for this. If our aphorisms don't stand the test of science as they've stood the test of time, then they aren't worth much. As it happens quite a few have now been proved or approved by recent research. Had any of my favorites not been borne out, of course, I'd argue that you can prove anything with research if you really want to. People usually believe that.

It's healthy to retain some skepticism about research. Research is like a photograph of a dancer—usually it shows just a part of the story, and often in a quite misleading light. I'm not one to subscribe to the view that cleverer people than me have produced this conclusion, so it must be true. If something contradicts the evidence of your own experience, my advice is, "don't believe it."

Lots of vested interests lurk behind some apparently respectable pieces of research, and much research is badly designed, executed, or interpreted—and often just unnecessary. Quite often research is structured to tell you what its producers want you to believe rather than what's true. For example, you could submerge me in reports that conclude most donors welcome and value fundraising direct mail but I wouldn't swallow a bit of it because I know what people tell me, time and time again.

Some Really Important New Insights

Faced with this sea of potentially useful (and useless) information I've decided to look at just a few specific facets of donor understanding that I think might be hugely worthwhile. Beyond that I'm going to cop out, other than to encourage fundraisers eager to learn more to get in touch with specialists such as those at Henley Management College or subscribe to learned international journals such as the *Journal of Nonprofit and Voluntary Sector Marketing,* something else that's valuable and wasn't around ten years ago.

Thanks!

One major body of research directly related to the theme of this book is covered in detail in Penelope Burk's book *Thanks! A Guide to Donor-Centred Fundraising,* based on extensive studies among donors in Canada. She describes the research that underpins her book as "the only statistically-based evidence of the measurable effect of meaningful communication on donor retention and gift value." I remember thinking on picking it up that maybe now I could stop saying "In my opinion—" and start substituting "As research has now definitively proved—"

Her endeavors are well worth studying. Lack of space prevents me from providing detailed summary, so with her approval I'll just lift a few of the nuggets from her book for inclusion here.

- Time is of the essence when saying "thank you."
- Relationship building begins the moment a donor's first gift is received.
- Nonprofits need marketers to acquire donors—and fundraisers to keep them. (The two are not synonymous.)
- The fundraiser's greatest challenge is to keep donors giving after they have made their first gift.
- Many donors have decided for themselves when and what to give and don't appreciate nonprofits trying to tell them otherwise.
- Sixty-nine percent of individual donors say none of the nonprofits they support call them without asking for another gift.
- Sixty-one percent of donors say they've received a request for a second gift with their "thank you." Eighty-one percent have been offended by this.
- A donor's prime needs are to know the gift was received, to know the gift was "set to work" as intended, and to know the project or program is having the desired effect.
- Individual donors like to be recognized but don't like to be singled out. Eighty-one percent of Canadian donors have attended one or more formal donor recognition events.

- It takes more time to keep donors informed of what their money is achieving than it does to ask them for it.
- There is enormous fundraising potential waiting to be realized, if fundraisers practice donor-centered fundraising.

This last point seems rather obvious, but I thought it nice to hear from a researcher. Penny's penultimate observation might seem equally banal but is actually a hugely useful observation, if fundraisers will only recognize it.

Understanding the Entrepreneurial Donor

Quite by chance, I recently stumbled on some research by two enterprising young Canadians, Guy Mallabone and Tony Myers from St. Mary's University in Minnesota, into the special characteristics of "the entrepreneurial donor." (Canadians seem to be quite good at this sort of thing.) Mallabone and Myers define the entrepreneurial donor as someone with proven ability to identify and pursue unique opportunities, find and take advantage of new resources, and make decisions on the direction of the enterprise while accepting and taking risks in the process. Do these people even have time to be donors, not to mention inclination?

Mallabone and Myers think so. Not only that, they soon came to believe that entrepreneurs generally make far better donors than others. (And not just because they also, of course, tend to have more than average of that other prerequisite of the donor class, spare cash.) To verify all this they conducted a detailed national survey across their home country that involved interviews with experts, focus groups, and the views of more than twelve hundred randomly selected donors, one in three of whom fitted their definition of an entrepreneur.

The survey set out to evaluate a range of donor characteristics around motivations to give or cease giving. Analysis showed much more clearly than either researcher expected that the more entrepreneurial the donor, the stronger the propensity to give a philanthropic gift. The following points also emerged from the research:

- When it comes to giving the next gift, when it comes to increasing a gift, and when it comes to making the ultimate gift, entrepreneurial donors are more likely to give than nonentrepreneurial donors.
- Key motivations for giving the next gift include vision and mission of the organization, helping those in need, giving back to the community, and the accountability of the institution.
- The top motivations for increased giving by entrepreneurs are that they are financially able to do so, the cause is consistent with personal values, the nonprofit has a strong reputation, and the performance of the nonprofit meets the donor's standards.
- The top motivations for giving the ultimate gift (the largest amount a person can give based on their current financial situation) are belief or trust in the organization, the results the nonprofit demonstrates, and the donor's desire to make a difference.

When it comes to understanding why people chose not to give in response to a specific donation request, no one reason stands out over another. It doesn't seem to matter how you alienate a donor. If a nonprofit alienates or turns off a donor, those donors tend to be alienated by the same factors, to the same degree and with the same intensity. The top two reasons why donors stop giving to a nonprofit are reduced credibility and lack of reliability (you didn't do what you said you were going to do with my money, so I don't believe you'll do it next time, either). Together, credibility and reliability add up to accountability.

Mallabone and Myers concluded that if a substantial part of our database (up to one-third) contains donors who qualify as entrepreneurs, then fundraisers need to consider how they treat this important segment, and to communicate with them appropriately and engage them more effectively. That sounds to me like advice worth taking, and yet another area that will repay further study.

Understanding Trust and Confidence

In the late 1990s, Stephen Lee and Adrian Sargeant began researching the importance of trust and confidence in fundraising.

This is perhaps one of the most crucial areas for fundraisers but one that, rather surprisingly, has been hitherto neglected. Confidence differs from trust, of course, in that confidence is rooted in specific knowledge or past experience, whereas trust is what we have to rely on (or not) when direct knowledge and experience is partial or entirely absent.

Lee's past life as director of the United Kingdom's professional association for fundraisers, the Institute for Fundraising, and Sargeant's long and distinguished career in researching the voluntary sector equipped them both well for this study, which set out to summarize the body of past research and academic findings in this area and to test the validity of the kind of claims I and others have been making over recent years, such as whether or not trust and confidence have the pivotal role we believe they have in driving the extent to which an individual might be prompted both to give higher sums and to give again over time. So, in essence, they set out to find whether we relationship fundraisers are barking up the right tree, or not.

The research basis and methodology for this study were complex and thorough and the samples studied were large, but I won't go into these here. Much of what Lee and Sargeant found is unsurprising, but not unimportant. Donors are generally much more trusting than non-donors. Reasons given for supporting and not supporting nonprofits were wide-ranging but predictable. Donors appear to believe strongly in the causes they support whereas non-donors feel there are simply too many to choose from. Non-donors felt more pressured to give than donors but not strongly so and fewer than 20 percent found nonprofit communications to be inappropriate or intrusive. Donors in this survey seemed to identify more with the causes they were supporting than with specific individual organizations.

When asked about how they trust different organizations, respondents in this survey were prepared to place nonprofits ahead of banks and utility companies but not by much, and even donors trust nonprofits less than they trust the police and armed forces. But in every case donors hold more positive views of nonprofits generally than do nondonors, and donors to specific nonprofits will trust their favored nonprofits substantially more than they will trust others they do not support.

All of which tends to suggest that trust is a fairly essential starting place for developing donor relationships. The researchers found confidence even more lacking than trust among their sample, although again donors are more confident than non-donors in nonprofits, particularly the ones they support personally.

But both trust and confidence in fundraisers and their organizations were shown to be worryingly low. Should and could we do anything about this? Well, Lee and Sargeant's conclusions from this study seem to point firmly to the importance of a more relationship-oriented approach.

So donors differ from non-donors in several important ways. I've always suspected it. And trust and confidence are essential requirements of fundraising relationships, with trust being the key to donor commitment. No doubt about that. And trust and confidence in our sector is not what it should be. As I've said, much of the value of this study is that it confirms what we already believe. But there are new insights too.

Of real significance from my point of view is Sargeant and Lee's conclusion that the quality of communication is the strongest factor underpinning donor trust and confidence—how appropriately and how often fundraisers give quality feedback that reflects outcomes and achievements—and the crucial factor is how donors perceive the various communications they receive from us. This seems to show quite clearly where fundraisers should be directing their attention and resources—into producing excellent and inspirational communications.

Lee advises nonprofits to undertake some form of communications audit, which can assess donors' likes and dislikes and help to make communications more responsive to their needs. "The only real way of building a bridge across the trust and confidence gap is through better communications" he says. "If we can do that, we will have even more trusting supporters and we'll find new people more easily as well."

The two also concluded that perceived quality of service, information on stewardship, and good judgment also have an impact on trust. This is clearly important work, and it is to be hoped that Lee, Sargeant, and their colleagues at Henley Management College will continue to push out the frontiers of our understanding of trust and confidence, while keeping levels of donor and public

trust and confidence under close review. All fundraisers will benefit if they do.

Men and Women Are Different

If ever there was a statement of the blindingly obvious, the observation that the sexes differ is it. It's something we all learned at age
five or younger. Yet this is exactly the kind of hugely valuable observation that just has to be proved by research before we fundraisers will take it seriously.

Of course men and women are different and may respond to
different messages, different stimuli, and different styles of communication. So why have all fundraisers habitually treated men and
women as one single, homogeneous mass?

It's one of the great mysteries of fundraising communication.
There is now a huge body of research on this subject, most of which
points to the advisability of our treating the two most basic of our
donor segments—the men and the women—rather differently.

The premise is that men and women use different language—so
will respond to different language. Men operate like fax machines,
women are like telephones—that is, men are more to the point,
brief, and factual, whereas women are more conversational, friendly,
and discursive. The sexes have different styles of socialization—boys
play competitively, girls play cooperatively. According to American
author Martha Taylor, women give to promote change, men give
to preserve the status quo. And this is just the beginning of how to
communicate differently with men and women.

I won't go into more detail on this here. The implications are
clear—and the same is rather obviously true for young and old
people also. This is part of the communication challenge facing all
fundraisers, to recognize and understand the differences that matter between people and so communicate with them more effectively. No more blanket mailings.

A book worth studying in this regard is John Gray's *Men Are
from Mars, Women Are from Venus*. But I suspect your own understanding of human nature and your donors will be your best guide
as to what might encourage your male donors to respond to your
appeals as distinct from your female donors. If your database will
allow you, of course.

Staying Ahead

I could go on, but I think the point is made. Fundraisers now have access to a wealth of new and valuable information that is soundly based and is growing by the day. Those who are serious about fundraising will acquaint themselves with what's available, sort the wheat from the chaff, and apply the best of this knowledge to guide their fundraising efforts. This will keep them fifteen minutes ahead of their competitors, if not more.

Action Points

▲ Be aware of all the useful research resources that are around and available to you.

▲ Don't do new research yourself if you can more cheaply access the information from others who have done it (and paid for it) already.

▲ Reexamine and improve your thank-you and welcome procedures.

▲ Use your research insights to inform your communications strategy and to guide your "experience" fundraising endeavors (see Chapter Thirteen).

▲ Identify your entrepreneurial donors and treat them accordingly.

▲ Ensure everything your organization does is geared to build trust and confidence in your organization and its mission.

▲ Particularly, make sure your communications with donors are up to the task of building trust and confidence.

▲ Create different communications for the men and women on your list, and the young and old, designed to speak to them in ways they will most relate to and respond to.

Donor Profile: Rachel Shapiro

Like many other young mothers, Rachel Shapiro finds life far from easy. Balancing the competing demands of her job, her husband, three children, and an aging mother all put such pressure on her, day in, day out, that she finds little time to even think about the needs of others.

She cares about the world outside her family unit, but it's just that the daily grind means that doing good beyond her immediate circle is something, by and large, that she has to leave to others better placed through financial or family circumstances to intervene. Of course, Rachel does help wherever she can, when another young mother at her local playgroup is stuck and needs moral or even financial support and she could lend a supportive ear or even a few dollars if she's flush that month. Or if one of the playgroup organizers needs a break, then Rachel will volunteer a little of her scarce time to provide cover so the playgroup won't have to close for lack of a supervisor. Rachel wouldn't think of that as anything special, and beyond that she gives to a few nonprofits from time to time, but not in any planned way.

This latter small generosity, of course, leads to her receiving a lot of unsolicited mail, which Rachel has learned to deal with in her own way. She never throws anything out unopened, storing it instead in a magazine rack specifically kept for the purpose, until the time she religiously sets aside each month for the purpose of "dealing with the mail." It's mostly from nonprofits—she doesn't get many letters otherwise, these days.

Rachel works only mornings on Fridays, so those days are usually a bit less pressured than most. Her plan is to get to that bulging magazine rack on the last Friday of each month, when she usually can create an hour or so to go through it between preparing the kids' lunch and tackling the mountain of housework that has piled up.

But the promised respite this Friday had not materialized because the playgroup leader was ill and Rachel had felt obliged to step into the breach. Despite her anxieties about how she could possibly squeeze all the demands on her time into the few hours available, despite the din around her and the constant barrage of little hands that tugged at her skirt seeking solutions to their worries and problems, somehow Rachel just couldn't shake off one disturbing image from the nonprofit annual report she had skim-read that afternoon. It was little more than a snippet, a short story that through creative design had leapt out of the page at her and had only taken a minute or two to read. It was a report about a little girl whose parents were always drunk. The youngster had tried desperately to look after her sister and baby brother, but it was the image of a little detail in this story, of the little girl feeding the other kids from a tin of cold baked beans in their dank bedroom, that kept nudging its way into her mind and disturbing Rachel's busy day.

Some days later Rachel gave her first big donation to the organization that had sent her that report, inspired by that single, unforgettable image.

Chapter Seven

Avoiding Common Errors and Pitfalls

I think the gentleman who created King Kong would have been more gainfully employed in making a set of concrete steps at the Ashton Road end of Bracechurch Street to help old people get to the bus without having to make half-mile detours.
LETTER TO THE EDITOR, *BIRMINGHAM EVENING MAIL*

Human beings are fallible—and fundraisers are just human beings in disguise. As in any other field, it is instructive to look at and learn from the mistakes of others—the mariner to sail with is the one who has been shipwrecked, for he knows where the reefs are.

I sometimes feel it's a pity that at most of the seminars and workshops on fundraising that I attend, the speakers seem to concentrate primarily on giving case histories of their successes. They rarely refer in any detail to their failures. Perhaps this is just human nature, but I am sure we could all learn at least as much from studying when, how, and why things went wrong as we can from looking at those few campaigns where, apparently, everything went right.

In the Heart of the Machine

Some years ago my long-time colleague George Smith presented a paper called "People to People" at the International Fund Raising Congress in the Netherlands, and I am going to quote liberally from it. His subject then was what he saw as the enemy of fundraising relationships—technology.

Most fundraisers would say that, correctly applied, technology is one of our very best friends and greatest assets, even our salvation (see Chapters Nine and Ten), but I agree wholeheartedly with Smith that in careless hands, there are few more certain and deadly foes. "First you are an individual donor," he writes. "Then you become an entry on a supporters' file. Then you are part of a database. . . ." You can almost hear the machine swallowing the donor.

It's not so much that the public resent their details being included in some gigantic anonymous lump of high technology—the fact is people rarely think about it. What they do notice, however, is when the machine gets it wrong. Usually that's because some flesh-and-blood being injected the frailty in the first place and the damn machine is too detached and clinical to stop repeating the error every time you decide to write to your donors.

Let's go back to that hoary old question of "how many times can you write to your supporters?" Imagine the damage that might be done to your precious relationships when every time you do write, you get your friend's name wrong! You can't say it'll never happen to you because every fundraiser knows it can, it does, and it will.

The Cold Hand of Technology

Take the example of a well-known environmental agency (names withheld to protect the guilty) which, within the space of just a few weeks, managed to allow technology's cold hand to come between itself and two potentially very valuable donors. The first instance was when a colleague of mine received four virtually identical mailing packs, different only in that three of them had at least one important component wrong in her name or address. Two of them had addressed her as Mr., a fairly basic gender insult. Such waste, particularly of paper, must have seemed doubly ironic to my colleague as the subject of all four appeals was nothing other than the campaign to save the tropical rainforests. (Even the sophisticated recipient who knows that tropical rainforests aren't used to make paper would nevertheless abhor this obvious waste from an environmental organization.)

Then, to add indifference to insult, the same organization wrote to another colleague of mine. This time the letter was a brilliant example of how not to say thank you (for a recent generous donation). Above his name my colleague was dismayed to see a long line of ten computer-generated numbers. This allows sufficient scope to allocate an individual number to very nearly two hundred times the entire population of the United Kingdom, or fifty times the population of the United States. But, not satisfied with this impersonalization, the nonprofit added a further line of seventeen more digits at the foot of the letter. For the recipient, this was the ultimate experience of being written to by a machine. But then, to compound the insult, instead of the director's own signature, the letter had been signed by some indecipherable person with the handwriting of a twelve-year-old.

Lost opportunities both, of course, but much worse. Offence could easily have been caused. Computers give rise to many amusing salutations that could also offend. Humorous examples include the legendary Mr. Obe, a fine old West African name that didn't happen to belong to the recipient (OBE—the Order of the British Empire—was just one of his decorations), and Mr. Prince, who in real life was (and still is) Prince Rainier of Monaco.

Some people have good reason to be sensitive about what we might do to their name. A nonprofit I once worked with received an irate complaint from a certain Miss Fishpool, because the salutation of their most recent letter had omitted the final "l" from her surname.

Funny, of course, but there is a serious problem for relationship fundraisers here. Such incidents can create lasting damage. The environmental organization in my first example should have been creating the kind of atmosphere that will encourage a donor's support, not polluting their prospects' mailboxes with the outpourings of machines.

This seems to be an example of the culture of mass marketing invading the culture of fundraising. Yet if the principles of relationship fundraising are practiced it can be the other way around. The culture of fundraising *can* invade the culture of mass marketing. Then much greater care would be taken to ensure duplicates are not sent out. List providers—the owners and the brokers— would be told in the strongest terms by a unity of substantial customers that unclean lists would no longer be tolerated under any circumstances. And removing those unsightly computer numbers, even replacing them with a discreet bar code or similar indirect identification device, would be simplicity itself. As would ensuring that the real person, or a facsimile thereof, actually signed the letter so that when it arrived it looked as it was meant to be—an individual letter of thanks, recognizing the gift of a friend on a personal, one-to-one basis (see Chapter Ten).

The Little Old Lady of London

The lengthy advice I presented in Chapter Five, to research the demographics and psychographics of your supporters so that you can prepare a donor profile, of course, also conceals a lurking danger in its wisdom—the tendency to suppose we are dealing with norms and caricatures and not real, individual human beings.

Your profile is a composite and must be treated as such. People are not composites. They are all different and need to be treated as individuals. Every one of your supporters is difficult to classify in their own way and if you rely too heavily on composite descriptions you might make some horrendous mistakes. Some will merely be annoying; others may cost you your relationship. Here's George Smith describing a potential donor, or maybe a client:

> She is a 77-year-old lady who lives in a pre–First World War house in inner London. Her four grown-up children have all left home and her husband has been unemployed for decades. She herself has never worked for a living. Her credit status is zero. In fact she lives in a part of London where mail order companies refuse to offer credit facilities.
>
> By now you will be feeling duly sorry for this sad remnant of urban society, this impoverished old dear shuffling sadly to the launderette and to the post office every week to pick up her pension.
>
> Let your eyes be undimmed with tears. What you have just read is a demographically accurate description of Her Majesty Queen Elizabeth II.

The story makes the all-important point, the one that makes fundraising such an unendingly interesting area. We may be using the most sophisticated of modern systems but we are communicating with people. To do this successfully we require warmth, humanity, understanding, and great care that we don't ever think of them as lists, or appear to think of them as lists, but we always think of them as people.

The Way We Talk to People

If we are bland in our descriptions and our views of the people with whom we communicate, it is inevitable that we will be equally bland in the language we use when we write to them. If we rely on formulas for the letters we use (the peeling—and unappealing—computer label, the four-page letter, leaflet, standard reply form, message on the envelope, and so on) will not our words be equally formula-driven and sterile as a result? Will we be sending formats instead of letters? Of course we will.

The way we talk to people is critical to our relationship with donors. For the most part we communicate via the printed word. That's how we express ourselves and depict our need. And it's how the donor is able to see what kind of people we are, whether we are honest and trustworthy.

Frequently the gurus of direct mail will tell us that copy doesn't matter, or that at most its importance is limited when considered alongside audience, offer, and format. This view may have some merit when considering the tiny percentage who respond to your cold mailings, but it is absolutely untrue and frankly dangerous when applied to your regular communications with donors.

Yet while fundraisers frequently employ professional copywriters to craft their cold direct mail packages, they often think nothing of relegating the crucial task of writing their warm mailings, their newsletters or information sheets, to enthusiastic staff with little or no qualifications or experience for the job. It is a curious reversal of logic.

If you still think copy is unimportant, compare and contrast the following two pieces of text from an annual report (again from George Smith):

I am raising funds for arthritis research. And I could say this. . . .

"Recent advances in clinical research bring the long-awaited cure for osteo-arthritis ever nearer. No fewer than 10 million people suffer from the disease and we desperately need your help to fund a long-term program of remedial work to reduce the terrible price paid by society for this most crippling of diseases. It is estimated that six million working days a year are lost through arthritis and that 95 percent of the population will be affected at some stage by the disease."

This is typical annual report text, but if I said that out loud to a potential donor I would risk boredom, confusion, inattention, and a lot of other fruitless reactions. But let's suppose I adopted the first person mode that comes instinctively with natural speech and said this. . . .

"My mother is crippled with arthritis. She can't get out of her chair now and she can't handle a knife and fork. There's probably someone in your family whose life has been made miserable by the disease. For there is not much we can do about it right now. The only answer is research and that costs money. Every pound you can give me goes to help. Can you please send us a donation? The cure will be too late for my mother, but it might not be too late for you or your children. Every time you get out of a chair and pick up a knife and fork, say a little thank you for your own luck and do something to help."

All right, it's corny, deliberately so in this case because it helps make the point. But does anyone doubt that the second piece of copy is more effective than the first? It sounds like someone talking, not someone going through the motions. The difference is always worth exploring. Read your message out loud. Does it survive the test?

The point is, words matter and they should be handled with care. Remember that you are trying to communicate a promotional message that you will then send uninvited in a free distribution publication. That makes it one of the hardest messages of all to get people to read. So they have to *want* to read what you say and the job of your writing is to make that happen so easily and skillfully that the reader will be happily and effortlessly drawn into your story.

The kind of writing that produces the best response in direct mail is concise, to the point, unpretentious, and unambiguous, for any style you attempt will most probably get in the way of the message. Avoid formality and any hint of self-satisfaction. Write to your donors in their language, not yours, and write with warmth and sincerity, featuring real people and describing the things that you do that influence their lives.

It usually pays to be brief, or at least not to waffle. I have some sympathy with Sir Winston Churchill, who sent the following memo to his First Lord of the Admiralty, "Pray state this day, on one side of a sheet of paper, how the Royal Navy is being adapted to meet the conditions of modern warfare." Concentrates the mind, doesn't it?

Good writing is quite a challenge and is rare in fundraising publications. But if it isn't good writing it won't be good reading and if it isn't good reading it won't be read. These days people have better things to do with their time. That's the challenge that makes good writing well worth working for.

The Mail Mountain

One major potential problem facing fundraisers and donors is that there is so much fundraising direct mail. Who would have thought just a few years ago that nonprofits would be using direct mail on such a scale and in such a variety of ways? This burgeoning growth started in the United States, but it is very much a fact of life in Great Britain and I believe it has also occurred in most European countries.

This contrasts with the situation in the early 1980s, when growth in direct mail fundraising began to accelerate, and many people resisted it because they suspected donors would not like it. The common cry was, "We can't mail our supporters more than once or maybe twice a year."

Not many fundraising organizations still feel like that. There aren't nearly so many organizations now who mail donors just once or twice a year. For experience has clearly shown that more regular mailing (usually) works very well. It does pay to mail your donors more often. Donors seem to feel, "We support ABC nonprofit, but we give our money to XYZ nonprofit because they write and ask for it." The same people support many organizations but they are likely to give most to the nonprofit that keeps in touch. So in a surprisingly short space of time nonprofit appeal mailings have grown . . . and grown . . . and grown.

But of course, the number of available mailing lists hasn't grown at anything like the same pace—certainly not the good ones. The last two decades also didn't see any substantial changes in either the number or the characteristics of the typical nonprofit donor—the little old lady from Des Moines, or from Tunbridge Wells, Fontainebleau, or Mönchengladbach, for that matter.

My colleagues and I used to say in hushed tones, "You know some donors in North America get thirty or more appeal mailings each month—incredible, isn't it? We couldn't ever imagine it happening in Britain." Now many people in the United Kingdom do receive fundraising mailings on a regular basis, if not every day then every week and often several times a week. What does this escalation mean to donors?

Quite simply it means they're seeing far more of it, they're recognizing it for what it is—a marketing communication—they're realizing that they don't want to be communicated with in this way and they're responding to it less and less. There is a limit to how many times we can sensibly write to our donors—but there are many different views as to what that limit might be. I believe we should only write when it is economically viable to do so and when we have something relevant and important to say.

If fundraisers don't take care to avoid overloading the mail donors will start to take their business elsewhere, or simply cease to be donors altogether, perhaps even striking one or two particularly offensive nonprofits out of their wills.

Perhaps the whole process is simply going through a phase of natural selection and will, in time, become automatically self-regulating. As more and more fundraisers subject a limited universe of prospects to more and more direct mail so responses begin to fall to the point that direct mail fundraising becomes uneconomic for the less "publicly appealing" causes. These then have to switch their recruitment to other sources, thus leaving cold donor recruitment via direct mail to the few most popular—and largest— nonprofits.

Junk Fundraising

There seems to be a silent conspiracy among people in direct marketing to expunge the term "junk mail" from our vocabulary. They appear to believe that by never mentioning the hideous phrase they will make the issue blow over, so the public will forget its irritation and perhaps even come to love direct mail, and the threatened disaster for direct marketing—regulatory intervention from on high—will be averted.

I think this is wishful thinking of the sort that ostriches do. If in saying so I am considered disloyal to the industry that provides my bread and butter then I am sorry but, like the little boy and the emperor with no clothes on, I can only own up that I see what I see. After all, the evidence that junk mail exists—and might even be on the increase—fills my mailbox every day of the week. By "junk mail" I mean inappropriate, irrelevant, badly prepared, and badly targeted mailings. In other words, unwanted and irritating rubbish.

This doesn't mean I am antipathetic to direct mail. Far from it. I think it is one of the most challenging and demanding of advertising media. When direct mail is done well it can be a joy to send and a joy to receive. But that happens too rarely. Unfortunately, most direct mail is mediocre and is met with indifference. Of the rest, quite a lot is junk, including quite a lot of junk fundraising, and that is causing damage to all fundraising organizations, particularly nonprofits. It is even threatening the continuation of direct mail fundraising as we know it.

One consumer described junk mail as "like a drunken stranger who comes up to you in the street and rambles on at you. You just want him to get out of the way as soon as possible." That's not the way fundraisers want their communications to be viewed, is it? That's not the way we'd expect donors to view us if we met them in the street. Why then are we making such a bad job of our written communications?

Lukewarm

Junk mail is just as much of a threat to warm mailing as it is to cold. Personal visits to donors are rarely viable in very large numbers. Large-scale telephoning of donors is often practical and very effective, but its value will be reduced if used too often. Perhaps because it's in its early days or perhaps because everyone hates "spam," unsolicited e-mail has yet to demonstrate potential for effective regular communication, at least with traditional donors. So direct mail remains the only practical means of communicating regularly with large numbers of donors on a long-term basis. If donors become even more resistant to direct mail generally (remember that your supporters also receive unsolicited mail from other nonprofits, from banks, insurance companies, travel firms, wine retailers, time-share operators, Uncle Tom Cobbley and all) then the outlook for fundraising communications, however relationship-oriented they may be, is bleak.

That's why I hate junk mail. I feel it has to be acknowledged, brought out into the open, and eradicated as quickly and as openly as possible so that the public can clearly see that fundraising, at least, has its promotional house in order.

"Junk" of course isn't unique to direct mail. You can have junk phone calls (we've all been on the receiving end of these) and equally you can have phone calls that make donors feel proud and happy and personally involved. Imagine you're a keen supporter of Third World causes. You learn on television of a disaster in the Horn of Africa and one of the nonprofits whose work in that area you have supported in the past telephones you at home that very night to say, "I know of your interest in this area and its people and I thought you would like to know what we, XYZ nonprofit, are doing to respond quickly to this situation." Most donors would be impressed and moved by such a personal report and would welcome the chance to help, if invited to do so.

Yet junk telephone calls cause most people to classify all promotional telephone calls in the same way. The public's natural reaction is to shoot first and ask questions later. As with direct mail, they'll resort to shooting all the messengers, whether or not they are bringing bad news, simply because too many similar-looking messengers have brought too much bad news in the past.

I don't blame them. But it doesn't have to be like that. The damage junk fundraising can do to our profession is easily imagined. Many people in our society are vulnerable to approaches from unscrupulous or badly trained and unsupervised fundraisers.

Imagine the confused and lonely old lady whose hearing is less than perfect, whose responses are slow and uncertain, who receives a telephone call from a nonprofit she is inclined to support. The nonprofit's emissary, recruited that afternoon from a nearby college or employment exchange, is following a carefully structured script designed to lead remorselessly one question after another toward an extracted promise to give, to give a large and specific donation, and then even to agree to give it regularly by automatic direct debit or electronic funds transfer, "the form for which, Mrs. Prospect, will be in tomorrow's post. . . ."

The difference between the two telephone calls I've just cited could not be more extreme. One is imaginative, relevant relationship fundraising. The other is junk. It doesn't bear thinking about. But it has certainly happened and will often happen again unless telephone fundraisers can be regulated by a respected and universally accepted code of behavior that can then be vigorously enforced. The United Kingdom's Institute of Fundraising and similar bodies in other countries have recently introduced such codes of practice for direct mail, telephone fundraising, and face-to-face solicitation. But they are not legally enforceable, and abuses do still happen. For these codes to be effective we need to devise some way of dealing appropriately with any organization that transgresses them. There are few things more futile than a toothless law.

All this may be soon entirely academic—throughout the past decade or more the threat of restrictive legislation from national governments or the European Parliament has hung over the fundraising community, designed to regulate how fundraisers store, exchange, and transmit personal data. If we don't get our act together the ability to determine our own response to these issues may be taken away from us.

The tragedy is that if restrictions are placed on our ability to use data, junk mail and telephoning is more likely to increase than to decrease. For accurate, up-to-date data enables us to *exclude* inappropriate individuals and to write or phone relevantly and in an informed way to the rest. With no access to such data, marketers will return to the bad old days of uncontrolled mass mailings—real junk.

Junk is not limited to the mail and the phone. We have all seen it on the television, on posters, press advertisements. It's everywhere. Let's not pretend it doesn't exist. That does nobody, neither consumer nor marketer, any good at all. It's like drugs or smoking. The best way to tackle the problem is to bring it out into the open.

The Final Solution

Although the public may not generally realize it, there is a ready-made and easy solution to the problem of too much junk mail from fundraisers. It is one we provide ourselves—the postage-paid reply envelope.

All an unhappy recipient need do is take the unwanted mailing and return it to the sender in the reply envelope so conveniently provided. Drastic, perhaps, but if enough of the public were to do this then the unwanted mail would have to stop, as nonprofits would be picking up an intolerable postage bill.

Low Organizational Self-Image

Some nonprofits make a number of mistakes brought on by their self-imposed tendency to wear sackcloth and ashes. They commonly say, "As a nonprofit we can't be seen to waste money," which is quite correct. But often what they really mean is, "As a nonprofit we can't be seen to spend money"—and that, as I have said before, leads to many false economies. It results in nonprofits' spending $5 and completely wasting their money when they could have spent $10 and achieved real value. Donors, of course, would much prefer the nonprofit to get value for money and if expenditure is clearly explained and justified will happily endorse the decision.

Nonprofits generally have almost totally failed to educate their supporters toward a mature understanding of the reality of their position, with the result that some of their supporters have been given quite unrealistic expectations of the organization's financial capabilities. So they make unrealistic demands such as "little or no administrative costs" and "expense ratio of 5 percent" and so on.

I don't blame the public for this kind of wishful thinking. The fact is that in the past nonprofits have done a poor job of explaining the commercial facts of life to their donors and to the public at large. It is this situation that leads nonprofits to present accounts designed to conceal rather than to reveal, charts and diagrams that show figures in a misleading perspective, and statistics that leave out any information that doesn't help perpetuate the deception. This kind of dishonesty by omission simply creates a rod for the nonprofit's back.

As always, the way people perceive what you say depends as much on how you say it as on what you are saying. That's what promotion is all about. But you have to be open and honest. Rather than tell a concerned donor that a part of each donation will go toward fundraising costs, is it not better to explain that by spending 25 percent of the gift on fundraising you can actually turn every dollar of that part of that gift into an extra $4 for the cause?

Of course it is. Donors think that's great. The need for positive projection of the facts was shown clearly long ago when a certain king required his portrait to be painted. He commissioned three painters each to try their different styles and the winner was to be handsomely rewarded with gold. Unfortunately, by a second accident of birth this young king was severely disabled. One of his legs was shorter than the other, his back was bent, and he was blind in one eye.

The first painter was absolutely honest and painted his king exactly as he was. The king was shocked and threw the artist in jail. The second painter portrayed his king as a dazzling Greek god. The king assumed the artist was putting him on and had him deported. The third artist painted a hunting scene—the king's favorite sport— in which his majesty was depicted with one foot on a tree stump (the shorter leg, naturally), his back bent as he took aim, and his blind eye naturally closed as he fired his rifle. The king was delighted, even though the painter had pictured him entirely faithfully, and the happy artist was duly awarded his bag of gold.

The moral of this story is that you must tell the truth, but it helps if you present it in an acceptable way.

A Neglected Public Face

Presenting things in a more acceptable way is a lesson many fundraising organizations could fruitfully take to heart when considering another area of common concern for relationship fundraisers—the public face of the organization. By this I don't mean the image projected to the media, I mean the face your public sees when they telephone or visit your organization with an enquiry or a request, or just happen to wander by.

Answering inquiries is an area many fundraisers overlook, but they do so at their peril. To show what I mean, consider the following results of anonymous tests. A colleague of mine once telephoned the top fifty nonprofits in the United Kingdom, asking for general information on behalf of a potential donor. Most were polite and helpful. Only one was downright rude, but several were hesitant, or suspicious, or asked awkward questions and made the caller feel uncomfortable. Ten out of the fifty sent very poor, ill-thought-out information. The material sent by many of the others was not very good. Only nineteen included some kind of clear response device. Worse still, having said they would, eleven out of the fifty failed to send anything at all. And most of the others took several weeks to get their dismal responses into the post.

Perhaps that is some indication of the quality of donor service among Britain's top fundraising nonprofits. Depressing though it is, it is a somewhat better picture than when we did a similar exercise five years earlier. Then only two out of forty-seven organizations approached made any further contact with the person who had requested their information.

Funny, isn't it? But it may not be quite so amusing when you consider how your organization would fare. I strongly recommend you to try this yourself. Next time you are out of the office subject your own organization to a "donor friendliness" road test. It can be very illuminating. If your voice is likely to be recognized, get a friend to do it for you—but do try to listen in. You may be very pleased and proud of your organization. But if not, think what effect that unhelpful voice is having when it answers your donors.

Ask yourself how well trained your staff are in basic telephone techniques, in answering the public, in making donors feel good, and in providing an accurate and speedy response to their requests. Are they familiar with the annual report, so that when asked can give a positive and helpful answer? If stocks are low, do they know how to get more, or whom to ask?

I work with many nonprofits. I know quite a few who are very hot in this regard. I know others who have never given it a second thought.

Your receptionist is a relationship fundraiser too, and needs to know as much as you do about what donors want and how to respond to them. Perhaps you could encourage this by buying a copy of this book for the reception desk. The voice that answers your telephone is often the public's first and sometimes only contact with your organization. It has a very special role to play in your relationship fundraising and can do a great deal of harm if it doesn't sound right or say the right things.

What Kind of a Reception Is That?

Another area at high risk of fundraisers' neglect is the reception area. Now your donor can not only hear but see the receptionist at work. What else can your donor see? A good display of promotional material? An intriguing set of press cuttings? Some interesting brochures to take away? A few copies of the annual report, some neatly framed posters? Somewhere comfortable to sit?

Chances are your reception area offers none of these things. Instead your donor will have to stand waiting for what seems an interminable time in a narrow corridor strewn with sundry leaflets, stacked with parcels, boxes, and the photocopier, next to peeling posters and paintwork with nowhere to put a cup of coffee. (A cup of coffee does, of course, come with the territory. This is just neglect, not abuse.) It has its own peculiar charm and it's appropriate for the church bazaar or the local youth club. But not for a nationally known fundraising nonprofit seeking to present a positive image and inspiring impression to the world of potential donors, all of whom might one day come to visit.

One national nonprofit I know has recognized that the people who come to visit are important and has constructed its reception area to create a good first impression. The focal point is a video and audio display unit containing short messages that are changed at intervals. Along one wall, neatly displayed, are all of the nonprofit's recent press releases and a display of press cuttings. A colorful target chart illustrating the progress of the latest appeal is also on show, as are a series of bright posters that surround the small library. And there is plentiful and comfortable seating. I like going there.

People tend to put a lot of emphasis on first impressions. Rightly or wrongly we judge people by the way they dress. What kind of an impression will your reception area make on your donors? Will it speak volumes about a successful, competent organization? Will it project an air of achievement and progress? Or will it present a depressing atmosphere of decay and decline?

Fundraisers from many organizations feel that the reception area is not part of their responsibilities, it is none of their business. But that is a mistake. A good reception area has an important part to play in your relationship fundraising. Ask your receptionist to keep a record of all visitors for one week—the people from the ad agency, the woman from Kansas, the computer engineer, the man who repairs the photocopier. . . .

They're all potential or current supporters. You might be surprised. Or maybe you think it doesn't matter because you don't get many visitors. Perhaps that's because you have a lousy reception area.

Make sure enough seats are available, train the receptionist, buy some flowers, get advice on mounting and maintaining a good display of leaflets and brochures. Have your posters framed. Keep your reception area clear and clean. And go and sit in it yourself from time to time.

The Importance of Nonresponse

The potential errors and pitfalls described thus far have all been visible and easily identified. It's not too difficult to create a mental picture of what happens in these areas when things go wrong.

I now want to consider an area that's of at least equal importance even though it's invisible: the danger of forgetting those who *don't* respond. By this I mean the larger part of every donor list, those who manage not to reply to most of our mailings, however appealing we may make them.

Fundraisers tend to ignore these people, despite having a universal and fanatical interest in overall response levels. "Wow," you may well say happily, "We've just got a 25 percent response to our Christmas warm mailing!" That's terrific. But that means the largest part of your donor list *didn't* respond. You achieved a 75 percent *nonresponse.* Why—what did you do wrong? What do your donors think of you? Did they mean to respond but not get round to it? Have they decided only to reply once a year? Will they ever respond again? Did they not like your mailing?

In fact, while most fundraisers could tell you whether they get, on average, a 15 percent or a 30 percent response to their mailings, many won't be able to tell you how many people on their list won't respond at all, how many only respond once a year, how many respond several times each year, how many respond every time.

Fundraisers have come to be so interested in the bottom line that it's easy to overlook those who don't reply. This is a serious error. Of course you can find some things out about these people through focus groups or, perhaps, a telephone survey, but how many fundraisers do? Wouldn't it be fascinating to know what nonresponders thought of the message? You can assume you know more or less what the donors who responded feel, but how about the rest? Are they really donors? Why didn't they respond? What changes, suggestions, or improvements could they make?

This subject is further complicated by the different definitions some fundraisers have of when a donor is a donor (after the second gift, say I), whether and when nonprofits decide to clean their lists, and at what point they decide to remove a donor who hasn't responded (after two years, I say) and put them on a tepid (reactivation) list. Of course, before any reactivation program is put into operation—see Chapter Nine—the relationship fundraiser needs to do everything practical to find out *why* a donor hasn't responded.

The question of "when is a donor really a donor" is a very important one. Before any individual can be usefully categorized as a donor there must be some concrete evidence of potential long-term support for the cause. A donor isn't someone who responds once as a knee-jerk reaction to a particularly emotive appeal. There must be at least a second gift as evidence of sustained commitment.

The difference between what one nonprofit and another refers to as a warm list can be quite staggering. One nonprofit my company prepared a questionnaire for received a 5 percent response, when others with apparently similar donors and appeal received 65–75 percent. What the first nonprofit referred to as its donor list of 400,000 names in fact probably came down to 20,000 real donors and 380,000 useless names it traditionally squandered its postage budget on.

The fact is that although a typical fundraising promotion may not generate a direct response from the whole donor file it almost certainly will have a considerable effect on a very large part of it. Research can prove this. Fundraisers need to know what that effect is, for the advertising impression made on nonresponders can be a crucial component of what you get for your expenditure on advertising. This doesn't just relate to direct mail but applies also to press advertising, inserts, and any other response advertising.

We should stop talking about direct response as if that were the only thing that matters. We are interested in "response." Whether it is direct or indirect is merely a matter of how long we have to wait to get our money. If we take the views and interests of nonresponders into account, surely that will influence the kind of response marketing materials—direct mail, press ads, and so forth—that we produce.

The Power and Perils of Emotion

Emotion, one of our greatest assets as fundraisers, is also one of our greatest dangers. There is no doubt that emotion pulls response. It opens checkbooks as well as hearts, but unbridled use or abuse of emotion can cause offense to the many while perhaps unjustly raising the expectations of the few.

The dilemma surrounding the use and abuse of emotion has been controversial as long as I've been in fundraising and probably since fundraising began. In fact, it is insoluble. There is no practical answer to this far-from-simple issue. But it is a subject that bears some further examination for it is fundamental to most nonprofits' communications with their supporters. Clearly, while bland communications don't work and are a great waste of money, some limits have to be imposed by those who frame our laws to prevent excessive use of emotion by fundraisers.

Emotion is essential to any appeal. Tests repeatedly prove that almost any audience will give more if the emotional lever is pulled. We all know the power and the potential in a child's eyes. Most nonprofits, by their very nature, have access to powerful emotive images and messages. The more emotive its appeal, the more popular and successful the nonprofit.

Would the public respond so generously to famines and natural disasters if they were not delivered directly into living rooms via the most powerful medium of all, television? Of course it wouldn't. Many of us can still remember the long lines of passive, starving children so movingly filmed at the time of the massive Ethiopian famines of the 1980s. In that situation, emotion is spontaneous and unstoppable. No one could see those scenes without being emotionally involved. It is right and proper that such suffering should be exposed, in its full and awful vividness, so that the scandal of starvation in a world of plenty can be brought home, and people be given the chance to act.

It is not the images or the use of the emotion that are obscene. What is obscene is the casual displacement of these images by other, more immediate news, such as the report of the sports scores or the latest share prices. What is obscene, I believe, is switching off or turning over in the hope that by so doing the problem, as well as the emotive images, will go away.

I don't see a dilemma in using to the full such clear and obvious images of suffering on the part of humans or animals. If your cause can draw on such legitimate emotion it will successfully raise funds. If it can't, it will have to try less basic and reliable means. It cannot tackle the problem without the funds.

Not everyone who works in overseas development shares this view. People who are starving still have dignity and rights. But development nonprofits also seek help for people who are not starving but who are poor. Where a question of acceptability arises is when images of poor people are presented as if they were starving, where images of black people are presented as if they were poor, and where poverty is presented automatically as unhappiness.

Programs of long-term development perhaps face these dilemmas more than appeals for disaster relief, where the need is immediate, obvious, and paramount. The people in need of development help still have the same rights, feelings, and dignity, but the dilemma arises when the fundraiser has to present their situation in the best way. The best way for raising funds will inevitably be the most emotive, but that may not be in the best interest of the people so pictured, for it may lead to inaccurate images, stereotypes, and ultimately to abuse of the very people the fundraiser exists to help.

European (and presumably North American) children are protected by law from potential exploitation by fundraisers. Parental permission is necessary before any photographs of children are reproduced and signed approval should always be sought. No such regulations protect the image of the Third World child. Any chance of protection is left in the gentle hands of the fundraiser, which brings me to the story of Mbazimutima.

When I was a fundraiser at ActionAid we recruited supporters via newspaper advertisements in the quality press. Because it was a relatively expensive exercise we were always testing—different copy, different sizes, different media—and our tests were rigorously scientific. We used photographs of African or Indian children waiting to be sponsored. As soon as one child was sponsored, we changed the photograph. No permission for this had ever been sought or given, but we had no complaints, mainly I suppose because the parents of these children weren't likely to read the papers in which we advertised.

One evening I was asked to approve a rush proof of an A/B split copy test we were running (a facility where two same-size versions of our ad appear in the same issue of a newspaper by being printed on different presses but mixed equally before distribution, thereby giving a valid split test). The only change in this particular test was in the child used. The relative pulling power of different children was being tested. Now there's nothing wrong with that. We all know that we need to use attractive, appealing images in our ads. In this respect nonprofits are no different from detergents. But one of my colleagues noticed that the picture captioned "Mbazimutima, aged eight, Burundi" actually showed a different child. Someone at the agency or the newspaper had used the wrong picture. I was very new at the time and was under some pressure from the newspaper and the agency to approve the ad quickly. No one would know the difference. If Mbazimutima's replacement were to walk down London's Oxford Street, no one would know he was the wrong guy.

We discussed it and agreed that whatever the consequences we would change the picture so the right name would appear under the right photograph. So Mbazimutima's name appeared under his photograph, as he would have a right to expect. I am sure that was the correct thing to do. As fundraisers we must never forget that we are dealing with real people who, if they were given the chance, would care about what we do with their image.

I once sent a photographer to India to document development work in Kerala. He came back with many stunning images but one of a ragged-haired, wide-eyed, naked boy was particularly dramatic and appealing. I used his picture in a small poster campaign and wrote a headline which was set across his lower torso, thereby covering his dignity. I never had his permission but it was a very popular poster and made him famous across the country. I don't suppose he ever knew.

Later our advertising agency selected the same picture for another national poster campaign, but here the headline wasn't so obliging and we had the problem of deciding whether or not to run a poster which showed in full a naked boy. I was very much against it, but was persuaded that rather than replacing the photograph, which wouldn't be easy, it could be retouched to remove effectively the offending part by blurring the image at the appropriate spot. In the end the retoucher transformed our stunning little boy into a no less beautiful and appealing little girl. But we had no right to do this and I have regretted it ever since.

Fundraisers for overseas causes have an awesome responsibility and not all of us discharge it faultlessly. When U.K. nonprofits such as the National Society for the Prevention of Cruelty to Children (NSPCC) and NCH Action for Children use images of children they have to employ models. These can then be art directed and made up as required and the public readily understands the need to protect the identity of the real cases. These nonprofits' promotions are no less effective because of it.

So if it is necessary in the United Kingdom, some similar rights and protection should also be given to people from other lands and cultures. This is a gray area for fundraisers. I don't know how it would work, but yet another code of practice needs to be devised to allow fundraisers to portray legitimate emotional images without demeaning, exploiting, or misleading either the public or the people whose images are being used but who can't give permission and can't protect themselves.

Domestic nonprofits also sometimes face similar dilemmas. I once took a photographer to a well-known London teaching hospital to photograph open heart surgery for a major heart research organization. The hospital was quite happy to allow us to take any photographs we wanted. The operation we were filming was on a middle-aged woman who was already unconscious on a slab. I remember thinking she looked like a lump of meat, she was so completely out of it. As we all, medical staff and photographers, went about our business, she was almost totally ignored. We took detailed shots of the operation which, it seemed to me, were the ultimate invasion of privacy. Later we discovered that the woman's permission had not been obtained so we correctly decided not to use any of the shots that showed her even though she herself would be in no way identifiable. Later she recovered from her operation and did allow the nonprofit to use her picture.

The dilemma posed by the images fundraisers use to portray people with disabilities is even deeper and more complex. Ann Macfarlane, writing in Arthritis Care's house magazine, *Arthritis News,* said, "The majority of disabled people believe that not only is much nonprofit advertising personally insulting, it also portrays untruths."

This observation may well be true and if it is, then the tragedy is that, just as with distorted views of overseas aid, damage is being done by fundraisers to the very people they are seeking to help. Somehow a solution must be found that enables fundraisers to present effective advertising that is positive, honest, and accurate. If it then still offends, perhaps the problem is more with the perception of the offended than with any actual offense.

Emotion can be used positively. It can make people think and so educate and inform where bland advertising would miss out. Disabled people can be consulted about the images fundraisers use, and should be. In varying degrees, in most of the nonprofits I work with, they are, although they may not always get their own way. The solution is consultation, fair representation, and even-handed discussion. As former British Prime Minister Harold Macmillan was fond of saying, "Slow calm deliberation untangles every knot."

Perhaps one way forward, as Ann Macfarlane goes on to suggest, would be the preparation of a set of guidelines and principles for good practice in nonprofit advertising. The trouble with guidelines, of course, is that inevitably they are also restrictions, they rarely cover all situations, and they sometimes create as many problems as they resolve. But it would be a start.

Boring, Boring, Boring . . .

The majority of nonprofit publications fail because they are dull. They present a picture of their organization as boring and ineffective, which is a sad waste because so often nothing could be further from the truth.

A few years ago I was invited to be one of the judges of the United Kingdom's Charity Annual Reports Awards. It was a sobering experience. More than four hundred organizations submitted their publications—and at least 90 percent of them were fit only for the wastepaper basket. Several clients of my company have won that award in the past but it is little consolation being the best of such a bad bunch. However, the awards have done a great deal of good and have made a major contribution toward elevating the status of nonprofit publications.

Things have improved in recent years and many more fundraising organizations now realize the folly of failing to invest time, care, and money in producing good, effective publications. But good intentions themselves are not enough. Another major danger is failing to listen to your donors. This can frequently be seen in nonprofits continuing to provide services that donors don't want to fund, but it's also frequently visible in a nonprofit's own publications.

From time to time I run workshops for fundraisers on publication design and production, particularly with regard to annual reports. One of my favorite devices for unfailingly attracting the audience's attention is to show some really appalling examples. It is rather wicked, I know, but I make no apology because once your annual report is published and distributed it is in the public arena and therefore is fair game for anyone to praise or condemn as they choose. The reason this device never fails to attract attention is that each member of the audience sits nervously through each ridiculed report thinking, "I wonder if mine will be next?"

It rarely happens, but one day, as I was showing a particularly dreadful, dull, and boring report, a hesitant hand went up in the audience and a timid voice confessed that she was, in fact, the originator of this dismal production. I, of course, began to backtrack like a mad thing but was stopped in my tracks by this woman, who now rather bravely stated that it was OK, she had no emotional stake in that production and had since read my book on annual reports. She felt she now clearly realized what was wrong with her first effort and had since introduced major changes. "Would you mind," she asked, "if I gave you a copy of my new report for your comments?"

After the seminar she did indeed give me her new report. It was certainly different. It was absolutely hideous—so overdesigned it was virtually unreadable and so far out in style that most recipients wouldn't want to try. Besides, its zany, unconventional shape meant it wouldn't fit easily in my wastepaper basket. I hurried off to make slides of it for my next annual report presentation. Such disasters are, thankfully, becoming quite hard to find.

The point is that she had certainly made dramatic changes, but they were all of the wrong sort. She had failed in the most important area of all: she hadn't listened to her readers.

Although most nonprofits have now improved their annual reports, many still neglect other important publications. For example, very few nonprofits produce a good welcome pack (see Chapter Eleven), yet the information sent as an introduction to a new supporter can be a crucial part of forming a long-term relationship. If your relationships get off to a good start, they are almost certain to flourish. If not they may never recover.

Personal Dislikes

I've developed a strong personal aversion to fundraising by collecting box. I know many organizations get worthwhile income this way, but I don't like it. It seems to me to be the antithesis of relationship fundraising.

With street collections people only give when they have to. They rarely even know the name of the cause and we, the fundraisers, have no way of explaining our purpose or going back later to solicit a further gift. Watch the eyes of passers-by to see how they loathe street collections. They smack of the begging bowl and do little good for fundraiser or donor in helping to enhance the position of either. They are a major contributor to the public's low esteem for nonprofits.

A research exercise in New York some years ago showed that people on the street are quite prepared to give to a fictitious cause (in that case called "The League of Two-Headed Babies"). The fact is that many people don't care who or what the collection is for, so long as the collector goes away quickly. Hardly positive fundraising. I did recently depart from my personal rule of avoiding street collectors because I was so impressed by the fortitude of a solitary woman collecting for one of the overseas aid nonprofits. She struggled in the rain against a sea of indifference while doggedly shouting her campaign slogan. That struck me as worth a pound of my money. Only later did I remember that collectors are not allowed to shout slogans or to do much other than just hold the tin and be there.

But that is an exception. Street collections won't win many converts, I suspect they are more likely simply to breed resentment. The late Cecil Jackson Cole (known as CJC), the remarkable man who founded Help the Aged, helped found Oxfam, and gave me my first job in fundraising, once said that a penny in the tin is a vote for the cause. I don't believe this is so. To win the hearts and minds of people you need a lot more time than it takes to pop a coin in the slot and perhaps a better place to do it in than a busy street.

CJC was right, however, in his basic assumption that encouraging people to give also encourages them to think about the cause they have given to—but street collections seem to me to be one of the least ideal ways of doing it. As far as I know, Oxfam was the first fundraising organization in Britain to commit resources to educating its donors, thereby echoing CJC's foresight.

On the positive side, street collectors do raise substantial sums of money and they are one of the few methods by which nonprofits actually reach the man and woman in the street. But I still don't like them. For much the same reason I am not keen on house-to-house collections, although at least then your collectors can leaflet, answer questions, and collect names, addresses, and telephone numbers of interested parties (see Chapter Nine).

I have similarly negative views of paper-based raffles, which tend to be propagated by coercion in that most people only agree to buy the tickets to get rid of the raffle-seller. I am also against much of the commercial selling of advertising space that nonprofits do in journals and programs. The reason for this is that they usually deliver very limited value for money so should be promoted as donations, not commercial advertisements. It is not always the case, I know, but too often professional advertising sales reps bludgeon small businesses into taking unwanted ads in tacky, badly designed publications that have no worthwhile circulation and because of their low quality are rarely if ever read. This breeds resentment among the advertisers and is certainly not a positive cooperation between industry and nonprofit. Some nonprofits have in-house advertising sales staff who are more scrupulous than the normal freelance ad sales outfit, but even these require more supervision than most nonprofits can give.

I also dislike any hard selling by nonprofits, however good the cause, and most potential sponsors and large donors would agree with me. Our business area is not appropriate to hard selling. Few businesses are. You don't get very far by pestering. All you do is queer the pitch for those who follow.

The Benefits and Risks of Marketing

Marketing imposes an essential series of disciplines on fundraisers. It enables the implementation of a planned series of tried and tested strategies and techniques, all of which are designed to help fundraisers achieve their ultimate aim—to raise more money.

Marketing helps the fundraiser organize research, identify prospects, target supporters and potential supporters at different levels, identify and test different products and propositions to put to them, and consider and evaluate price structures and public awareness and perceptions. It encourages and enables fundraisers to segment their donor list into a host of relevant subdivisions and then to approach each of these groups in a relevant and economical way. It causes fundraisers to evaluate each and every area of promotional endeavor and constantly seek to improve cost-efficiency.

Many fundraising organizations can dramatically illustrate the improvements that successful introduction of marketing techniques has made to their bottom-line figures. Most of the next chapter is devoted to describing how to do it. But marketing can also enable you to screw up your relationship with donors completely.

A Dangerous Love Affair

Nonprofits' love for marketing is still in relatively new bloom and, although one or two little indiscretions have sullied the initial idyllic expectations, there is no real sign that the affair is anything like over. In fact there is every hope that, given a few steadying outside influences and a little knuckling down to realities from both sides of the relationship, a long and happy marriage may result.

I hope so, for there's no doubt whatsoever that effective marketing can do a great deal for nonprofits. And there is reason to expect that fundraisers can do a great deal for marketing, too. I just wish we could call it something other than marketing, something that would mean more to our donors. For marketing for a nonprofit is very different from commercial marketing, and donors don't like to be marketed at.

There are clear dangers and considerable risks in nonprofit marketing. Before nonprofits plunge into too deep an embrace, these must be carefully considered. These days, it pays to take precautions. Also there are a number of siren voices, particularly those of direct marketing agencies, currently urging nonprofits to undertake more aggressive marketing activities. Beware the marriage guidance counselor who also rents tuxedos. Beware also of the tendency among agencies to see direct mail in the abstract, in terms of marketing theory or mounted on display boards for a presentation, rather than as donors see it, arriving uninvited to pile up in jumbled heaps. It is unlikely, perhaps, that your direct marketing agent will have been a fundraiser, but it helps a lot if you can work with someone who has at least been a donor.

Marketing Damage—and How to Avoid It

One definition of marketing for fundraisers might be that it is the process that enables fundraisers to target the needs and wants of donors and potential donors and to satisfy them through the design, pricing, communication, and delivery of competitively viable fundraising products and services. It enables fundraisers to plan, prepare, and view all their strategies on a regular basis and to allocate resources according to the needs thus identified.

I think if you read the preceding paragraph again you'll see the danger that I am referring to. The definition is couched in the language of marketing, but it isn't in the language of fundraising. If you use that kind of language with donors you'll pretty soon come unstuck. And many people from marketing backgrounds do use that kind of language when talking about and to donors.

I think that's a shame and it should be discouraged. We don't want to "educate" donors so that they understand the terminology and issues that involve fundraisers today. The unique relationship between fundraisers and donors will only be protected and strengthened if fundraisers accept that we should talk to our donors in their language, not ours. By language I don't mean just words but pictures and the combination of words and pictures together that, if presented carefully, can be five times more powerful than either words or pictures on their own. Language also means gestures and the way we present ourselves generally.

If donors feel they are being sold to or addressed by a marketing machine they will quickly cease to be donors. Therefore, we should not be treating our donors in the same way as our commercial counterparts treat their customers. That fundraising is different must be recognized in all our communications with donors. This means we need a different language, the language of fundraising, not the language of marketing.

Fundraising has taken many spectacular leaps forward in recent years, but these were almost always technology-based or marketing-based. We borrowed the systems and processes of commercial product marketing. We perfected the techniques of direct mail and began to write to our donors far more vigorously and far more often. We set up databases to enable us to contact our donors with mathematical precision. Our fundraising programs came to rely on the cold hand of technology. We introduced bland generalizations about people; we called them our targets, our prospects. We classified them and we gave them profiles. We even started to address them as "Dear Friend." How bland can you get? "Dear Friend," I ask you!

In the 1980s the culture of mass marketing began to invade the culture of fundraising. We can see this invasion in the rigid formulas that inhabit the letters we send to our donors—the window envelopes and computer labels, the obligatory underlining, phony postscripts, and so forth. We see it in all the imperfections, blips, and blemishes that inevitably creep into our databases. We see this invasion of mass marketing when we no longer think of our donors as people but as lists and numbers.

It also matters that we should show appropriate respect when we refer to donors. Labeling people as "lapsed" donors or "failed" donors is bad enough, but I have heard otherwise nice, considerate fundraisers refer routinely to unproductive segments of their database as "the residue" and even "the sediment." This won't do.

Following the Crowd

A famous advertising copywriter once claimed that the beginning of success is to be different, the beginning of failure is to be the same. If this is true, fundraisers are failing their donors.

Take, for example, the way nonprofits have embraced the techniques of selling by direct mail, and the formula we have adopted to carry our sales message to our customers. Commercial direct mail appeals to the lowest common denominator. Only a small percentage will reply so go full guns for them, the rest don't matter. If it works well once, keep milking it until it stops working and then move on. We have taken over the commercial direct mail formula with only a few minor adaptations and fitted it for fundraising's needs. It's a formula we're all familiar with—the standard-size outer and reply envelopes, the carefully laid out four-page letter with lots of underlining, the obligatory P.S. and photograph of the writer (when did you last include your photograph in a letter you wrote to a friend, or underline anything, or even write a postscript?), the ubiquitous appeal leaflet and reply form, the handwritten return address on the reply envelope, and so on.

We've all seen hundreds of them and they're all beginning to look very alike. Now of course this formula is tried and tested. It can be trusted. It still works well and so has more than earned its place in our affections. But isn't it a fact that most donors can see through it? Therein lies the danger.

The bottom line indicates that only sales matter. Relationship fundraising says this isn't so. If we can show our donors that there is more depth, substance, and sincerity in our communications than they've come to expect from other sources, then I am sure we will benefit in the long term.

If we are not to compound the errors of the past and fall into some of the traps we've fallen into before, then we fundraisers are going to have to be different, and distinctly different, from all the rest. In that way the culture of fundraising may indeed begin to invade the culture of marketing, rather than the other way round.

Action Points

▲ Try to learn from mistakes—preferably other people's.

▲ Beware of the modern machine. Use it wisely and cautiously.

▲ Banish computer numbers from your correspondence. Try bar codes instead—people don't appear to notice bar codes but they can be very put off by computer numbers.

▲ Treat donors as individuals. View your composite descriptions as useful indications and generalizations only.

▲ Avoid the bland and the dull. Inject passion and life into your copy so your enthusiasm and commitment come shining through.

Similarly, steer clear of formulas, or producing anything that might look just like everyone else's production.

▲ Don't hide from the problems of junk mail. Confront them. Don't do junk marketing and don't let anybody else get away with doing it either.

▲ Be honest and open with donors. Don't conceal problems. Tell the truth in a positive way.

▲ "Road test" your nonprofit. Phone in posing as a donor and check the response you get.

▲ Check your reception area and monitor everyone who answers the phone or meets the public. If their performance is not exemplary and their training faultless, introduce simple guidelines and explain why things must change.

▲ Find out who visits your reception area. Go and sit in it yourself from time to time. Phone in and out through your switchboard.

▲ Find out from your readers how good your publications are. If they're not doing a first-class job of selling your cause, make changes. Dull publications are rarely read. Make yours reflect your cause.

▲ Think carefully about how you use images in your advertising. Balance emotional impact with honesty and integrity.

▲ Don't forget your nonresponders. Find out how they feel.

Donor Profile: John Collins

John was angry. He put the phone down, not quite with a crash but very firmly.

"Honestly," he said out loud, although he knew he was talking to himself. "Why can't these people check their facts. Talk about inefficiency. . . ."

Having got that largely out of his system, but still inwardly mumbling about too much spent on administration and what are they doing calling at this time, anyway, John went to the fridge and poured himself a drink. Balancing his microwaved pizza on top of his foaming beer he shut the fridge door with his boot, a technique that over the years had worn away the enamel on the door, and swayed into his living room. He flopped down on the sofa, flicked on the TV, and forgot about it.

Meanwhile, the telephone fundraising organization that had rung John to solicit the long overdue renewal of his membership in a well-known environmental organization was preparing to query this lapsed renewal—among others—with the client. The caller noted that John had informed him that he was still a member and had renewed his membership quite recently. Mistakes do happen and the telefundraising organization wasn't going to take any chances of creating offense.

But John wasn't a current member. He hadn't renewed his subscription for more than two years. If you had stopped John on his way to work the next morning and asked him he would have told you with absolute conviction that he was a fully paid-up member not just of that environmental organization, but of several others, all in similar areas.

John cares, make no mistake. He really cares. The only thing is, it's more than a year since he renewed *any* of his subscriptions. He thinks he's a member, they think he's lapsed. John never reads appeal mailings but he knows he still gets quite a lot, so he must be a member. And he gets quite a few newsletters too.

As John would say, "How am I supposed to know?"

Chapter Eight

Building Better Friendships Through Marketing

You have to be the change that you wish to see in this world.
MAHATMA GANDHI

According to Stan Rapp and Tom Collins in their excellent book *MaxiMarketing,* the late 1980s saw the beginning of the most important business development of the twentieth century. They described this event quite simply as the death of mass marketing and the birth of individual marketing.

Arguably, this shift represents the greatest single opportunity for fundraisers ever. But there's more to it than that. All kinds of businesses throughout the world are finding that their relationships with customers are changing. In the last few years we have seen a shift from "get that sale now at any cost" to the construction and management of customer databases that can create a complete record of relationships with customers throughout their lives.

Most marketers have yet to realize the opportunities this represents. Fundraisers should respond to the chance they now have to make the prediction come true. They have the once-in-a-lifetime opportunity to take the kind of lead that will make relationship fundraising a model for the rest of the marketing fraternity.

It is somewhat ironic that fundraising has in the past two decades just begun to embrace conventional marketing techniques and wisdom and to employ trained marketing people, at the precise time that marketing itself is undergoing a fundamental metamorphosis. Some nonprofits are caught in a dilemma. They have begun to appreciate the power of commercial sales and marketing techniques and have enthusiastically embraced aggressive sales tactics, particularly direct marketing techniques. Now they are being told that maybe they are being a bit short-sighted.

A central theme of this book is that the traditional approaches of product marketing were in many respects inappropriate and counterproductive for fundraisers and that, while the old marketing was clearly bringing many short-term gains, it was also stirring up a host of problems for the future. In fairness, the value of customer relationships has always been recognized in professional marketing, but practitioners often underestimate its importance or overlook it in their drive for increased profit.

The new marketing need have no such in-built destructive tendencies. The new marketing, based as it is on the cultivation of individual direct relationships, is ideally suited to fundraising, and fundraising is the perfect area in which to show how well the new marketing works.

Marketing—and relationship fundraising for that matter—is only of value to fundraisers if it helps them to raise more money more efficiently. There is no value in getting carried away with the idea of a mutually supportive relationship with your donors unless the ultimate effect of that relationship is to increase the flow of funds for your cause.

What Is Marketing?

Marketing involves finding out what consumers want or need and then supplying it at a profit. Research, strategy, product design, advertising, public relations, communication, and even after-sales service are all part of marketing. Marketing involves constant monitoring of consumer reactions to product, price, and delivery and enables you to establish whether or not your product is viable. Any strategy for marketing should be conceived against a background that takes full account of internal resources such as your own management and staff, the existing external market of current customers and prospects, your competitors, and local, national, and perhaps international media. It also includes macro considerations such as the economy, demographic shifts, politics, and so on. Analyzing these various elements is the first step in preparing a marketing plan.

Everybody in your organization should be part of your marketing plan. From the chief executive officer to the person who answers the switchboard, everyone has an important role to play in marketing your organization and should be clearly aware that they do.

The marketing plan for fundraising may well be part of a larger strategic plan for the whole organization that covers such areas as service provision, associated organizations, campaigning, staff policy, and other activities not normally part of fundraising. If so, fundraising planning has to adapt to fit in with that overall strategic plan. From here on, however, this discussion of the marketing plan relates only to marketing for the fundraising operation itself.

Marketing for a fundraising organization is inevitably and irrevocably different from marketing products such as detergents or motor cars. This may be less significant for fundraisers in a hospital or university, where a clearly defined product or service exists, than it is for a nonprofit or cause promoting a less tangible need or service to a disadvantaged third party.

Fundraisers will only succeed in marketing if they start by recognizing these differences, capitalize on the strength this gives them, and plan their marketing to take the differences fully into account. This was always the case. But the new age of individual marketing means fundraisers have to be even more aware of the underlying factors that contribute to their unique relationship with their customers.

The Age of Choice

The old mass marketing is indeed dead. Gone are the days of the Model T Ford, when you could have any color you wanted as long as it was black. Choice now is almost limitless and customers themselves are being involved more and more in deciding how they want to make their choices. So luxury car manufacturers already offer buyers more than just the opportunity to choose internal and external color schemes—they can also select the upholstery materials used, some internal components, and an endless array of optional extras. Just around the corner is the day when prospective car buyers will virtually be able to design their own cars to be manufactured to order by computer-driven robots.

Every one an original. That suggests some very satisfied customers.

Choice is not just the province of car manufacturers. Revlon makes 157 shades of lipstick, 41 of them pink. Whiskas cat food offers 30 flavors. *Catalyst,* the leisure industry customer loyalty package, offers customers the opportunity to choose which editorial areas interest them in their free quarterly magazine—travel, motoring, cookery, business, or whatever. So, instead of receiving the bland, generalized content typical of most airline or hotel magazines, *Catalyst* readers choose their own reading matter, thereby guaranteeing their interest (in theory).

This kind of individual choice was impossible before the development of the computer database (which enables the publisher to solicit customers' views and store them for easy access) and the technology by which that database can be applied to select, print, and bind each individual copy of the magazine according to the choices stored in the database. These are the components that make individual marketing possible to tens of thousands of people simultaneously. It is these that fundraisers must now use to best advantage.

Databases are not a recent development. Businesses have kept lists of their customers since selling began and many, notably corner shopkeepers, have not only known their customers by name but have known all their family member's names and all about their private affairs. What is different now is the computer and the potential it gives us to instantly remember names, addresses, dates, donations, frequencies, amounts—facts and figures by the millions. Computers can also find out about your donors by matching, cross-checking, and analyzing the data on hand, and the cost of all this is going down all the time.

Marketing has moved full circle. Potentially the personal service of the village shopkeeper is now in the hands of the national fundraiser.

Some Marketing Considerations

Sometimes good intentions can frustrate a nonprofit's marketing activities—and few good intentions are as frustrating as those of dedicated nonprofit employees trying to protect their donors. I had an early example of this at ActionAid. Two of my colleagues, when asked why they were failing to keep records of the names and addresses of people who had sent in money, explained their fear that I would use their addresses to write and pester these good people for more money, and that would upset them.

Crazy and misguided though it seems, there is a germ of truth in this argument and I suspect it is still a view shared by many nonprofit boards. I would certainly have written to those good people, but I hope I wouldn't have upset them. As it is, potential donors were denied the opportunity of helping a cause they obviously were interested in. They weren't even given the chance to say no.

The other classic that happened at about the same time—and I swear this is true—was when the head of the mail room asked that if I must run a Christmas appeal could I organize it at some other time of the year as the mail room was always very busy anyway in the few weeks leading up to Christmas?

As a first step toward preparing your marketing plan it is necessary to carry out a marketing audit to evaluate and record the current state of your organization's marketing. I suspect that even nowadays many organizations would find, as I did all those years ago at ActionAid, that formal marketing is nonexistent, or worse. (I didn't know any of this at the time. With hindsight it was a case of the blind leading the blind—but we were successful in spite of that.) It's all changed now, of course, and ActionAid's marketing department is one of the most sophisticated to be found anywhere. But even if no marketing apparatus exists in your organization the exercise is nevertheless worth doing and can be very illuminating. From the lessons thus learned the next step is to construct your plan. This essential preparation done, then all you have to do is implement it!

Here are some considerations for fundraisers, questions you might ask yourself when contemplating your marketing audit:

- What is different or unique about us and what we do? Are we first, or best, or biggest? Can we find a niche that is uniquely ours?
- Who are our major markets? Research by the American Heart Association showed that it wanted to address forty-one different markets, so you'll probably be talking to more than one.
- What is our position in relation to other causes, similar appeals, or services?
- What are our objectives?

- What is our product and what are its benefits (for example, a television station might produce programs but it gives customers entertainment and information)?
- Different people react differently to different propositions. How do people react to ours?
- How can we change the proposition to improve the response (without necessarily changing the product)?
- What is our pricing policy (if it exists at all)? Are we controlling how much donors give or are we leaving it to them? Is our price high enough for our needs, or too high for our donors' pockets?
- How are we packaged—that is, what is our reception area like? What do our visible communications look like?
- Do we have a brand image or identity? How do our donors, our prospects, and our service users perceive us? (See Chapter Five.)
- How do we perform on after-sale service—speed and quality of response, thank you policy, and the like?
- Can we make any special offers, promotions, or incentives, such as invitations to open house sessions, visits to centers, and the like?
- How good is our promotion—advertising, use of media, publications, displays, personal presentations?
- How effective is our distribution—volunteers, local groups, shops, regional staff? How do our distributors use our materials?

And so on. An even more basic question, to top the list, might be "what business are we in?" Mary Parker Follett, America's first management consultant, had a client that thought it was in the curtain business. She persuaded its managers they were in the light control business, and transformed their entire approach. Similarly, leading marketing professor Theodore Levitt quoted the decline of the American railroads to illustrate an organization that failed to understand what business it was in: "The railroads did not stop growing because the need for passenger and freight transportation declined. In fact, that grew. The railroads are in trouble not because the need was filled by others (cars, trucks, airplanes, even telephones) but because the need was not filled by the railroads themselves. They let others take customers away from them because they assumed they were in the railroad business, rather than in the transportation business. They were product-oriented, instead of customer-oriented."

As fundraisers, we are in the donor development business and not, as you might think, in child care, or Third World development, or higher education, or whatever.

How to Turn Change into Innovation

Most people resist change and many fundraising organizations go out of their way to avoid it. But the opportunity to change can be just what your marketing needs and your marketing plan can help you achieve it. Here are some guidelines:

- See change as an opportunity, not a threat.
- When your organization is at its most successful is a good time to refocus and to change. Don't become complacent; that leads to decline.
- Find the right person to lead change. Any new initiative needs someone who loves it.
- Challenge people who say, "We've always done it this way."
- Identify specific objectives. Measure them before and after. Get everyone involved to agree on these objectives.
- Change your people's behavior, not their attitudes. The change in attitudes will follow.
- Recognize your different publics. Develop and exploit any niches that are special to you.
- Test your changes at every stage. Remember that noncustomers will always outnumber customers, so research what they want too.

The Marketing Mix: Creating an Effective Marketing Strategy

An organization's marketing strategy will flow from the earlier stages of marketing audit and preparing the goals and objects. The strategy is important because it translates all the information and insights that emerged from the initial process into a workable long-term plan.

An effective strategy will be customer-centered, distinctive, innovative, sustainable, and flexible. It should be easy to communicate the basics of the plan to others and should be capable of motivating everyone involved into enthusiastic commitment. It will identify the markets being tackled and the products that are right for each segment of the market, and it will use, as appropriate, the whole range of fundraising methods available: direct marketing, of course, but also personal solicitation, events, major donors, big gift campaigns, joint promotions with companies, local groups, and the whole arsenal of tools.

The Marketing Plan

The process of planning is as important as the plan itself, if not more so. So savor the task of preparing your plan. It should be fun, challenging and approached by all with open minds. Donors should be involved in your planning too—they'll love it, you'll learn, and the bond between you and them will strengthen. But don't overplan—beware of paralysis by analysis.

How to prepare the plan itself is beyond the scope or purpose of this book. However, there are a few reasonably accessible books that are recognized guides to marketing planning. These include McDonald and Leppard's *The Marketing Audit: Translating Marketing Theory into Practice*, *Marketing Plans* by Malcolm McDonald, and *The Twelve-Day Marketing Plan* by James Makens. One of the easiest to use is *The Marketing Plan: A Pictorial Guide for Managers* by Malcolm McDonald and Peter Morris—which, as its name suggests, is not only useful but is about as much fun as marketing planning can be.

If not always fun, marketing for fundraisers should nevertheless be accountable, appropriate, acceptable, affordable, and action-oriented, and it should give added value—all the A's.

All marketing starts with the prospect. But before you can reach people who might be receptive to your message you've got to know where to find them.

Targeting

Targeting is described as the art and science of identifying, describing, locating, and contacting one or more groups of prime prospects for whatever you are selling. (Here is the first hidden danger of marketing. It's full of unnecessary complexity. Everyone knows what targeting means. It neatly says in one word what a marketer will describe less well in twenty.)

Fundraisers build their donor bases by effectively targeting those individuals and groups most likely to give to support their cause. Target marketing can involve combinations of geographic, demographic, and psychographic consumer characteristics to narrow down potential prospects. To target accurately we not only need to segment consumers according to the full range of their attributes (geographic—regional, economic, cultural, geographical; demographic—age, sex, race, education, religious background, family size, residence; and psychographic—social values, beliefs, attitudes, interests, opinions, lifestyle), but also to anticipate social change (see Chapter Five). If this information is available, and increasingly it is, computers can now easily overlay it—drawing on numerous interactive databases—and come up with not just a profile of your most likely targets but also a list of their names and addresses.

As mentioned earlier, nonprofits should be paying particular attention to targeting "the new old," the healthy, vigorous, and often affluent younger end of the fifty-plus market who own so much of the Western world's disposable wealth and control so much of its enterprise.

Segmentation

The idea of segmenting a database is not new (few ideas are) but it is one that can pay enormous dividends for those nonprofits who do it properly. More than a few nonprofits have yet to get round to it, but it makes enormous sense.

People are different. Even though many donors will conform to your typical profile, you'll have some who are young, rather left-of-center working women, and you'll have some elderly retired military types. It doesn't make much sense to treat all these different people in the same way, particularly as modern technology has given you the means to individualize on a large scale.

Effective segmentation is the key to making personalized marketing work because while we can't (yet) write truly individual letters to everyone, we can write different letters to each segment. (After targeting, I'm not going to attempt to define segmentation. We've all eaten grapefruit, and we all know what a segment is.) In the context of your database for relationship fundraising a segment is a group of like individuals separated and kept distinct from the others because in some way or other they are substantially different. In the past, we have divided our lists into crude historical segments based on how people performed in the past: by their most recent gift, by the size of their last gift, by how often they've given, by what they've given to. This is immensely useful information. But it is also possible to segment by interests or by personal attributes such as lifestyle and beliefs. All this information can be gathered with your donors' permission and can go into your database. Another way to segment is by choice: how and when donors choose to hear about you and what they wish to hear about. Some organizations farsighted enough to segment their donors in this way are reaping considerable benefits. Which do you think will work best: if we send donors what we want them to have or what they would like to receive?

Perhaps in the future a Third World development nonprofit will be segmenting its donors into groups such as well traveled or lived overseas, young families, enthusiastic about changing the world, old sentimentalists, lonely seekers of friendship, and so on, and writing to each of them different, more appropriate letters.

This takes us into a difficult area. I feel comfortable about technology's ability to enable us to write fewer, better, more relevant letters to our friends. But I feel uncomfortable about the obvious potential for cynical abuse of information. This is a dilemma all fundraisers will have to address in the near future—how far do we take segmentation and at what point does personalization become deliberate deception?

When preparing reciprocal mailings, for example, most nonprofits will run a de-duplication program with the other nonprofit's list. This is good commercial sense, but few organizations keep a note of which of their supporters also support other nonprofits. Would it be useful to know which of your donors are also donors to other nonprofits? I think so. Taken to its conclusion, you could then build a list of superdonors who appear not just on two nonprofits' lists but on three, four, five, or more. You could then swap your three-nonprofit supporters with another nonprofit's three-nonprofit supporters, and expect correspondingly better results.

In fact, reciprocals could be much more segmented than they generally are at present. Instead of the simple swap of donors, you could also suggest swapping your three-time givers with another nonprofit's three-time givers, and so on. (This assumes, of course, that reciprocal mailing will continue to be a permitted option— see Chapter Nine.)

How long will it be, I wonder, before someone constructs a national database of nonprofit donors with all this information on it? Then it would be possible to select all the "little old ladies from Tunbridge Wells" from one central source. Alarming thought, isn't it?

Product

"Give a man a fish and you'll feed him for a day. Teach him to fish and you'll feed him for life," the old adage says, probably attributable to Confucius, as most of them are. It is, of course, true even if a bit patronizing, and has been quoted ad infinitum. The sage didn't say, "Ask a supporter for a donation and he'll give you a low-value one-off gift. Present your request as a product and he'll regularly give you larger amounts regularly over several years." But he could have and without being at all patronizing it would have been just as true.

Fundraising "products" are of increasing value. Sponsoring a child or adopting a granny are examples of high-value ongoing needs. Sponsoring a brick or joining a low-cost membership scheme may be the other end of the scale. Recognition and reward schemes are also products. For £104 per year (about US$150) you can become a cultivator sponsor at Ryton Gardens. For £20 ($30) per year you can be a friend of the NSPCC. Such schemes may not be huge money-spinners themselves—though they can be. But they do guarantee the long-term involvement of the purchasers, who can be sold other things now they're "in the store."

In the late 1990s many nonprofits switched from soliciting one-off donations to asking donors for a small, manageable monthly contribution. In the United Kingdom and other countries this has now become the favored fundraising entry product. How much money this concept has raised for nonprofits is open to calculation, but it is certainly huge. This trend toward offering committed giving products led directly to the current trend for face-to-face fundraising (see Chapter Thirteen).

I know of one nonprofit that encouraged its supporters to give monthly gifts by regular funds transfer, which most chose to do on a monthly basis (because British people are paid monthly). As these donors were already giving so substantially and so often, the fundraising staff felt they couldn't ask for any more. In fact the opposite turned out to be true. These good regular donors responded very generously to special and emergency appeals, proving what most retailers know very well—your most likely new customer is your existing customer. And the easiest way to extend your customers' involvement is to offer a new product, provided it is appropriate to their needs or desires.

When designing your product, consider what its benefits will be to your customer. Will the product sell? You can only find out by testing. More often than not it's the product, not the marketer, that determines success or failure. At ActionAid we couldn't fail with child sponsorship but, whatever we tried, we couldn't succeed with "Village Neighbour," a lower-cost scheme where donors were linked to a village project rather than a particular child. We failed because "Village Neighbour" was a product the public didn't want to buy, even though it was a brilliant idea and entirely appropriate in development terms. Design your product to fit the marketplace, because the marketplace won't alter itself to fit your product.

Product is one of the key marketing considerations known as the five P's. The others are price—what your product costs; place—which really means distribution but that doesn't start with a "P"; promotion—which is all your advertising and packaging, that is, the physical appearance of your goods or services; and people, perhaps the most important "P" in marketing. People are mentioned throughout this book and promotion and packaging are covered in other chapters, but the others are each worth a mention here.

Price

Few nonprofits are used to thinking in terms of price in the way that for-profit companies do. Many commercial organizations have come to realize, often painfully, that the real secret of success is not sales, supply, or service, it is getting the price right.

Nonprofits generally could benefit from a review of their pricing policy. At worst there is no guidance on price and donors are left to fix their own giving level. This usually results in small gifts and also to lowered response as potential donors are afraid to offend by giving a gift the organization might think too small. In membership and similar schemes, where there are fixed price levels, nonprofits tend to aim low so as not to discourage the poorer end of their market.

This is ideologically commendable but not very sound commercially. Those nonprofits that have priced their proposition competitively, such as the child sponsorship agencies, are among the most successful nonprofits today. In Britain, a sponsor's minimum annual contribution nowadays is around £180 (most give via the government's Gift Aid scheme, which enables the nonprofit to recover the tax already paid on the gift, and many donors also make one-off donations on top). The average donation for many other nonprofits that aren't asking for a specified regular amount tends to hover around the £10–£15 mark. Think about the implications of that for a moment.

In many cases nonprofits seem to be in quite elastic markets and their products are often not noticeably price sensitive. When I was at ActionAid we increased the cost of sponsorship several times, but it seemed to have little or no effect on recruitment rates. In some areas there is price sensitivity, as between various membership schemes. Supporters might not expect Greenpeace to charge more than Friends of the Earth, for example, although I can find no logical reason whatsoever why what they charge should be affected in any way by, say, what the National Trust charges or the National Asthma Campaign.

I have also found that when the reasons behind a price increase are explained in detail to donors they invariably understand and respond positively. Whether they donate $10 a year or $10 a month makes little difference financially to most donors if they believe enough in what you are doing, but it will make an enormous difference to you. (See also Chapter Eleven, where price is discussed further as a major opportunity for fundraisers.)

Place

Place, although important to most commercial marketers, is really of limited importance to relationship fundraisers, unless we consider the importance of taking our marketing out of the office and into the homes of our donors. While fundraisers continue to do much of their marketing by mail or electronically, place has little importance because the Postal Service and e-mail give us almost immediate access to all corners of the globe. So it is with the telephone.

There are just three principal ways to approach your prospects—by mail (snail or electronic), over the phone, and in person (eyeball to eyeball, as they say, or belly button to belly button). According to some fundraisers, the mail is sixteen times less likely than a personal visit to be effective. Many nonprofits already do lots of individual visits, but these tend to be organized on a regional or field basis so are often overlooked by headquarters, which so far has probably not even considered marketing in person, because of the prohibitive costs (and inconvenience) that would be involved. What a shame we can't send volunteers round to visit our donors, rather than mailing them—we'd do up to sixteen times better. Now there's a thought. . . . Perhaps place *is* important after all.

Ten Marketing Questions

While we are in the mood for asking questions, here are ten marketing questions all relationship fundraisers need to ask themselves:

1. How many different types of prospective donors can I identify and describe?
2. How can I reach these donors and persuade them to support my cause?
3. How many "offers" could I make?
4. How can I avoid wasting money on current promotions?
5. How can I test my promotional messages?
6. How good is my organization at answering inquiries? (Test this one yourself; see Chapter Seven.)
7. Do we save names? What do we do with them?
8. How can existing supporters help us find new supporters?
9. Can I think of ways to get my advertising to do double duty? This is where a single effort is used to accomplish two or more different jobs. That is, can you promote organizational or brand awareness while recruiting donors, demonstrate your commitment to a particular campaign while raising funds, and so on? In certain circumstances this multifunctional approach can make a limited advertising budget very much more productive.

10. Do we have ways of ensuring that we listen to what our prospects are saying?

These questions should be considered alongside those previously raised in the planning stage (discussed earlier in this chapter).

Search for the URG!

Marketing is full of jargon. But often there's a good reason why a new word is created to express a hitherto unknown idea or process unique to a particular business area. Most professions have their jargon—from prostitution to the clergy. So it pays to understand some of marketing's jargon and to borrow it for your own purposes. But don't allow your donors to hear you doing it, for they are hardly likely to approve. The best way to avoid the risk is to create your own donor-friendly terminology appropriate to your own individual business area.

One of marketing's most powerful pieces of jargon is the notion of the USP—the unique selling proposition. Finding your USP involves searching your product or service to find the one thing no one else can offer and projecting it as unique to you. Polo Mints achieved this remarkably with its "mint with the hole" concept. Imagine buying a sweet because it has a great big hole in it! People did, and still do. The mint with the hole has been a market leader for years, largely thanks to its unique selling proposition. The term "unique buying proposition" might be more appropriate, because that expresses the concept from the customer's point of view.

An example of a fundraising organization that has exploited its USP is Greenpeace, those people in inflatable boats who put themselves between the harpoons and the whales. Their USP is not the slogan "Thank God someone's making waves," it is the idea of peaceful direct action to protect the environment.

Donors respond to Greenpeace because secretly they'd love to be in that fragile inflatable themselves, taking action to save the planet. Greenpeace offers them the opportunity to be there from the safety of their armchair. (A substantial proportion of their supporters, however, actually do volunteer for active service and this gives Greenpeace quite a logistical problem in handling all these would-be rainbow warriors with tact. Or perhaps it's an opportunity?)

But the term USP is not appropriate for fundraisers even though the concept certainly is. I prefer to use a term that says the same thing but is directly relevant to fundraising—URG—the unique reason to give. I advise fundraisers to search for their URG.

Personality Problems

Another piece of marketing jargon that fundraisers might usefully adopt after suitably changing its name is the concept of brand and brand image. Imagine what your donors would think, if they heard you talking about that! But a strong, easily recognizable brand identity is important for fundraising organizations. It is your personality as a cause among all the other nonprofits they might support. A strong and even unique brand image might be your organization's only hope of distinguishing itself from other apparently similar nonprofits operating in the same field. Some nonprofits—for example, the Royal National Lifeboat Institution and Save the Children Fund—have very strong personalities, or brand images, while others have not. Greenpeace, Amnesty International, Oxfam, Médecins sans Frontières, and Habitat for Humanity are all truly international brands—the number of which is growing as more and more organizations set up fundraising programs as well as projects overseas.

Has your nonprofit, or organization, got a personality? Or is it bland, anonymous, or just as yet largely unknown? Could it benefit from a strong, clear personality? How might it go about getting it?

At this point, cue the charlatans from corporate design division who'll descend with a whole load of baloney about positioning, market profile, identity research, and the need for massive investment in a new logo. Fine, if you can afford it. A logo is important, as is consistency of style and color, but you don't get personality from a snazzy suit of clothes. That is not to say that brand image doesn't have any value. For example, it is the big "brand name" nonprofits that attract most of the floating bequest income.

My favorite bit of logo nonsense is the story of Pirelli, the tire (and calendar) people, who, apparently, commissioned a top international design consultancy to make recommendations for the change of their logo worldwide. Off went the top design agency and several months later back its executives came to air their proposals. Pirelli's management were apparently shocked to be presented with a very slender document, not much thicker than the invoice that was underneath. The shock deepened when they read that the agency's recommendation was that their current logo was doing a very good job and shouldn't be changed at all. Rigor mortis set in when they read the invoice. It was for $1 million.

Pirelli paid, of course, or so the story goes. In fact, the design agency had conducted extensive research in the 139 (or however many) countries where Pirelli was represented and no doubt its people tested a lot of alternatives and did a lot of work. It still seems like rather an expensive piece of self-indulgence. The Pirelli story is now part of advertising folklore and may or may not be true. Some version of it probably is, and there are a few equally cynical stories going around involving the amounts spent by different nonprofits on their logos.

Some organizations have got great logos that are a real asset to their cause, but the best logos are simple and immediately clear. Creating a new logo is rather like creating a new letter of the alphabet. Imprinting it indelibly on the public's consciousness is a rare achievement, a task that should only be attempted by those with substantial resources of time and money.

The big brands—McDonald's, Nike, Coca Cola—are an inescapable fact of daily life and we all know and recognize them instantly. This has obvious value. But branding for a nonprofit, even more than a commercial enterprise, is not just about appearance. It's about values, beliefs, aspirations, what your organization stands for. . . . Even the smallest of organizations can have a clear and appropriate brand and although it won't be known to everybody, you can make it very well known to all the different types of people that really matter to you. Many corner shops have identities and values (friendly, helpful, reliable, good conversationalists, open late) that are strong enough to persuade patrons to shop with them even when wider choice and lower prices can be found within easy reach.

Your brand identity is not about what *you* would like to be, or even what you think you are. It is what *other people perceive you to be.* Successful brand management is about taking control of this process rather than leaving everything to chance. Your brand is, in fact, an essence. It has to pervade your organization from the chair of the board to the switchboard operator, from your most distant outposts to the very core. It follows that it has to permeate through all your communications—verbal and visual, printed and electronic.

In case a definition of the word brand would help you, here is my favorite: "*Brand* is the set of ideas, images, feelings, beliefs and values that are carried around in a person's head." That shows how important the concept of brand is.

Strong beliefs and values are what set nonprofit organizations apart from commercial brands (although many companies now are looking seriously at occupying this territory). Given the strength of our belief systems, nonprofit brands should be much, much stronger than others. Yet there are few strong nonprofit brands, and a host of trivial and superficial products are much more readily recognized and liked than we are. Maybe it's just a question of the relative size of budgets, but I suspect that's only part of the story. The simple truth is we haven't told our stories very well.

Fundraising by Phone

Telefundraising (or, preferably, fundraising by phone) is another of those areas that has such an impact on relationship fundraising it transcends all the artificial divisions of any chapter headings, so I mention it briefly here and also come back to it in more detail later. I've already outlined some of its pitfalls and problems in Chapter Seven. As with direct mail I didn't wish to give telefundraising a chapter on its own because it has a relevance in almost every aspect of donor service and development.

Telephone fundraising is yet one more of those marketing techniques that just over a decade ago almost everyone in fundraising said would never happen in the United Kingdom, despite the spectacular success it was then enjoying on the other side of the Atlantic.

Events have proved almost everyone to be wrong. Telephone fundraising did rather well in the United Kingdom and, in fact, brought in a lot of money for a number of quick-off-the-mark charities and universities.

The telephone is the third-largest advertising medium, by expenditure, in the United States, after television and magazines. There's no doubt that the growth of telemarketing *is* impressive, even frightening, although resistance to telemarketing has also increased and consumers, aided by new technological developments, are becoming much more skilled at screening unwanted callers out of their lives (see Chapter Thirteen). So perhaps the unbridled growth of telemarketing will be short-lived.

The reason for this growth is that telemarketing works. Calling to sell is only a part of the story—the telephone has many more uses than that. Like many other useful techniques or tools, telemarketing can be dangerous in unprepared or misguided hands, but undoubtedly the telephone offers enormous benefits to fundraisers. So it pays to collect your donors' phone numbers. How to communicate with donors via the telephone is covered in detail in Chapter Ten.

Relationships with Companies and Foundations

Although they have much in common, companies and foundations should be dealt with separately as they have different motives and starting points that inform their decisions, and different strategies and tactics are therefore likely to be needed to attract and keep their support. Even if you're a fundraiser for a small organization and are charged with raising money from both, you need to understand the differences and develop a distinct approach for each.

But clearly it is just as important to develop strong, lasting, and productive relationships with commercial donors and foundations as it is with individuals. The techniques, prices, and products may be different but the same principles of relationship fundraising still apply. The people who work in companies and foundations are, after all, just individuals doing their job.

Some of the differences are worth considering. People at work don't have as much time as most people at home. Therefore, make your communications shorter and more to the point. Do your homework beforehand to ensure you don't waste your time or theirs. The decision makers in these places are also not so likely to conform to any of your typical donor profiles, so you may have to work a lot harder for them. For one thing, senior managers are still most likely to be men. They will also often be younger than the average individual donor and their motivation for agreeing to their organization's support of your cause will most probably lean toward self-interest and mutual benefit rather than pure altruism.

So don't under any circumstances be apologetic when asking for a donation from a commercial organization or foundation. Companies only give when they want to, and most have a budget specifically for that purpose. And a foundation's sole reason for existence is often to give money away to organizations like yours. Your function as a fundraiser, therefore, is to help them do their job. Show them your marketing plan (or offer it). After all, the people you are talking to do business plans. They'll be impressed to see you do as well.

Companies and foundations get many applications for funds. Those with very specific areas of interest will tend to get fewer. A few years ago Allied Dunbar, then one of Britain's most philanthropic companies, received just fifteen hundred requests each year because it had carefully publicized its procedures and requirements. But that was still six different proposals to consider every working day. The Carnegie Trust got twice as many. The Boots Company gets fifteen thousand requests each year—that's roughly one request for money every seven-and-a-half minutes. Even that is small beer compared to many companies. In the United States the Atlantic Richfield Corporation reckoned that on average, it receives one application for philanthropic support every *second*. These numbers will most likely have increased over recent years rather than declined.

Of course, the smaller, local companies and foundations don't get nearly so many requests and it's there that fundraisers will be most likely to find opportunities. To stand any chance of success against such a volume of competition you have to be very good.

Read the first paragraph of your letter out loud. Does what's different about your proposal stand out clearly? Or could that first paragraph have been written by just about anyone else? If you can make a good, relevant individual application and follow it up efficiently by telephone, make an effective impression at a meeting, and, once given the donation or grant, follow that with well-documented, well-presented, and fully supported feedback on the progress of the project, then you have the beginnings of a successful relationship with that company or foundation. But you must provide regular, relevant feedback and, to maintain the relationship, you must have a constant need of sufficient size and type to merit their further support.

The most important part of any appeal to a company or a foundation is the *idea*. Be sure your idea is properly thought through and fully worked out in all its detail before you go anywhere near the potential donor. It must be an idea relevant to the organization you will present it to. Then your application must clearly, simply, and persuasively present the idea. Explain in human terms what the support will achieve, not just the millions you need for a large-scale project. The people who will be involved, the work they will do, the children they will help, the kind of land that will be reclaimed, the pain that will be replaced by smiles, or whatever. . . . Make it human. Most of the applications that compete with yours will be boring their prospect's pants off with endless reams of statistics and impenetrable pages of gray type. If your application sparkles with individuality, achievement, illustration, and human interest it will stand out, and that's more than half the battle.

Many foundations and companies expect very considerable after-sales service. Be sure to find out what information each prospect will expect from you and only go after the grant if you can be sure to meet those conditions.

Among the major changes in corporate sector assistance to nonprofits recently have been the strengthening of "cause-related marketing" and the development of a more "holistic" approach to corporate social responsibility, that is, the bringing together of sponsorship, charitable giving, employee involvement, mentoring, and such into a more cohesive approach, which is often referred to as "social marketing." Both these changes—which often go together and are not just restricted to the biggest national and international companies—mean that a fundraising strategy focused solely on securing donations is unlikely to generate more than a token response. If bigger and sustained support is the object, then an applicant nonprofit is now likely to have to identify a diverse menu of mutual benefits that could grow from a relationship with a company.

According to David Carrington, formerly CEO of PPP Healthcare Medical Trust (Britain's third-largest grant-making foundation) and now an independent consultant, grant-makers will also increasingly be interested in being more flexible in the ways that they support a nonprofit—going beyond the project or appeal-specific grant or donation to get involved in "core cost" grants, loans, or underwriting. That may be in the future for most foundations, but a pioneering few are keen to go this route now.

David is convinced fundraisers need to be aware of the diversity among foundations in their policies and ways of working. "It's not just that their aims, focus, criteria, types and sizes of grants, terms and conditions are different," David says, "but that the way they process applications varies a lot." He continues,

> I'm always amazed when fundraisers turn up to a meeting with a trust and make a "standard" presentation—often impressively techie and glib about the wonders of the specific appeal or project—and then get in an awful tangle when the questions start. The grants officer may know a lot more than the fundraiser about the policy context within which the proposed project is being set (how statutory agency contracts work) and probably ought to be talking to the people within the not-for-profit who actually negotiate with the purchasing authority so that the role of charitable funds within the "jigsaw" of how the project's finances are to work is clear. Or the fact that the meeting is taking place is because the trust has already decided it's keen on the project idea but wants to know if the applicant organization is best placed and organizationally healthy to do the job—so the questions to the by now glazed-eyed fundraiser are not about the glitzy message but about the not-for-profit's balance sheet and governance!

> At the other end of the spectrum, the small family trust will probably behave just like an individual donor—their interest being sparked by a family situation, or tragedy, or crisis, or a personal approach from someone they trust who is committed to the non-profit. Glitzy presentations from smart fundraisers are not the key for those potential donors, either.

David illustrates this point with a personal anecdote. "Our family's latest donation is to help our local family center—which we helped to set up twenty-three years ago when we were among the first service users!—to cope with the consequence of losing almost all their play equipment when their storage shed was burnt down last week. Now that's an example of sustained relationship funding!"

David Carrington also feels the diversity of "donor care" practice for trusts and foundations is sometimes inadequately recognized by fundraisers. He says,

A fundraiser who relies on a standard reporting format will quickly come unstuck and will probably fail to get the support renewed. In a similar area, over the last fourteen years of running grant-making trusts I've been regularly surprised and dismayed by the lack of diligence among fundraisers (and their finance officers) in reading the trust's terms and conditions before they sign them on behalf of their organization—or observing the requirements subsequently. The worst possible donor relationships are ones when the donor has to remind the grant recipient of the reporting conditions; or when the donor hears secondhand about a significant change or development within the grant recipient organization; or when an actively engaged donor finds that they have been put on the database that churns out those standardized appeal letters every couple of months.

Despite his enthusiasm for relationship fundraising and the advent of a more customer-conscious approach to fundraising, David Carrington knows from experience that bad practice is still widespread in fundraisers' approaches to foundations. "It's often down to a lack of basic common sense or courtesy; and so the quality of the practice could be improved easily if well managed and supervised."

David's version of my earlier advice about reading the first paragraph of the appeal letter aloud is to suggest to fundraisers that they get a close friend—who is not as intimately involved in the nonprofit as they are but whose friendship is strong enough for it not to be wrecked by a row about the fundraiser's grammar—to read the letter that accompanies appeals to foundations simply to see if it is easily understandable. If a friend can't immediately summarize what the appeal is about, what chance has the busy foundation or corporate affairs officer?

Publicity and Public Relations

Publicity and public relations are a little outside my scope here, but I can't resist relating one example of a publicity campaign, the National Children's Home Birthday Campaign. It raised a great deal of money for its nonprofit sponsor, the publicity that was generated lifted the sponsor's profile considerably, and lots of people had lots of fun. It is also a good example of how a lot of planning, initiatives, and hard work led to a classic success story.

But I particularly like the story because it involved an idea—what advertising guru David Ogilvy would term "the big idea." And in this case, the idea was rather an unlikely one. In fact, NCH's then director of fundraising, John Gray, whose idea it was, told me about it before the campaign was launched and I remember thinking he was crazy—it seemed such an obvious and simple idea I didn't think anyone would latch onto it. I should have known better.

A few years before, John had attended a CASE convention in America. That's where he picked up the idea, and that single idea certainly would have paid for his trip many times over. At the convention John was in a group that was asked to come up with some long-term objectives for their organizations, things they would like to see their organizations doing in two to three years' time. John realized as he thought about it that very soon his organization would be celebrating some significant birthdays—the organization itself would be 120 years old, it was 150 years since the birth of their founder, Dr. Thomas Stevenson, and the eightieth birthday of their eminent and much-loved chairman, Lord Tonypandy, better known as George Thomas, former speaker of the U.K. House of Commons, would take place.

"Right then," thought John. "We will announce this year to be NCH Birthday Year."

Then John uncovered the most startling piece of overlooked obviousness. Everybody has a birthday, every year. That made his campaign relevant to everyone. All companies have anniversaries. For many, their special anniversary would coincide with NCH's series of birthdays. What better reason to give a thank you gift?

By sheer good fortune, NCH's three birthday dates were evenly distributed throughout the year—one in January, one in June, one in December. Each would be the cue for a host of linked publicity and PR events. Now John had a campaign. All he and his team of fundraising professionals had to do was get behind it, maximize and take advantage of all the opportunities they could create, and wait for the public's enthusiasm and generosity to do the rest. (Of course, it sounds easy with hindsight.)

The Birthday Year did succeed in involving huge numbers of people, in mounting a vast array of publicity events and in achieving enormous national and local coverage—all for something as everyday (or every year) as a birthday. NCH is a family organization and it appealed to family businesses, particularly those with families as customers where the link of supporting a nonprofit that helps the family could be most easily seen or was most obviously beneficial. It produced and sold mugs, T-shirts, and other memorabilia, all marked with the birthday year. It persuaded supporters to stage events on their birthday—from the man who raised £25,000 by cycling on his birthday to the man who rappelled down a mountain on his birthday. A nationwide chain of drugstores pledged to raise £150,000 in its tenth anniversary year. British Telecom, which was twenty-one that year, held a birthday party for children hosted by singer Stevie Wonder at the top of London's Telecom Tower. And lots more birthday-linked events were organized. In a remarkable direct marketing initiative NCH sent all its donors a birthday card, asking them to send it on to Lord Tonypandy, with a gift. Despite the fact that this mailing went out just six weeks after NCH's traditional Christmas appeal mailing, thirty-two thousand people responded and sent £180,000 with their birthday good wishes.

To crown the year NCH launched a special "super-donor club"—the NCH George Thomas Society—which raised a further £500,000; the launch was attended by many of the most eminent stars of stage, screen, and politics. A major feature of NCH's publicity success was its ability to involve celebrities, from all the major Royals down to and including current, past, and even future prime ministers (the year straddled the changeover from Margaret Thatcher to John Major, and both supported NCH).

So although the Birthday Year was described as a publicity event, NCH involved many different facets of relationship fundraising— all of which contributed to its success. In all, NCH's birthday campaign raised over £1.2 million extra income and a research survey showed that the enormous publicity that had been generated had raised NCH's prompted awareness from 51 percent to 78 percent. Not a bad result from a single idea.

Success in any publicity event can depend on being in the right place at the right time, knowing the right people, and being able to respond very quickly to situations that can arise completely out of the blue. Another necessary quality of the fundraiser at times like these is the ability to seize initiatives, to take risks, to get others enthused and involved, and, of course, to drop everything and work round the clock until the campaign's success is assured and the need—or the opportunity—is no more. These are high-adrenaline times and can be the most exciting and rewarding of any fundraiser's career.

One further point—publicity and public relations are inextricably linked with fundraising. There is never any reason for separating the two. They must both be related parts of the same division within any fundraising organization.

Action Points

▲ Recognize that marketing to raise funds is entirely different from marketing detergents, motor cars, or any other product.

▲ Carry out a marketing audit and create a marketing plan. Make it part of your organization's strategic plan. If you haven't got a strategic plan, find similar-sized organizations who have and ask them how they go about it.

▲ Turn change into innovation. Avoid complacency and see change as an opportunity.

▲ Find the right person or people to lead change. Involve everyone and get them to change their behavior as a prerequisite to change.

▲ Decide whether you are a supermarket or a specialty store. Exploit your niches.

▲ Don't neglect the views of your noncustomers.

▲ Encourage individual choice. Tailor your fundraising programs to give donors maximum choice and opportunity for participation.

▲ Design your product to fit the marketplace, rather than expect the marketplace to fit your product.

▲ Get the price right.

▲ Don't use marketing jargon when speaking to donors.

▲ Identify your "unique reason to give."

▲ Everybody in your organization is part of your marketing strategy. Make sure they all know it and know their role.

▲ Every time you get a donation try to get a phone number and e-mail address too. Give the opportunity to add a number in your coupons and reply forms.

▲ Don't be apologetic when asking for corporate donations.

▲ Make sure your proposals are professionally presented and well written. Make them sparkle with originality and powerfully presented needs.

▲ Look for the big idea.

▲ Cultivate the right contacts. You never know when you will need people but at some time or other you certainly will.

Donor Profile: Marsha Robbins

"If I get another one of those charity mailings, I'll scream." It was at least the third time this week that Marsha had found herself saying or thinking something similar. She seemed to have got on every single mailing list there had ever been and she couldn't understand how.

It bothered her. She disliked being written to by nonprofits or anybody else trying to sell her something. Nowadays it just seemed as if all the mail she got came from somebody trying to sell her something.

She remembered the time she used to get letters from her boyfriend—when she used to look forward to getting mail. A young woman should look forward to getting letters, she thought. Because so many of them came from nonprofits seemed to make it worse. She told her friend Elaine down at the dance center that she really hated getting so many requests for money and felt bad that she had to say no so often. Also, she thought they all looked too much alike. None of them were very believable. Elaine hadn't a clue what Marsha was going on about—she never got any letters, not from anyone. "I'll pass you on some of mine," said Marsha.

Marsha was still thinking about it as she came home. Even before she removed her key she could feel the mail delivery piled up inside the door, crumpling as she pushed it open. "More begging letters, I expect," she thought and stopped to pull them out.

Later that evening Marsha went for a walk as usual, just to the mailbox. She dropped in only three envelopes and as usual they were rather similar. On the front of each one some text explained, "This letter does not require a stamp but if you stick one on it will save us money."

Chapter Nine

Making and Keeping Friends

*I thought that our government couldn't fail to listen to us
when so many people were insisting that something should
be done. . . . We may never have met, yet I think we all
showed the same aim, worked together in the same spirit
and shared the same joy the day John was released.*
JILL MORRELL, OF THE FRIENDS OF JOHN MCCARTHY
(BEIRUT HOSTAGE)

All fundraisers appreciate the importance of finding new donors.
Some indeed seem to spend more time and money trying to recruit new blood than developing the potential of the donors
they've already got. (Everyone knows that it's easier and cheaper
to get donations from existing donors than to find new ones, but
that still doesn't stop nonprofits spending much more on acquisition than on development.)

But every fundraising organization needs to be recruiting new
supporters constantly, if not for reasons of growth then to replace
those lost through natural (or unnatural) wastage.

What Is a Donor Worth?

What constitutes a *donor* differs from one nonprofit to another. For
some organizations receipt of a single gift qualifies the giver as a
donor. For others it is receipt of a second gift, of any size, that dif-
ferentiates the genuine donor from the casual, spontaneous, uncommitted responder.

As only about 50 percent of first-time givers go on to make a second gift when left to their own devices, adopting this second definition would immediately cut many fundraisers' recruitment statistics in half.

This seems to me to indicate a need to split the warm file in two—responders and donors. New responders should then be encouraged (via a welcome pack, thank you letters, mailings, newsletters, and telephone calls) to move as quickly as possible to the donor file. Responders that didn't give a second gift would be subject to various reactivation approaches before ultimately being rested on a dormant or "once a year" file if justified.

Reactivation: Don't Lose Your Friends!

At ActionAid I learned the value of each new donor through the sufferings of a sister organization in America. At that time we were a young, developing organization and we had discovered that we could use press ads and inserts cost-effectively to recruit sponsors (donors who give a substantial gift, usually monthly, to sponsor a child overseas). Through adroit use of direct marketing techniques we were adding between ten and twelve thousand new sponsors a year and because we hadn't been going long enough (or our administration wasn't alert enough) we hadn't yet noticed any significant drop-outs. But my counterpart in the U.S. Foster Parents Plan, George Ross, told me his agency had just spent $750,000 on advertising to recruit six thousand new sponsors, during a year when they'd lost over six thousand sponsors who had dropped out. So they'd spent three-quarters of a million dollars and hadn't even managed to stand still.

A fundraising product such as sponsorship clearly has built-in problems with drop-outs. However successful you are at extending the donor life cycle, as sure as they joined you, donors will one day leave (unless you can persuade them to pass their commitment to donate on to their children). But this restriction may well be outweighed by their longevity. ActionAid now reckons that those regular donors who do become sponsors will continue giving, month after month, for about twelve years on average.

The time in between joining and leaving is the "lifetime" of your donor, and that average figure is vital for you to know. (The ideal donor gives to a large-scale proposition over a long period of time—or, in other words, has a high lifetime value.)

For some organizations that time will be very short, just a year or two. For others, like ActionAid, it will naturally be much longer. But whatever the donor's lifetime is, there is a lot any organization can do to extend it.

A New Lease on Life

As new donors cost around five times more to recruit than lapsed donors cost to reactivate, why is it that nonprofits usually persist in spending the vast bulk of their promotional resources on finding new supporters?

The first rule in finding new donors is, in fact, to do everything you can to extend the life of your existing donors. First remove anything that might make them want to leave you in the first place—discover through research every conceivable reason there could be why anyone might want to leave you, and work to eliminate those factors. Then introduce a series, up to five or even more, of reactivation initiatives. These might range from personal letters through to a phone call, even to a personal visit from you or your chairman and may include a letter direct from one of your projects either at home or overseas. Whatever you do, don't talk about previous supporters, lapsed members, departed donors. Don't give the impression that they have already left you. Most of them haven't. They just haven't got round to renewing.

Like most people, I rarely pay bills until I get the red reminder and I don't renew magazine subscriptions until I get at least three calls for renewal. This is not a deliberate policy—it's just that there are some things I only get round to when I have to. Once, however, I failed to fill in the first renewal reminder for my favorite magazine, *New Scientist*, and they never sent me another. My subscription lapsed and I haven't got round to going into a newsagent to buy a copy so I can get a new subscription form even though I'll probably get a cut-price introductory offer. So, through my own inertia, I lost out, through doing what lots of people do. But so did *New Scientist*.

In theory you can keep on sending reactivation mailings to a given section of your lapsed donor file until responses from that segment become unprofitable. Political organizations in the United States have been known to send forty or more reactivation letters to one donor over a period of months. I wonder what kind of an impression that gives the recipient?

One kind of reactivation initiative that I'm less than enthusiastic about is the approach that suggests "make a once-only gift of £100 and we won't ask you again." I dislike this on two counts. It implies that by asking a former donor you are bothering them, so it runs against the basic principles of relationship fundraising. And organizations that say they won't write again almost invariably do—succumbing to the "I know we said we wouldn't ask you again, but you'll never guess the latest disaster that has hit our program in Guatemala" syndrome.

Any reactivation program has to be sensitive to the donors' wishes and each communication, however presented, should allow people a comfortable way out. It should even give them the option to remove their names from the file. A cold mailing to lapsed donors often works very well, which shows that donors frequently don't think of themselves as donors.

Finally, if every practical initiative has been tried and nothing has worked, accept it and say goodbye nicely. That often works.

Recognition and Rewards

Without doubt donors like their support to be recognized. The simplest, most usual, and most important recognition device is the thank you letter (see Chapter Ten). At the other end of the scale, a lifeboat or even a building can be named in a donor's honor. In between these extremes there are many other valuable ways of recognizing donors' contributions (and thereby increasing their loyalty and commitment). Some are surprisingly easy and inexpensive to introduce.

Recognition devices come in many forms. Several nonprofits are already using privileged phone lines (only promoted to one particular group of donors), commemorative plaques in appropriate sites (for example, a day care center), the award of voting rights, listing in the annual report, access to privileged information, and so on. Some organizations have created specialist societies or clubs for larger donors, such as NSPCC's Benjamin Waugh Foundation and National Children's Home's George Thomas Society (described in Chapter Eight).

Special events that recognize donors' substantial contributions can be both interesting and rewarding. One nonprofit I know invites all its donors to an open house. Most cannot come and many write declining the invitation but saying how pleased they were to be asked. Some enclose a check simply as a gesture of goodwill. Those that do attend enjoy a fun day out, see their nonprofit at firsthand, and meet the people involved. If it wasn't their favorite nonprofit at the start of the day it probably will be by the end. And many valuable donations are made as a result.

Another nonprofit hosts regular receptions for donors and staff. Drinks are served and modest refreshments provided, usually underwritten by one of the organization's suppliers. Front-line staff give interesting presentations and the director makes a short speech. Those donors who come usually go home with their batteries recharged and the staff who attend have had a perfect opportunity to talk to donors and find out what they think and what makes them tick.

One nonprofit I worked with used to hold regional supporter conferences on Saturdays, one every six to eight weeks on average, in different parts of the country. Every supporter in the local area was invited. Ostensibly the purpose was to explain the nonprofit's policies and activities, but inevitably those who came brought friends (attendance was always remarkably high) and we enrolled many new supporters on the day. Again donors went home highly motivated and recharged but, equally important, so did the staff. We never had any trouble recruiting staff for these information days, despite their being held on a Saturday. People enjoyed it.

Donor recognition events should be planned into your agenda for the coming year just as frequently as you can manage them. Renewal schemes will also help you to hold on to your donors. Donors like their support to be recognized. Why not introduce long-service awards for people who have supported you for, say, five, ten, fifteen, twenty years? Choose intervals that help to extend the "lifetime" of your donors. Structure your awards so that reaching one level automatically encourages the donor to go on to the next, as in bronze, silver, and gold schemes. The "club" concept is well proven in fundraising terms and although recognition for long service needn't be so formal—it could be just a personal letter from your patron or president—it can be just as effective in extending and upgrading your donors. Clearly the use of different levels of certificates or tokens depending on the amount raised will have wide application in local group and volunteer fundraising.

Most fundraisers in Britain are still a little reticent about using incentives or rewards although these have been shown to work in other countries and can be very helpful in finding and motivating new donors. According to Ted D. Bayley, author of *The Fund Raiser's Guide to Successful Campaigns,* as few as one in a hundred people might object to donor recognition pieces, but research proves the other ninety-nine are genuinely motivated by the recognition. Some will even increase the value of their gift if it is tied to larger, more attractive, or more publicly visible recognition. On some college campuses in the United States, there are ornamental gates and arches that have different names on each side—for example, "Donor A Memorial" from the west and "Corporation B Gate" from the east—so twice as many donors can be memorialized.

One area where rewards are appropriate is in "member-get-member" schemes, where your donors find friends and neighbors who are just like them and who might also be interested in your cause.

If you want to know how effective this is, ask American Express. They recruit thousands in this way, but then they do offer genuinely valuable rewards such as half a dozen bottles of wine or a leather-bound personal organizer. One American Express cardholder introduced over a hundred friends in one year. He either leads a very organized life or has a bad liver.

Nonprofits have to think what incentives might be appropriate to them. Perhaps a gift of merchandise from your catalogue, or something small made by one of your projects, or a badge or lapel pin, or perhaps a certificate of recognition for special achievement—possibly for introducing five friends—and so on. If every supporter were to bring in just one new friend you'd soon double your donor list virtually without cost. Try inserting a simple member-get-member leaflet in your next mailing. Test it on a segment against the remainder of the list to see if it has any impact on the basic levels or values of gifts and if it covers its cost of inclusion.

To do this properly, of course, you'll have to have a clear idea of what it normally costs you to recruit one donor. Surprisingly, many nonprofits don't know this figure, just as they don't know what a donor is worth to them. Yet without this information the only way you can build a donor list is by accident.

Member-get-member schemes are widely used by nonprofits but I know of few that work really well. I suspect this is something to do with donors' feelings of privacy and reticence about telling others about their generosity. Most prefer to support their favorite causes in relative anonymity and few are prepared to evangelize for their nonprofit.

Some years ago, when we devised loose magazine inserts using built-in reply envelopes for an overseas aid nonprofit, I found that we had a bit of white space left over on the inside of the coupon. (Normally we have to squeeze information onto coupons, but in this case the way the paper folded meant that we had more space than we needed.) We added some address panels for "introduce a friend," more in hope than anticipation. Response was surprisingly good. Of the thousands of people who completed the coupon about 8 percent gave the names of others, providing us with a large pool of potential new supporters. When we sent our (specially prepared) follow-up welcome pack, a very encouraging number converted, giving us one of our cheapest recruitment methods.

Reciprocal Mailings

Reciprocal mailings are the simplest and most cost-effective way of increasing your donor base. Contrary to popular expectation there are few howls of protest from overexposed donors. They get lots of other mail anyway and generally have little idea or interest in where it all comes from. Nor is there any sign that it reduces your supporters' likelihood of responding generously to your next appeal. However I suspect that if donors become aware that their names are being swapped in this way they may be somewhat less than enthusiastic. It is certainly good practice to allow donors to opt out of reciprocal mailings—and even when they don't, it's worth monitoring their opinions on the practice to ensure it's not doing as much harm as good. (And make sure it's legal before you try setting up a reciprocal arrangement; in Germany and several Scandinavian countries, reciprocal mailings are prohibited by law.)

Reciprocals work because nonprofits are not usually *directly* competing with each other, not even similar causes. This is another difference between us and most other kinds of business. Of course this is only true up to a certain point. Donors do feel that they can't support every cause and will stop giving, or give selectively, if they think they are getting too many requests.

Reciprocal mailings produce response levels somewhere between what you would expect to get from your cold mailings and your warm (one nonprofit I know achieved 17.5 percent response to a reciprocal). Whereas cold mailings rarely break even these days, reciprocal mailings almost always make a substantial profit. There's no list rental cost and with every response you add a new donor to your list, which of course you don't get from warm mailings.

Donors recruited in this way will be worth more because they tend to make higher than average donations and to stay with you longer. And, as these donors cost less to recruit in the first place, reciprocal mailings tend to be good news for fundraisers.

It is very important to give donors that chance to opt out of reciprocal mailings if they don't wish to participate. In Britain there is a code of practice on reciprocal mailings that can be obtained from the Institute of Fundraising, which explains the care and precautions fundraisers must take to protect list security, to avoid upset, and so forth. The threat of restrictive legislation looms particularly large over reciprocal mailings and this avenue for finding new donors may be closed to fundraisers in the very near future. Few of the remaining alternatives will be as affordable or as attractive. I am told by fundraisers Rich Fox and Harvey McKinnon that reciprocal mailing is also an issue in North America, although there is no immediate threat of legislation.

Reciprocal mailings continue to increase in popularity with fundraisers in the United Kingdom thanks to the almost universal decline in response and increase in cost of cold mailings. Nevertheless, despite its rising cost and increasingly unacceptable image with the general public, cold direct mail still remains one of the most cost-effective methods of recruiting significant numbers of new donors—donors that you can be sure will be mail-responsive.

Cold Direct Mail

There are many proven techniques to increase the effectiveness of your direct mail, both cold and warm, and most of them are not secret. I don't have space to go into much detail now, but it would be impossible to look even superficially at fundraisers' relationship with their donors without considering the extraordinary impact direct mail has had on the fundraising business in recent years.

Fundraising by direct mail is not new. In 1887, Dr. Barnardo's Homes were mailing 200,000 appeal letters a year using very emotive, well-written letters, well laid out over several pages, with indented paragraphs and lots of underlining. They also used quite sophisticated member-get-member mechanisms, leaflets, even handwritten postscripts.

There's very little that the current generation of direct mail fundraisers has originated, but we did certainly help direct mail to proliferate. In Chapter Seven I looked at the dangers of the direct mail explosion and the potential damage badly prepared, formula-driven, and badly targeted direct mail might do to a fundraiser's relationship with donors. So here I will try to restrict discussion of cold mail to practical ways of amending current practice to limit any negative effects it might have on your prospects and to increase its chances of getting your relationship off to a good start.

That's not easy. The most obvious way is to avoid slavish adherence to any established formula even though you know it, at least, has a proven track record. The trick is to devise an original or individual approach—more individual at least than the formulas that most other fundraisers follow—but it has to be one that you can show, through testing, works at least as well as or better than the traditional direct mail approach.

Difficult though this may be, it's not impossible and some nonprofits have done it. One way is through the facsimile letter. The Muscular Dystrophy Group of Great Britain and Northern Ireland used this effectively for several years. It all started because the chief executive of MDG at the time, Paul Walker, felt mailings failed with him because they were immediately recognizable as direct mail appeals—and were treated accordingly. So the Group's agency devised a mailing pack that didn't look like a mailing but instead looked like a real letter, the kind you or I might send to a friend. Why not? People like to receive letters. They don't like to receive mailings. That is good relationship fundraising thinking.

The main letter wasn't on MDG letterhead. Instead it came from a well-known and much-loved supporter, television celebrity Richard Briers. It was handwritten on cream-colored personal stationery and Richard Briers, a third party speaking on behalf of children with muscular dystrophy, was able to invest his appeal with far more urgency and emotion than many MDG staff would have felt comfortable with. And since its source was not associated with the MDG, the message was also more credible coming from Briers.

There was a discreet lift letter from Paul Walker. This was folded so recipients simply read on the outside, "if you have decided to help. . . ." Of course, once they opened it they were hooked because Paul was already thanking them for their decision to support the cause. A photo card with Richard Briers's handwritten message was also included and a handwritten reply form completed the pack.

One of the most controversial aspects of this mailing was the outer envelope. This was high-quality stationery, with a closed face (no window), the type of envelope people use to send letters to friends. Addresses were typed by hand. Instead of the ubiquitous preprinted postage-paid notice, a real postage stamp was affixed. So on arrival, MDG's appeal mailing looked just like a real letter, the kind you or I might get from a relative or friend. (I hate the postage-paid notice. It so clearly identifies letters as mass mailings; as soon as that mark distinguishes the content, the whole package goes in the trash. The public, I regret to say, tends to regard the postage-paid notice as junk mail's logo.)

Once opened the nature of the appeal was obvious, but its authentic and compelling presentation guaranteed readership and response to this pack substantially exceeded previous cold mailing efforts. It was Muscular Dystrophy Group's banker pack for years.

To test whether the personal touch of the individually typed and stamped letters was worth the extra cost, MDG's agency carried out a carefully structured five-way split test. Segments of several mailing lists were sent identical contents inside five different types of outer envelope: a window envelope with postage-paid notice (the conventional fundraising letter); a window envelope with a stamp; a non-window laser-addressed envelope with postage-paid notice; a non-window laser-addressed envelope with a stamp, a non-window hand-typed address with a stamp—the conventional personal letter format. Since then I have asked many groups of people which envelope they felt would most likely achieve the best response. The answer has always been the same—the one that looks most likely to contain a letter from a friend. Yet fundraisers persist in sending out appeals that look like mass mailings.

In fact, the typed and stamped envelope did achieve a much higher total response than all the other segments. Even when the increased cost was taken into account, the banker pack still worked best. But it was a lot of trouble to organize, so in time this particular mailing pack was dropped. Perhaps some other enterprising organization will come along and give the idea new life.

Different from the Herd

Many organizations have now put thought and effort into making their warm and cold appeal mailings different from the herd. One of the most effective departures in recent years came from the Henry Doubleday Research Association, for Ryton Gardens, the United Kingdom's National Centre for Organic Gardening. Their appeal to members (all organic gardeners are likely to be fiercely opposed to junk mail) raised eight times its target, largely because it broke almost every "rule" of the direct mail industry.

The appeal package consisted of a plain brown envelope inside which was another (reply) envelope and a single, large (A1) sheet of brown wrapping paper that was printed on one side only. The mailing immediately addressed recipients' assumed aversion to direct mail by explaining that, once read, the entire sheet could be recycled as seed pots for use in the member's garden. The rest of the sheet was taken up by some letter copy, a map of the gardens, a list of the problems and immediate needs at the center, and a structured hierarchical offer inviting members to become either gardeners, cultivators, seedsmen, or sponsors (at different price levels). This unusual mailing was completed by a reply mechanism consisting of donation form, banker's order form, deed of covenant, and a panel describing how to assemble the seed pots, *after* it had been read, by simply folding sections of the sheet.

Innovative though it was, the Ryton Gardens mailing had what skeptics would regard as a built-in flaw. If the reply forms were detached, the HDRA member could make six seed pots, but keeping the reply forms would let the member make *eight*. But despite this disincentive, the response far exceeded expectations and generated the kind of enthusiastic fan mail that direct mail fundraisers dream about. Most of all, HDRA members seemed to appreciate that their interests and concerns had been taken into account, so they were glad to help.

If the beginning of success is to be different and the beginning of failure is to be the same, then it will pay fundraisers in the future to ensure that all our mailings are individual and different, not clones from a formula. I think we owe that to our supporters.

Off-the-Page Advertising

Press advertising does bring some direct response but nowadays the cost usually far outweighs the income. This means that, apart from a few rare exceptions, press or off-the-page advertising is not a practical way of finding large numbers of new donors. This wasn't always the case.

The Oxford Committee for Famine Relief, the forerunner of Oxfam, was regularly advertising in Britain's daily and Sunday press from the early 1950s through to the late 1970s. Although the advertisements used look very dated now, they embodied many of the ingredients of a good fundraising press advertisement—newsy style, use of newspaper setting, listing of well-known supporters, mention of specific amounts to give, and so on.

Today's fundraiser might find such advertisements naive, but these ads really worked. Oxfam achieved returns of up to £31 for every £1 it invested in press advertising. Even in those far-off days, Oxfam's pioneering press ads showed an understanding of off-the-page fundraising techniques that is frequently lacking in today's ads.

Nowadays, few nonprofits can claim to recover even their direct costs from fundraising press appeals. Yet in the United Kingdom more nonprofits than ever before continue to spend more money than ever before on press advertising. In 2000 U.K. nonprofits spent a total of £46.1 million. That's a lot of money. And these nonprofits are using the press in an increasing variety of ways for fundraising and fundraising-related purposes, including donor and member recruitment, image-building, campaigning, promoting events, and much more. But, I wonder, how many of them are getting value for money, or anything like it?

For the majority of nonprofits the most practical and measurable use of the press is to recruit new supporters, albeit often at high cost. But millions have been spent trying to create awareness and much of it has been wasted. How much awareness can you create for half a million pounds? Not a lot, as many nonprofits are now realizing.

Conversely, some hard-headed nonprofits are giving clear instructions to their agencies—find us new supporters at x pounds per response. The agency's brief is to buy space accordingly and tightly monitor results. In the United Kingdom nonprofits such as Help the Aged, Sightsavers, and ActionAid have all used this system effectively. More nonprofits should follow their example.

Many of the lessons Oxfam learned in the 1950s and 1960s still apply, although if you look through a selection of Britain's daily papers you'll quickly spot how many nonprofits are unaware of them. Here are a few of these basics of press advertising:

- Fundraising ads only work in the "quality" press.
- They work best in special positions.
- Small spaces are generally more cost-efficient than large ones.
- Short, clear, readable copy gets the best results.
- Make an offer, make it in the headline. Eighty percent of your investment should go into picture and headline because four out of every five readers will read no further.
- Show where the money goes. The simple proposition linked with the sensible use of funds works every time.
- Make response easy.
- Clever buying in space, timing, and position are certainly more important than cleverness in copy. Most newspapers need to fill odd spaces in their page make-up from time to time and will offer very special terms to nonprofits that can provide appropriate copy as a filler. This is usually referred to as "distress" space.

Perhaps expenditure in press advertising will fall in coming years as more nonprofits realize the long-term nature of press advertising. Perhaps the specialist uses to which fundraisers put the press will become sharper-edged and more clearly focused in terms of measurable results achieved, as more and more nonprofits realize that press advertising is just too expensive for anything short of absolute precision.

Do I sound cynical? I am a bit. Nonprofits misspend more of their promotional budgets on press advertising than on anything else. But perhaps in the future, as direct mail acquisition costs increase, off-the-page advertising will reemerge as a cost-effective way of finding new donors. That would open up some new potential—but if so it is unlikely to stay cost-effective for long.

For me an early advertisement from the British charity Help the Aged provides an excellent example of the classic fundraising ad, which works as well today as it ever did. This small advertisement, about eight inches across two columns, carried no illustration, but the bold headline made a simple and very direct proposition:

MAKE A BLIND MAN SEE—£10.

What an offer! Where on earth could anyone get such value for money? This simple, clear advertisement got straight to the point. The text was typeset to look as if it had just come off an old manual typewriter, which made the whole ad look as if it had been put together by two old ladies working in a leaky garret. But what came across was their passionate belief in the urgency and rightness of their appeal.

Fundraising ads *must* work. They've got to. After all, for the cost of that advertisement at full price in one issue of a newspaper such as the *Daily Telegraph,* Help the Aged could have restored sight to 264 people. If the media buyer has done the job properly, that price could be reduced by 50 percent or more. Still, even at that cost the ad has to work hard because, instead of buying the ad, Help the Aged could have chosen to restore sight to more than 100 people. That kind of thing puts quite a responsibility on those of us who would use the press to raise funds.

Inserts

Magazine inserts fall somewhere between direct mail and off-the-page advertisements. An insert can be thought of as unaddressed direct mail delivered via your prospect's reading matter rather than through the mailbox. Or it can be considered a loose advertisement that rather than being fixed to the page falls out immediately when the magazine is picked up, thereby at least increasing its chances of being noticed.

Inserts were very popular in Britain a few years ago, with many nonprofits using them extensively in weekend newspapers and specialist magazines. The development of the technology to create the all-in-one mailer complete with reply form and envelope transformed direct response advertising for some nonprofits, as inserts provided a cost-effective way to deliver a detailed message to a specific audience *and* gave an immediate and easy way to respond. But here again the donating public showed its sales resistance. Inserts became overused in the United Kingdom; they lost their novelty value and now are generally only effective for high-priced fundraising propositions or, exceptionally, for a membership organization such as the Royal National Lifeboat Institution, which promotes its low-cost membership scheme successfully using very simple and inexpensive inserts.

Inserts are something of a shotgun approach when compared to well-targeted direct mail, but they have some advantages including high impact, opportunities for creativity and originality, and the chance to tell a detailed story through long copy and good photographs. In addition, they provide cost-effective opportunities for testing different formats and copy (one insert my company prepared involved ten simultaneous tests and a print run of 1.3 million). Inserts are also very flexible and will offer challenging opportunities to whoever designs and produces them. The disadvantages of inserts include high unit cost and quite high minimum quantities, so they can be expensive particularly in the development stages. RNLI's annual campaign in one year totaled 18 million inserts with fifty different copy and design tests. Production and organization can be extraordinarily complex so it is important to know what you are doing.

Recruiting Face to Face

Face-to-face fundraising, or direct dialogue, is one of the most significant recent development in large-scale donor solicitation. Given its importance, I describe it in detail in Chapter Thirteen, which deals with recent developments. Because of its significance in donor recruitment I'll summarize the benefits and shortcomings here.

Benefits of Direct Dialogue

- Allows the donor to have a two-way interaction, to ask questions prior to committing to a gift
- Provides a good return on investment
- Offers flexibility (unlike mail, direct dialogue lets you test different average gifts, different selling approaches, or instantly alter the amounts or information gathered)
- Minimizes renewal costs because all donors are signed up to an automatic payment method
- Offers at least the potential for a very positive experience for both the donor and the asker
- Can be a good way of publicizing your organization to new types of donors

Drawbacks

- Requires a big up-front investment, unless your face-to-face agency covers initial costs
- Selects donors who have only proved that they are responsive to face-to-face solicitation, and who may not be responsive to mail or phone upgrade, or to renewal if they lapse
- Tends to have higher attrition than mail-sourced automatic donors
- Can be a nuisance if done badly

Assuming it's allowed to continue without restrictive regulation there's no doubt that face-to-face fundraising as practiced by the proponents of direct dialogue will be one of the most important recruitment methods for fundraisers in the early part of the twenty-first century.

The Internet and E-Mail

The Internet is certainly a powerful communications, campaigning, and fundraising tool—and as it wasn't even mentioned when *Relationship Fundraising* first appeared, I think it's worth at least a mention in this book's penultimate chapter, which is about recent developments. So I'll only include brief reference here to its role in attracting new donors.

I was drafting this section in late 2001, at the time of the September 11 terrorist attacks on New York and Washington. The phenomenal effect the response to those catastrophes had on the culture of on-line giving in North America has in itself moved the Internet to a whole new level as an effective giving channel.

There are several good sources of information for the Internet fundraiser, and some of these are listed in the Bibliography. One of these, *Direct Response Fundraising*, edited by Michael Johnston, has a specific contribution about on-line fundraising from my old colleague Jason Potts, who as head of New Media at Burnett Associates taught me much of what I know about relationship fundraising via the Internet. Jason passionately believes in both the Internet and relationship fundraising, and has become something of an expert in how they can best work together.

Another useful source is a book called *Fundraising on the Internet,* edited by Mal Warwick, Ted Hart, and Nick Allen. A lot of money can be wasted by those who don't know their way around this complex medium and this book is a useful guide (although it's a fast-changing field, so you'll have to budget for frequent updates). Visiting the sites of successful on-line fundraising organizations such as the American Red Cross (http://www.redcross.org) and Greenpeace International (http://www.greenpeace.org) is also a useful first step.

But how good is the Internet and e-mail for recruiting donors? According to Nick Allen, CEO of donordigital.com and one of the brightest e-fundraisers around, donors don't usually go in search of nonprofits to support. They support organizations they already know and trust, or ones that successfully invite them to support their mission. So fundraisers have to get back to basics on the Internet like anywhere else. They will have to acquire donors by driving them to their site and creating compelling appeals, easy donation systems, and effective acknowledgments and repeat solicitations.

Jason Potts tells me that where the Internet differs from other communications channels is that it has the ability to recruit, provide a simple way to give, and personalize future correspondence to the donor's requirements, all at the same time. Combining marketing strategies to encourage people to see and complete a donation form with a simple secure way to give, a tailored e-mail follow-up, and of course a personalized thank you, is quite a compelling set of tools for the relationship fundraiser. Getting individuals to use those tools is the challenge. While the Internet and e-mail will clearly never replace a one-to-one conversation as the most effective of fundraising media, they do offer fundraisers the potential to communicate on many levels (words, pictures, sounds, and moving images) and offer donors choices in the type and frequency of information they'd like, following their first gift.

Most nonprofits are investing more and more into on-line acquisition and although returns haven't been startling as yet, they are growing rapidly year by year for most organizations. Nick Allen believes that as the cost of acquiring and retaining donors grows for just about every other medium, particularly mail and phone, the Internet looks better and better.

Jason Potts points out that as more people around the world go on-line, this creates both opportunities and threats for fundraisers around the world. These opportunities can be very culturally specific. For example, in contrast to European anxieties around Internet security for on-line giving, donors in Latin America are in many cases happier to give on-line as they tend to be very mistrustful of their postal system. The threat comes through a lack of ready understanding of this sometimes complex environment. Unlike the wealth of data on offline fundraising letter writing, as yet there is very little science available on what increases or reduces response in fundraising on-line.

Increasingly fundraisers are targeting professional people with money but little time. The Internet and e-mail may be their preferred methods of communication. If you can communicate your needs effectively and set up easy-to-use payment or debit facilities, then new supporters and their donations will flow in. Nonetheless, fundraisers will still have to treat their donors well, to be quick in response and very service-oriented. In short, to make the most of the Internet a new, donor-oriented approach is needed, which is good news for relationship fundraisers though it will confound anyone who thinks of on-line interaction as a rapid route to fundraising riches.

You'll also need to get your donors' permission for anything you do with them on-line, as this is an area where so-called permission marketing should come into its own. E-fundraising is an ethical minefield, so if there isn't already a code of practice on e-fundraising in your country I suggest you get hold of one from somewhere else quick. Try the Association of Fundraising Professionals in the United States or Britain's Institute of Fundraising.

Although many fundraisers are sinking most of their investment into their Web sites, this may be a mistake. According to Michael Gilbert of *Nonprofit Online News* in the United States, e-mail is the killer application of the Internet. It is, Gilbert asserts, person-to-person communication, the one thing that breaks down barriers faster than anything else on the Internet. His advice is to stop waiting for people to discover your Web site, and start discovering their inboxes. Oh, and e-mail is, of course—for the present at least—cheap. But beware: if there's anything the public hates more than junk snail mail, it's junk e-mail.

Gathering Names

You can recruit potential donors without paying for lists of names. Names (qualified leads) can be collected in a variety of ways—but the conventional wisdom of the fundraising craft is that if a donation hasn't been given, or even if it has but not through the mail, then that new name is unlikely to be as productive as that of a new donor recruited by direct mail. Your new donors will be less likely to be "mail-responsive," in the jargon of the direct marketing industry. However, some nonprofits are now reporting that donors recruited via press advertising are more rather than less responsive than those found through cold direct mail. The theory is that people on mailing lists have been overexposed to appeals, whereas those who respond via the press are often new blood, not to be found on anyone's database. This seems to me to be another sign of the times, yet more of a clue to the limited life expectancy of cold direct mail.

But fundraisers have to be careful. You can't gather names from just anywhere. Some lists will be a liability rather than an asset and may respond less well than if you had mailed the telephone directory. Of course, names can be tested at low cost and common sense will probably guide you as to what will work and what will not. (If you are gathering names, addresses, and telephone numbers you also now obviously have to add mobile phone numbers and e-mail addresses too.)

If you do house-to-house collections, an effective way to gather names for free is to print a space for name, address, and telephone number on the back of your collecting envelopes. The resulting names are already responders and if you add an offer of further information describing your work, then the hook can provide useful members or new supporters. By flagging their source on your database you can then track these names over a period of time to see if they are cost-effective additions to your list. Even if they don't respond to mailings, it may be worth trying a telephone call.

You can try collecting the names of swimmers, walkers, and runners from sponsored events—and even the people who have sponsored them. However, some nonprofits that have done this are not very enthusiastic about the results they achieve. This doesn't surprise me as so often runners and their sponsors are reluctant donors and may feel they've done enough already. They may, however, simply be a different kind of supporter and may well help you again if treated appropriately.

A friend of mine recently told me about a barbecue party he went to, given by a friend he used to go cycling with. Midway through the party the host was called into the house to take a phone call and left his guests for about half an hour, which was rather longer than he should have. On his return the host explained that the call had been from an environmental nonprofit for which he and my friend had recently done a sponsored cycle ride. They had telephoned to see if he would consider becoming a member. My friend's host wasn't in the least put out by this interruption of the feast. He was delighted and very flattered to have been asked. His pleasure at the prospect of joining this group was evidenced by the length of the phone call, but he would never have joined if left to his own devices.

Names can also be gathered via the telephone. This can be done through direct recruitment off the page, as in Greenpeace's small-ad campaign, which rode on the back of the "green revolution" of the late 1980s. This surge of public interest in all things environmental allowed the nonprofit to place tiny single-column ads that simply said "Join Greenpeace" and gave a phone number. No explanation or selling message was needed and hundreds phoned in to join.

Even small ads can be costly in the wide-circulation press, however, and results have to be measured carefully. Despite the organization's high profile, name-getting by telephone wasn't particularly cost-effective for Greenpeace when compared to other methods.

Unfortunately for Greenpeace, a few years later some of these spontaneous joiners are proving quite hard to renew by mail, but recent tests in telephoning renewals have produced very encouraging results. According to Rich Fox, a Malibu-based telefundraising specialist, this is not surprising. His experience in telephoning lapsed subscribers in the United States and in Europe indicates that the telephone is particularly effective at overcoming the biggest inhibitor to subscription renewal—inertia.

You can do a local variation of Greenpeace's small-ad campaign by sticking up posters or getting free or concessionary coverage in your local paper. Names can also be gathered by phone if you have an advice or information line—provided you let callers know that's what you're doing.

The telephone is also an indispensable means of taking credit card donations in the simplest and most convenient way. Callers can simply read their card number, expiration date, and amount they wish to give over the phone—and while you have them on the line you have a chance to discuss your work, find out more about them, and perhaps increase the size of that donation. If you don't offer donors the chance to support your cause in this way you are almost certainly losing both money and potential donors. Note also that credit card givers tend to give up to 25 percent more than those who just send in a check.

Television has also been regularly tried as a method of adding names, but the cost of advertising on television deters most and those who have tried it rarely sustain their campaigns, which indicates questionable cost-effectiveness. And even when TV response rates are high, quality is often low. Responders recruited by television often fail to make a second gift and the people who ask about your services too are more likely to waste your time than have serious interest.

Membership

If you work for a cause, consider launching a membership or similar type of scheme. People who join as members will often quite happily pay an annual membership fee and respond regularly to warm appeals for funds, as well as buy merchandise, leave legacies, and do all the other things good donors do.

Just because you call them members doesn't mean you have to grant them voting rights. (Check your by-laws first.) But for many people the word membership has connotations of shared control so an alternative may be preferred, such as key supporter, club donor, or friend, although these are often not felt to be as good. One thing about members is that they do belong. It's that sense of belonging that your scheme needs to cultivate.

You can offer a hierarchy of members (or supporters), recruiting ordinary members at, say, $30 per annum, family membership at $40, lifetime membership at $250, and so on, with special concessions for students, retirees, and people who are unemployed. These amounts are roughly typical of those charged by national membership nonprofits in the early 2000s and are probably a lot lower than they ought to be in terms of relevant value for money. Getting the price right is obviously crucial—too high and you'll put people off, too low and you'll lose money and also give out the wrong signals in terms of value for money.

It is quite possible to further subdivide your membership and create usually purely nominal sublevels. Some fundraisers are adept at this, successfully dishing out meaningless titles that sound slightly more grand the more you are prepared to pay. But it helps donors find their ideal giving level and, of course, the member who pays you most in membership fees is the one most likely to give you most in other ways such as special appeals, capital gifts, and legacies.

The Information Line

An information service, of course, doubles as a very convenient avenue for supporters' complaints, doubts, and criticisms. By advertising your hotline, action line, or information line you appear anxious to please and donors respond very positively to this. You are, therefore, able to smoke out any concerns and anxieties among donors easily and, as I said earlier, many nonprofits have found that complaints often turn into valuable donations. Once established your hotline service can be easily advertised at no cost in all your promotional materials, newsletters, and even in your direct mail (see Chapter Ten).

The Video Party

In the mid-1950s, Tupperware—an enterprising American company with an overpriced and ordinary product range—hit on a marketing idea that transformed its fortunes and turned both company and products into a household name. The firm recruited local agents who sold its plastic airtight containers by the million at Tupperware parties.

These were no ordinary sales demonstrations, no mere repetition of Avon calling. Tupperware parties were major social events. Just to be invited was an accolade and to be allowed to buy was almost a privilege. Women went along just to touch Tupperware's plastic containers and talked about it for weeks afterward.

Well, it seemed like that to me, a mere boy at the time. A friend of my parents was awarded the position of South West Scotland regional representative for Tupperware and she introduced my mother to this elevated social activity. Somehow in time Tupperware disappeared from the scene—overtaken by cheap imitations. The product lingered on, however—many of my mother's original Tupperware containers are still in use and I'm sure some pieces, particularly the zany salt and pepper set, are now collectors' items. But what has really lasted is the memory of those parties and Tupperware's distinctive and successful marketing method.

The U.K. naughty nightie queen, Ann Summers, revived the idea in the permissive 1970s to market far more salacious products in the privacy of the prospect's own home, where intimate items could be demonstrated and bought in the company of half a dozen raucous and not quite serious friends and neighbors.

Does this strange concept have applications for the fundraiser today? I think it does. Hence the video party. The concept is delightfully simple and essentially follows the Tupperware formula. You need to find competent and willing volunteer hosts, recruited from your donor file, who will agree to hold an XYZ (insert the name of your nonprofit here) party in their own homes. They provide the coffee and cookies, you provide a suitable short video of your work (ten to fifteen compelling minutes) along with supporting leaflets, a stack of enrollment, membership, or donation forms, and some guidance notes for the host. The host selects and invites suitable friends, some of whom will already be XYZ donors.

The objective for the evening is clear and single-minded. Your host wants to recruit at least five new donors to the cause. That'll make sending the video and support material worthwhile. Some hosts will organize brilliantly, recruit lots of friends, and go on to run lots more XYZ parties. Others will do less well and may need encouragement. For the most successful, their XYZ party will soon pass into local legend and attendance at the next will be a must. But don't neglect their effectiveness at recruiting new donors and even as a way of thanking and encouraging existing ones. Everyone will enjoy the video.

The President's Task Force

The following case history makes a fitting end to this chapter, for it really is recognition par excellence, proof that donors really do like the hierarchical schemes that I mentioned earlier. Even if they clearly understand it as a device designed to secure their involvement, they appear not to mind at all.

Donors want to be involved in their favorite causes. The joining of a structured scheme gets them in on the inside, usually at a very modest cost. Fundraisers should capitalize on this compulsion to belong. Voluntary organizations have a clear and very desirable product in involvement schemes, one that is often underdeveloped.

A classic example of how completely this can work in practice was the launching of the President's Task Force, an elite donor group established by Ronald Reagan's office shortly after his election in 1981 as president of the United States. Of course, the qualification to join the President's Task Force was that you should give a minimum donation—$10 each month—to campaign funds. Large numbers of patriotic Republicans rushed to do their duty, trading a small amount of their disposable cash for the recognition and reward that went with being able to tell friends and neighbors that they were on the President's Task Force.

Various pieces of commemorative paraphernalia were produced and distributed in case members had to prove their status to doubting acquaintances who needed physical evidence of their friend's small but important role in affairs of state. These included "presidential medals of merit," presidential medal of merit lapel pins, model American flags (which had been dedicated en masse at a special ceremony in the White House), and inscription of the donor's name on the "presidential roll of honor." There was even an exclusive "members only" Task Force telephone hotline.

Donors, of course, loved it. For just $10 a month this was real value for money. Most of all, to encourage the authentic feel of the campaign, the fundraisers had produced stationery that was the exact facsimile of President Reagan's writing paper. Color printed and embossed, laser personalized and signed, it looked exactly as it would had the president himself taken time out from his busy schedule to write a personal note to acknowledge the donor's individual contribution and stress its importance to America.

More than a few of these letters were framed and hung in a prominent place in the family home so that visitors could be easily subjected to an hour or so's dissertation on the donor's sacrifice for America.

Across the length and breadth of the United States, thousands of Republicans took their membership of the President's Task Force very seriously indeed—and the dollars rolled into the president's office as a result. Sustained by a brilliant direct marketing campaign of record and reward, the President's Task Force gave its donors something beyond price—the prestige of practical involvement in something they believed in. It simply used the best of technique and technology, plus a forgivable amount of kitsch, to establish the ideal relationship fundraising proposition, an ongoing relationship where both donor and recipient could benefit in equal amounts, at the end of which a clear financial and practical target could be reached.

In relaying the case history of the "President's Task Force" at the International Fund Raising Congress in Holland, John Groman of Epsilon Data Management provided an anecdote that summed up the power of the campaign:

Late one evening a motorcycle patrolman flagged down a speeding motorist on one of America's interminable interstate highways. With customary leisurely grace he strolled up to the driver, who appeared to be in something of a hurry, and proceeded to ask him to provide his driving license and evidence of insurance. Without a word, but inwardly seething at the delay, the driver got out of his car and led the patrolman firmly by the hand round to the back of the car, to the enormous trunk of his Cadillac. Still without a sound, but with a gesture of magnificently righteous indignation, he flung his hand dramatically down to point out the large and very official-looking bumper sticker that prominently proclaimed the "President's Task Force" and indicated that the driver was, in fact, nothing less than a member.

The patrolman was astounded. He stammered a fulsome apology, saluted, swore it wouldn't happen again, and waved his distinguished visitor happily on his way. I don't know that the patrolman escorted the task force member across the state line with lights flashing and sirens wailing, but I like to think he did.

Action Points

▲ Don't emphasize finding new blood unless you are already doing all you can to keep your existing donors.

▲ Find out the average cost of recruiting a donor for your organization. Then find out how much, on average, each donor is worth. Costs will differ according to recruitment method, but you may also find that, for example, a donor recruited by a press advertisement will, on average, be worth more to you than a donor recruited by direct mail.

▲ Differentiate between donors and responders. Prepare material to upgrade responders speedily.

▲ Set up a logical program of reactivation for lapsed donors. Test it.

▲ Introduce appropriate schemes of recognition and reward, where relevant.

▲ Hold a donor recognition event at least once each year.

▲ Test your donor-get-donor recruitment methods. See if you can offer an appropriate incentive.

▲ Take advantage of reciprocal mailings while you can. Follow the reciprocal code of practice.

▲ Consider whether you can make your appeal mailings individual to you and different from the rest, while retaining their effectiveness. If you must rely on formulas, try not to make it too obvious.

▲ Test the value of gathering free names, such as event participants. Don't forget to collect telephone numbers and e-mail
addresses too.

▲ If you haven't already got one, consider the benefits of setting
up a membership or similar scheme. Choose membership price
levels carefully. Try to structure the scheme so that members'
activities are purely charitable, thereby avoiding possible tax
liabilities. (In Britain, this will enable you to recover income tax
already paid on the majority of your subscriptions; in the United
States, it will encourage greater participation as the members will
be able to deduct their payments from their own taxes.)

▲ Make your involvement schemes special and worth joining.

▲ Establish a telephone information line.

▲ Try organizing some video parties.

Donor Profile: Kevin Tuckwell

Having just given his destination, the mild-mannered gentleman in the pinstriped suit had hardly settled into the back of the cab when his driver launched into a breathless tirade.

"Did you see that piece on the news last night about the havoc caused by those anti-globalization protesters?" Kevin the cabby had opinions on this and most other issues of the day. "Absolutely sickens me, it does," he went on. "Who do they think they speak for then? Not me, I can tell you. Bunch of yobbos looking for trouble if you ask me—just football hooligans out for some aggravation during the quiet season. I'm sure they couldn't give a **** about free trade or genetically modified food, they just want to create grief, that's all."

The pinstriped gent looked mildly uncomfortable. Cab drivers today, he was thinking, are either downright uncommunicative or they never stop, and it seemed that for the duration of this trip he was stuck with one of the latter. It had dawned on him that, in this traffic, he might have to listen to Kevin for the next twenty minutes or more so he decided that the best tactic was a moderate response, and merely observed that it was only a tiny minority that had caused the trouble and the large majority were peaceful, and even had a point.

But Kevin would have none of it. "Bleeding foreigners if you ask me. It's the foreign agitators that are always behind these things, you take it from me. They plan it over the Internet, I'm tellin' ya. It's the same with all those asylum seekers. They're all run by Chinese gangs who make millions out of shipping truckloads of the poor sods into the country. And the asylum seekers always pay up, see, 'cos they know they're onto a cushy number here with social security, free hand-outs, and what have you. And they'll jump the housing queue 'cos they have so many kids. You see if they don't."

This was all too much for the mild-mannered gentleman. He leaned forward in his seat and delivered an impassioned response through the grill that connected him to his opinionated cab driver. Perfectly controlled but not so mild-mannered now, he told Kevin something of the reality faced by asylum seekers, the poverty, degradation, and persecution they might have been subjected to in their homeland that had caused them to uproot, to leave their homes and friends and risk everything for the chance of bringing up their children in a better environment. The mild-mannered gentleman concluded by saying Britain had little enough to boast of in its treatment of refugees and should be proud if it could offer safe haven to those in desperate need.

"Blimey . . . what do you do then?" inquired Kevin, a bit non-plussed at this outburst. He thought he was the only one entitled to voice strong feelings in his cab.

"I'm chairman of. . . ." replied the gent, and he mentioned a nationally known and respected human rights organization.

"Well don't sound off at me, then," said Kevin, clearly hurt. "My daughter's a regular supporter of your lot, you know, and I've been known to chip in the odd five bob meself when she's asked me to. Last time," he retorted with some indignation, "I gave your lot 50 quid, I did, just last month!"

Just then the cab drew up at its destination. As he got out the mild-mannered gentleman thanked Kevin for his ongoing donations and reassured him that without such generous and committed sup-porters the organization couldn't possibly continue. With that he paid his fare, but didn't leave a tip. Kevin, feeling very pleased with this unexpected recognition of his philanthropy, didn't even notice. Just as the mild-mannered gent turned to go, Kevin's next fare chanced along and jumped into the back. Kevin obligingly let him settle down before pointing to a recumbent youth in the doorway opposite and without a backward glance at the mild-mannered gent launched into his next tirade. "D'you see that young bloke begging over there?" he snarled. "Beats me why the hell young blokes like him don't. . . ."

Chapter Ten

Keeping in Touch
with Your Donors

*We cannot create feelings. We must learn how the tide is
running in people's minds, and float our messages on the
surface.*
DRAYTON BIRD, *COMMONSENSE DIRECT MARKETING*

Floating a message on the surface of people's minds is an extremely challenging and expensive business. It's also too often hit
or miss. To ensure we get a reasonable return from our limited
promotional resources, we fundraisers have to be more than a little circumspect in our choice of promotional media and our
choice of messages. Most important for fundraisers is getting our
messages regularly and consistently to our warm lists, our established and newly recruited donors. But it's also important to promote our messages to less proven audiences—the cold general
public—and inevitably there will be considerable overlap between
the two. Don't forget that the most demanding critics of your
donor recruitment advertising will be your existing donors.

I learned this early on from public reaction to the first fundraising loose insert inserted into one of the United Kingdom's leading Sunday supplements, the *Observer*'s color magazine. I was
involved in organizing this innovation for an international development nonprofit. Our insert was a then-unique format leaflet with
built-in reply form and envelope. The response was quite overwhelming but the loudest and most enthusiastic comments were

from the organization's existing supporters (the majority of whom had been recruited via the *Observer*) who, along with nearly a million other people, had seen this strikingly different communication fall from their Sunday magazine. Thankfully the calls were universally favorable. Donors were greatly encouraged to see such a surprising, positive promotion. Although our new insert had been entirely directed at potential new donors, its impact on existing supporters was considerable. This effect applies equally to all forms of communicating with donors—direct mail, press, television, posters, and everything else.

General Awareness Advertising

Donors will certainly see your press advertisements and posters, as will volunteers, staff, even board members. So, of course, will you. This may be regarded by some as sufficient justification to make up for the desperately poor response and income that most nonprofit off-the-page advertising generates. I find that hard to accept. In the absence of direct response many fundraisers justify press advertising through its indirect benefits, although these are usually vague and notoriously hard to measure. Advertising does put the organization's name about and it does help to pave the way for other initiatives, but press advertising now is so expensive, the public's consciousness so hard to penetrate, and competition for your reader's attention so substantial and sophisticated that most fundraising organizations simply haven't got the resources to make any noticeable impression.

Therefore they can very easily waste a great deal of money. All but a very few nonprofits have extremely limited budgets for advertising. By "limited," I mean that these days, anything less than an advertising spend of £1 million a year in the United Kingdom or several million dollars a year in the United States would almost certainly not be enough to sustain an already established brand image on its own, or make any lasting impression on public recognition. Many nonprofits are established household names but few, if any, have achieved this solely through press advertising campaigns or similar vague attempts at achieving awareness, even though press advertising may have played a part.

Selling Like Soap

People sometimes complain that nonprofits are being sold like detergents, or cornflakes, or margarine. Well, in 1990–91, Radion (a laundry detergent) spent just short of £10 million on advertising in the United Kingdom, Kellogg's Cornflakes spent £5.82 million, and Flora margarine spent more than £4 million. (My son Joe, who was nine at the time, thought there was something seriously wrong with his family because we didn't use Radion, so I suppose advertising must work to some extent.) Yet after investing many millions in TV and press advertising Radion then disappeared almost overnight from supermarket shelves and public memory, even Joe's.

By 2001 these figures (for the survivors) had increased considerably. According to Media Expenditure and Analysis Limited, Unilever's total advertising spend in 2001 was nearly £160 million in the United Kingdom, including £21 million on one brand, Persil.

Against this kind of expenditure, how can nonprofits compete? These figures show that nonprofits are not being sold like soap at all—nowhere near it. I know that much of this commercial expenditure goes on television—and in most countries nonprofits have already shown that they can't spend enough to make television work for direct response. As costs escalate and responses fall it seems likely that most other mass media will become equally uneconomic. Recruiting new donors via paid-for mass promotion as we know it—television, press, direct mail—might soon be a thing of the past, except perhaps for very special propositions.

Support for field fundraising activities, to inform and announce, to raise money, to recruit members are all valid uses of advertising. But while paid-for advertising still has a place in many large nonprofits' marketing mix its role is generally a supportive one. It should never be seen as a panacea for all messages, covering fundraising, image, identity, information, education, and all the rest. Fundraisers often think advertising will solve all their marketing problems because the amounts of money spent appear to be so large, but of course it is a mistake to equate expenditure with value.

And broad awareness alone will not make an appeal successful. Sometime back several London-based medical nonprofits were led down this particular garden path. They spent millions of pounds on awareness campaigns in the press and on posters in the hope that they could buy into the public's consciousness or create some kind of donor "brand awareness." Sadly, almost all this money was entirely wasted, public consciousness was hardly stirred, far less shaken, and when the money ran out these nonprofits were left with next to nothing to show. You can't bank a five-point temporary increase in awareness.

Most nonprofit "brands" have been created over many years. To shorten the process, if it is possible, would take more money than is likely to be available, yet many nonprofits attempt awareness advertising with pitifully limited resources. For most fundraising organizations it is like firing a peashooter at a battleship, the budgets just don't match the objective.

But remember David and Goliath. Perhaps it's just a question of getting the approach right, of deploying your limited resources with cunning and strategy so that a very little can go a very long way. That's what most effective nonprofit advertisers do. Press, poster, and even television advertising are seen as reinforcements of other methods of keeping the nonprofit and its messages in the public mind, including local and national publicity, public relations including media relations, special events, regional staff and volunteers, and so on. And, of course, your own direct communications with supporters.

Disaster Advertising

Direct-response off-the-page advertising plays a very important part in how many international nonprofits respond to a disaster overseas. While public attention—and sympathy—is focused on the plight of the victims, the fundraiser has a brief chance to be of immediate and practical help. But it's essential to react with extraordinary speed, implementing a probably prearranged plan of action at a pace that would be unthinkable in normal times—information to be gathered, advertisements written, copy approved, positions negotiated, and space booked in hours rather than the usual weeks. Successful disaster advertising has several other important aspects:

- *Judging the scale of the disaster.* Ads will only work if they are supported by major press and television coverage.
- *Courageous booking.* Media owners and their representatives have to be persuaded to displace already booked advertising, often from regular customers, to make way for your appeal. For some unknown reason disasters usually seem to happen on weekends and this means finding the personal phone number of senior advertisement sales staff and ringing them at home (a good justification for having a strategy in place in advance).
- *Good media selection and appropriate copy.* An urgent, newsy style usually works best. And media owners, even at short notice, will discount space for nonprofits at times of disaster.
- *Sustained TV and press coverage.* If the disaster is dislodged by subsequent news, ads can die.
- *Absence of any conflicting disaster.* Two simultaneous disasters tend to cancel each other out.

Communicating by Letter

Direct mail is one of the most challenging of media, creatively and organizationally, and it can and should be a lot of fun. In the first edition of this book, I pointed out that although it was possible that the future would bring some other and more effective means of floating messages regularly before donors, but I couldn't imagine what it would be, unless the technology could be found to beam fundraising messages via our prospects' central heating systems or something equally unlikely. Since I made this pronouncement ten years ago, e-mail has arrived. OK, so it doesn't come via the central heating, but it's close—many U.S. donors get it with their cable television hookups. However, e-mail still seems unlikely to supplant direct mail, though we could perhaps make much better use of it than we do. But I would hesitate to say anything so categorical again.

Meanwhile, we have to make effective use of the Postal Service to deliver in reasonably good time and shape the unique messages we can create, print, and insert into mailbox-sized packages. Direct mail remains our most frequent and most important communication with donors, so it's important to consider how fundraisers can approach their use of frequent postal contact so as to best develop and exploit their relationship with donors.

Let's switch away from marketing theory and abstract concepts to perceiving direct mail the way our donors see it—as it arrives, uninvited, in the mailbox. Most people I meet are excited by the receipt of mail, particularly if it's unexpected. So the fact that your communication is uninvited can even be a plus. But excitement can easily turn into disappointment and even dismay if the unexpected message is a bill, or a tax demand, or bad news of any kind. Or that notorious felon, unwanted junk mail.

We all know this. What's the point of going over it here? Just this: most fundraising marketers plan their communications by thinking of themselves, what they need, what they want, what they have to say. The relationship fundraiser starts by thinking of the donors, what they want, what they need and what will interest them.

So perhaps our first objective should be to bring only good news. Something good for them, rather than good for you. They're already irritated by the inescapable frustrations of daily life. If you can brighten their day rather than add to the irritation, your communication will have a much better chance of working. If not, then first glance is all you'll get.

But be aware, as with everything else, there are exceptions to this. Some people will *always* respond to the cause, however the message is packaged. Sometimes bad news, or the threat of it, can have a positive effect on response too. As part of the United Kingdom's code of telephone fundraising practice it is now customary in Britain (and in most of Europe, though rarely in the United States) for fundraisers to send what's called a "pre-call opt-out" letter before a telephone campaign, giving donors the chance to decline to receive the phone call. The letter helps build relationships by giving the people the opportunity to not receive an unwanted call. It also saves the cost of calling those who decline the call and the time in dealing with complaints they would have made about the call, and it keeps the fundraiser from hurting the organization's relationship with them. Giving donors the opportunity to make their gift in order to avoid the call greatly increases the mail response, getting in gifts at far lower cost. In tests conducted in the United Kingdom this type of letter has brought in about twice as much money as an identical direct mail letter that did not mention a possible phone call, but just asked for a donation.

Whatever the message, every fundraiser should have the scene in the donor's home in mind when preparing any mailing. Whether it's an appeal, a questionnaire, a thank you letter, a pre-call opt-out, or an invitation. Whether you're writing to thousands of people or to one individual. Stand beside them at the mailbox and imagine how your letter will arrive and will be received. Watch how your partner reacts to incoming mail. Go and stay with friends, and watch them. Know what it's like when the mail arrives. Build the presentation of your package around this activity.

It's at this point that your understanding of your donors will be really valuable. You can then write to your donors where they are, not where some marketing agency thinks they should be, or wants them to be.

You cannot claim any depth of relationship with your donors if when you write to them your letter has the appearance of a mass-produced, mass-mailed communication employing obvious computer technology and techniques. You don't write to your friends like that. If it looks like a sales pitch, the same negative applies. You don't sell to your friends.

And you don't write to friends at well-spaced, convenient intervals that fit in with your marketing plan and preconceived notions of when to write. You don't write ritually on quarter days—you write when you have a good reason for doing so. So that tends to negate Easter appeals and Christmas appeals and so on. I'm not saying these are not the best times to write, they probably are. But try not to let donors see that as your reason for writing. Otherwise their response may not be what you wanted.

AICDA: *attention, interest, conviction, desire, action.* This is one of the first memory aids I learned as a copywriter. It used to be AIDA, and still is for most direct marketing copywriters, which might be a more memorable mnemonic. However someone who knew a little about fundraising clearly felt attention, interest, desire, and action were insufficient for fundraisers, and so added conviction. I don't know what an "aicda" is, but I find the word just as easy to remember. You need to give that kind of directed structure to all your communications. I also learned a lot of other things, sometimes the hard way, about what does and doesn't work in direct mail.

I'm going to make the rather risky assumption that you, the reader, have also had these tenets of fundraising-by-mail thrust at you in various parts of your training and education for your fundraising job, so I will just go through the checklist very quickly. It always pays to go over the basics and the checklist may even be of more use to you without the usual verbiage to describe what's often fairly obvious.

Like every other aspect of direct mail, the addition of a message on the outer envelope should be rigorously and regularly tested. In cold mail a message on the envelope almost always reduces response largely because it acts as a signal that an appeal is inside and so reduces opening. Any exception to this is usually a singularly clever or appropriate message, and these are rare. Or perhaps something so intriguing it almost forces the recipient to open the envelope. In warm mail the envelope message usually makes little difference either way, presumably because most donors are prepared to hear from organizations they've supported before. However, this is not tested often enough. (I would be interested to hear from fundraisers who have information on envelope tests.)

Constant testing of every aspect of direct mail really is essential because society is changing dramatically and people's understanding and opinions are evolving rapidly. What worked two months ago won't necessarily work next month. I especially advocate that you test concepts such as letter length, use of a leaflet or lift letter, the almost obligatory use of a postscript on a letter (surely donors are beginning to see through such devices?), underlining, use of a Johnson box, salutation, and so on. It pays to keep testing constantly so that your message is as sharp as possible.

I advocate anything that makes your message seem individual to you and to the donor—to your relationship. Start with "you" and not "we" and don't start by asking for money. Treat donors as family. Let them recognize your need as their need. Share the problem. Tell your donors what you want them to do, give a clear and easy course of action (see "The Ideal Reply Form," later in this chapter). Remember that emotion always outsells intellect and get in plenty of little human details, action, case histories, and first-person quotes. Use simple, everyday language and write in an informal, friendly tone. Avoid all jargon, and don't assume that your readers know all that much about what you do, or will have read your last letter or even any of those that went before. Be sure all your materials stand alone. See to it that your letter looks like a letter, not a page out of a book. It should look like something that could have been typed on a typewriter. And don't use justified lines. Remember that in fundraising direct mail, neatness costs money.

Decide also not to refer to your written communications as mailings or even appeals. Mailings and appeals are impersonal and presuppose a request for funds. Instead, talk about letters, news, and special messages.

Personalize your warm letters. Of course, you can test this against a "dear friend" letter, but the personalization will almost certainly cover its cost. Even if it didn't I'd still advocate its inclusion as worth the money. What kind of person writes to a friend as "dear friend"? What kind of friend can't be bothered to use my real name? Sending a circular is not what relationship fundraising is about.

The key word in regular letter writing to donors is *relevance*. Make your letter relevant, interesting, appropriate. Don't appear to take it for granted that they will respond every time. Talk about what their involvement enabled you to achieve last time, why it was needed then, and who benefited. Let third parties tell their own stories of what that benefit meant. Give donors many different ways to help. Keep it interesting, short, readable, structured. Remember the mailbox. Make it a letter you'd like to receive yourself.

The Ideal Thank You Letter

I think thank you letters are a much underestimated fundraising tool. Many fundraising organizations might benefit from paying them a little more attention.

A short while ago, I set myself the task of writing a multipurpose thank you letter for one of my company's clients. Because this was for a quite small organization, I decided to produce it on a single piece of business-size stationery. In true copywriter style I borrowed several components from other letters I'd seen, most noticeably from a superb new customer welcome letter I came across from a firm of U.K. publishers called Wyvern Books. That letter, although addressed "dear business manager" rather than personally, struck me as a really well-thought-out, user-friendly communication that in a short preprinted panel to the right of the page summarized everything I needed to know about how Wyvern Business Library could help me and my business. A short description of the service was included with details of the company's mission, its administration, its mailing policy, and even the chance to introduce a friend. It was almost a mini-welcome pack on a single letter-size sheet. The bit I really liked—so much so that I copied it—was the box that asked, "Do you want a word with someone? We are just a phone call away. . . ." Then it listed who's who at Wyvern Books and what they did, and the final line before the number said, "But we're all here to help. Call us." The whole thing was very comprehensive and businesslike, yet it was done in such a friendly, helpful tone that I decided to plagiarize it mercilessly. Its approach is altogether appropriate for fundraisers, and it is an example of brilliant relationship marketing. I'll buy Wyvern's books again.

The other inspiration I borrowed was an idea Oxfam had many years ago of simply printing donation and tax receipt forms on the back of the letterhead. It costs next to nothing yet is a constant reminder of Oxfam's need for funds. I wonder how many of Oxfam's suppliers and business and trade contacts have covenants with Oxfam as a result.

In my model thank you letter, the text is individually laser-printed for each donor. The stationery is in two colors, and the information panel is printed in gray, so the letter text really stands out.

This letter works hard for the cause. It is economical, logical, and accessible. Yet many nonprofits still have pompous and impenetrable stationery—on which they write pompous and impenetrable letters. How welcoming are *your* thank you letters?

Newsletters and Magazines

Several nonprofits I know have tested the bottom-line value of including a newsletter or magazine with supporter mailings. Results have been mixed. Sometimes a publication adds interest, increases readership, and lifts response. Sometimes it seems to make little difference or may even distract from the appeal, and its costs of preparation and insertion clearly indicate that the nonprofit is losing money by including it. To be reliable these tests have to be done on a large scale over some time against a control group and even then the results can be misleading. Nevertheless, as a result of this kind of research, some organizations have stopped sending their newsletter or magazine and so have cut an important means of communicating with their donors in the interests of immediate cost savings.

In relationship fundraising some form of regular platform for communicating with donors is essential. It needn't be a frequent full-color magazine. It can be a low-cost four-page newsletter printed in two colors and sent out just three or four times each year. (But bear in mind that the cost of full color printing has come down a lot recently, and donors perhaps expect it now more than they once did.)

The newsletter is an automatic reason to write to your donors. You need no other excuse. It must be interesting, relevant, exciting, short—an attractive and highly readable summary of what the organization is doing, thanks to your—the donor's—help. It can have features of value and interest to the reader, such as tips on exercise or health from a medical research nonprofit, news on legislation and advice services from a disability group, and so on, as well as reporting directly on the progress of the organization. In a relationship that can easily seem one-sided—you asking and them giving—the newsletter is a gift from the nonprofit to interest and involve its supporters in the work they believe in.

From the organization's point of view a quality newsletter repays its investment as it serves as an effective, low-cost way of involving people in your organization's mission. But so many nonprofit newsletters are appallingly done. They either neglect their readers entirely, drown them in too much information, or subject them to archaic or virtually absent design and unimaginative copy. A good newsletter will have a range of stories of different lengths and styles. A typical A4 (eight and a half by eleven inch) newsletter might have ten to fourteen different pieces from a short feature to snippets of a few lines, including a strong lead story taking two-thirds of the front page. And, of course, it will use several photographs— excellent ones, not blurred snapshots.

Donors don't want waste paper. But they will really appreciate a good newsletter and you will be able to use it for all sorts of productive purposes—to explain your philosophy, your new ideas, your latest campaign, how you use bequests, your helpful new booklet, to report on the last appeal, to give a brief trailer for the next appeal. . . . The list of uses is endless.

Magazines more elaborate than the four-page newsletter are perhaps more likely to fulfil a role for the nonprofit, at a cost, than to make any direct contribution to fundraising income. However, that doesn't mean to say the informative, well-designed color magazine cannot be readily justified. Many organizations need to keep donors informed of the people and the stories that make up their work, and a regular magazine can be the ideal vehicle. It can also pay you to inform your supporters in detail and to educate them in the issues and dilemmas that your organization sometimes faces.

But magazine production is demanding and expensive and too many nonprofits do it badly. A bad publication does a lot of harm. Yet a really good magazine can make a unique contribution to relationship fundraising. This is one area where bottom-line considerations certainly apply but where the accountant's cold logic needs to be balanced by the fundraiser's flair, imagination, and enthusiasm for the long-term benefits of good donor communications.

A good newsletter, or magazine, forms just a part of your communications with donors, but it is a crucial and highly versatile part. If it's well done it gives you unique opportunities to float your messages on the surface of your donors' minds, and ultimately into their consciousness.

The Annual Report

The annual report is the one chance you have each year to present the entire story of your organization, its news, its philosophy, its character, its commitment, its style, and its methods of working. For the techniques and methods of annual report production, see *How to Produce Inspiring Annual Reports,* which Karin Weatherup and I coauthored. Your annual report is your case statement—for staff, for volunteers, for your board, for all your different types and levels of supporters, for other nonprofits, for businesses and foundations, for the media, for suppliers, and for many other specialist audiences. Consequently, its content, design, text, illustration, presentation, and use are all vitally important.

The annual report can be very valuable for donors, particularly larger donors. You need to assess its cost-effectiveness for smaller donors and if you do decide to send it to them they will need to be told why they are receiving it. It is also worth considering research into how your most important publication is viewed and used. Training is essential for all staff who will use the report. Whatever you do, don't send your annual report to any donor without a personalized cover letter. You must also provide some means of response and some compelling reasons to do so. Any publication without a cover letter is just a circular and will be treated as such.

Reader response doesn't just prove that your message is getting through, it can pay for the whole publications exercise—and even show a profit. The Royal Star and Garter Home, located at Richmond in Surrey, England, is a residential nursing home for disabled veterans. Each year, it produces an illustrated annual report—a moving, well-written, and well-designed document full of dramatic human interest stories. One year the report carried a shopping list of high-value items the Home needed. Within days of sending the report out, the Home had received a pledge for the top gift—£20,000 for an ambulance. Encouraged by this success the next annual report contained another shopping list, this time with a top gift of £60,000 for a day center. This time it took only three days for one generous supporter to pledge that large amount.

To test the value of the publication further, the Royal Star and Garter Home ran a split test, the only difference being that one-half of the test segment received the annual report, while the other did not. The results, shown in Table 10.1, speak for themselves.

Significantly, inclusion of the annual report didn't increase the number of donations, but it did encourage donors to give more. This

Table 10.1. Royal Star and Garter Home Test Results.

	Total Mailed	Responses	Percentage	Total Income	Average Donation
Without annual report	1,473	379	25.73	£15,917	£41.99
With annual report	1,473	368	24.98	£22,383	£60.82

Source: Royal Star and Garter Home.

is not conclusive evidence of the value of sending a good report, but an efficient annual report or review can do a lot to encourage response.

Eight Suggestions for Encouraging a Response

1. Always send your publications with an explanatory cover letter.
2. Include a reader inquiry form listing multiple ways to help.
3. Encourage response in your editorial at every practical opportunity.
4. Include a coupon or donation form.
5. Enclose a postage-paid reply envelope.
6. Include the name of an individual to write or send to.
7. Invite calls to a telephone hotline or information line (ideally staffed, not an answering machine).
8. Use a hook, if appropriate—a relevant incentive device, such as closing date, free offer, competition, introductory subscription, or invitation to a special event or reception.

The Ideal Reply Form

Perhaps there is no ideal reply form, but certainly some are more appealing than others and many suffer from being downright unfriendly to the user. These discourage response and so are expensive and wasteful. The following sections (based on a more detailed version my company used to ensure that reply forms include all important details) may be a useful general guide, which you can adapt to suit the particular needs of your individual communications. Please don't stick rigidly to any formula you may find in this list. The worst thing for the whole fundraising community would be if all appeal forms were identical. We already suffer from this to some extent.

Reply Form Design Considerations

The reply form has to be the hardest working piece in any fundraising communication. Its function is to provoke the most generous possible response from the potential or existing supporter. It is up to the design and copy to make this possible. The objectives of the form are straightforward.

- To reiterate the appeal
- To confirm the action the donor should want to take, including suggesting clear gift amounts
- To guide the reader easily through all aspects of information both on the front and on the back of the form
- To allow for the fact that the majority of the donors are middle-aged to elderly

Size

The form must be large enough to feature the information but tie in with the size of the outer envelope. Normally it will be the same size or double the size. If the form is folded it must be along the bottom so that it can be inserted mechanically. It must fit the reply envelope or should have to be folded no more than once to do so.

Appeal Message

This should be a concise, emotive reiteration of the appeal described in the accompanying letter.

Action to Be Taken

There should be a line saying "Yes, I want to . . . " or some appropriate variation.

Donation Values

Have a line in a large typeface saying "I enclose my donation of . . . " before inserting check boxes if you intend to use these (consider whether the amounts suggested should be descending or ascending).

Method of Payment

This can be by check or money order made out to the nonprofit's name. In Britain, make sure the nonprofit's branch (if applicable), bank, and account number are shown; in the United States it's enough to make sure that the name is the same as the one on the bank account. Donors can also pay by credit card (check to make sure your organization accepts credit card payments and which ones)—specify the types of card accepted and leave sufficient room for at least sixteen digits for the card number and four for the expiration date. Then leave space for the signature, name, and address of the cardholder.

Address Label

Leave enough space for the address label to be placed or for laser printing. Do not print corners or a rectangle as when the label is affixed mechanically it does not always cover the position guides and looks unsightly. Make sure there is enough white space around the label so that if the form moves in the envelope the print never shows through the window. On a warm mailing ask the donor to notify you if any of the details on the label have changed or are incorrect. If you can you should include space for donors to add their home phone number, mobile phone number, and e-mail address. If you wish to carry out reciprocal mailings the form needs an appropriately worded clause allowing donors to opt out if they don't want to take part in reciprocal mailings.

Additional Giving Options

Many donors like additional detail. Any of the following steps might enhance a donor's motivation to give.

- Create a shopping list explaining what the donation values featured can either buy or achieve. This will help donors decide how much to give. Make sure that any check boxes on the donation form correspond to your shopping list.
- Add a photograph of the appeal subject to round off the message. Unless the identity of the subject is obvious the picture should be captioned.
- If your form uses both sides of the paper, add directional instructions, reminding the donor to complete the back of the form.
- Include a friendly explanation of how easy the forms are to fill in, what benefit they give, and what the nonprofit's tax status means for the donor. It may be signed off by the person who has made the appeal in the letter.
- Always allow sufficient space for an older person to fill in the requested information. Reversed panels can help guide the reader to the sections that need to be filled in.
- Always feature the nonprofit's name, address, and registered number.

- If the address is not on a label affixed on the reply form, add codes to identify the various list segments being tested. This is most commonly done as a scratch-off code (ABCDEFG and the like).
- Say thank you.
- Always stop and ask yourself whether your grandmother or a favorite elderly friend would fill in this form. If your answer is yes, then you have the right reply form.

The function of the form is first to sell and second to make buying easy. In a way it is unfortunate that in order to do this it has to be written and designed. Neither of these requirements entitle it to be regarded as a work of art. You don't buy because of a sales rep's pithy delivery of lines or eloquent gestures, you buy because you are convinced by the message and because the rep makes it easy to purchase on the spot. Think about that before you write or design your next form.

The Coupon

The least helpful coupon I ever came across was in a French magazine. The ad appeared on the right-hand edge of an early right-hand page—a very good position, from a response viewpoint. The problem was that the entire ad, including the coupon, had been reversed white out of black. Now, reversed type is a bit silly for any ad, because it's more difficult to read and should only be used for effect in short, bold copy. But a reversed coupon implies either a jest on the part of someone who wanted to resign anyway or an agency that deserves to lose the client's account. Unless, of course, that particular magazine's readers all have pens with white ink and routinely write on black paper. Even without going that far wrong, many fundraising ads do fall down at the coupon and again lose response and waste money as a result.

All my advice for reply forms also relates to coupons—but with the coupon you have much less space. So only the absolute essentials can go in as you still have to leave enough room for handwriting. And, of course, coupons should only ever appear at the bottom outside edge of the page for access and ease of removal.

Creative Use of the Phone

Talking to your donors on the telephone is the next best thing to being there. This will continue to be true, whatever legislation might do to curb telefundraising. Whenever anyone mentions telemarketing, both fundraisers and donors tend automatically to think of invasions of domestic privacy—some intrusive, pushy student stumbling through an ill-thought-out script in an embarrassing attempt to pressure people into buying something they don't want. "I always hang up on them," everyone says, and wonder how on earth they can possibly make a decent living.

If fundraisers generally are held in low public esteem, then telefundraisers have sunk out of sight. I felt enormous sympathy with Robert Leiderman when I read the opening chapters of *The Telephone Book,* his entertaining explanation of how to use the telephone to find, get, keep, and develop customers. Robert could clear a room at parties even more quickly than I can, just by announcing his line of business.

Yet most objections to being telephoned are apocryphal or imagined. People think they don't like telemarketing calls because that's what they think they should believe or they've been led in the media to believe. Someone who receives a call that is personally relevant will not consider it to be either unsolicited or telemarketing. The calls people object to are almost all the classic—and objectionable—pushy telesales calls.

Why is it, I wonder, that so many nonprofit boards consider the telephone to be intrusive and unacceptable but have no objections at all to collecting house-to-house? In practice house-to-house collecting is far more intrusive and more difficult to deflect. Yet I've never known a board object to house-to-house solicitation in the way so many object on principle to using the phone. The method of approach is neutral. It is how it is done that is either good or bad. The key is relevance. In that regard, telefundraising is no different from direct mail.

No sensible fundraiser concerned with the building of long-term relationships would wish to jeopardize a relationship by making unwelcome junk phone calls. But short-term opportunists might. The potential for considerable damage and distress obviously exists.

A tiny point: fundraisers and board members should be aware that many of the major gift solicitations that they believe volunteers are undertaking in face-to-face meetings are, in reality, being done on the phone. So it might be wise to train volunteers in phone skills.

It's for You

One piece of professional conduct that should be enshrined in any code of practice for the telephone is that fundraisers should not make calls to any potential donor at home unless they already have a relationship. Another is that as soon as the phone is answered callers should be required to ask if now is a convenient time to call—and should politely and promptly end the conversation if it isn't.

When it rings, it's answered. That's the power of the telephone. It's a power that has to be wielded with great respect. Some years ago I saw a presentation Robert Leiderman prepared for fundraisers to demonstrate the potential of the phone. When comparing the phone to direct mail he said, "When did you last get out of the bath to answer a direct mail letter coming through your door?" meaning you would get out of the bath to answer your phone.

This didn't convince me. I enjoy my bath. I would try to drown the sound of the phone ringing, perhaps by singing more loudly or by splashing my rubber duck. If the caller persisted, then I suppose, very reluctantly, I would get out and, dripping wet, clutching my towel, I'd trot downstairs to answer the wretched thing. How do you think I would react if the caller was someone trying to solicit a donation? Few things could be more calculated to dent my relationship with that nonprofit, believe me!

So this power also has to be wielded with caution. Every time the phone is answered, telefundraisers should think that it might be me, or someone a lot bigger than me, who just climbed out of the bath to answer it.

But Robert's point is a good one. When did you last stop a meeting to read a magazine ad? You did, to answer the phone. When did you last tell someone to ring you back because you were watching a TV commercial? When it rings, it's answered. That makes the telephone the most intrusive advertising medium. Visiting by phone is exactly like visiting in person. As Robert Leiderman says, why should we be any less respectful of our hosts just because we are visiting by telephone? The key is to ring the right people on the right subject at the right time with the right offer.

Relevance

Just as it is an irresistible method of contacting donors, the telephone can also be irresistibly persuasive in the hands of an effective user of the medium. A good telefundraiser raised on relationship fundraising knows just when and how to use that power to develop and extend donor relationships. Fundraisers too often think they are dealing with a yes or no. Most donors and potential donors haven't thought it out so clearly. The telephone is an ideal vehicle for approaching the maybes, the nearlies, and the lazies.

Don't be afraid to prepare a detailed and comprehensive script. Scripting is just preparing what you want to say in advance. Like any publication or direct mail shot, what you want to say to potential donors will be more effective if it is carefully structured and well presented. A good telefundraiser will use the script as a base, departing from it effortlessly as the need and the conversation dictates, returning to it when required to keep the focus of the call and avoid lengthy, expensive, and unproductive chats. If you use outbound telefundraising to any extent it will pay to have your script prepared by experts.

Leiderman gives delightful advice about scripting in *The Telephone Book*, such as, "Write the way you talk, not the way you write." "Cut the first three paragraphs, because almost inevitably it takes about three paragraphs to get the rubbish out of your brain." (The second is also often true for direct mail.) "Forget the rules of grammar." "Ask your granny if she understands the script." And lots more.

Inbound or Outbound?

So far I've only mentioned outbound telefundraising—when you call them. Telefundraising can also be inbound, when they call you. And you can also use the telephone for events, research, lobbying, and for other important purposes.

A word of caution: if you store research information on a database, be careful to let your donors know. You may be infringing data protection legislation if you don't. Similarly, if any research information is to be stored for later use in sales or fundraising, that could be infringing your country's codes of practice. This doesn't mean you can't use research information for fundraising purposes, but you have to let donors know beforehand that this is what you are going to do.

I said in Chapter Nine that one of the best uses of outbound telefundraising is in reactivating lapsed donors. Most donors fail to renew or continue their support simply through inertia. But however inert they may be, when the telephone rings, they answer it. As the calling nonprofit already has a relationship and if the caller can represent its case cogently and compellingly, the donor will agree to renew, and will accept and sign the completed donation form that the caller will send the next day (note that to close the deal the telefundraiser still has to rely on the post or e-mail to get confirmation, unless the donor has given a credit card number). Often donation averages pledged by telephone are much higher than those achieved by mail. In Britain, many recipients of phone calls can be persuaded to allow the nonprofit to recover tax on their gift. And where reactivation mailings are achieving percentage response levels in low single digits, a well-conducted donor reactivation campaign by telephone can achieve reactivation rates of 60 percent or more of successful contacts.

Each outbound telefundraising call will cost around ten to fifteen times as much as a direct mail shot, but provided an established relationship exists the results can easily be ten to fifteen times as successful. The benefit for the telefundraiser is that at the end of the campaign there will be more donors and many times more net income, providing the campaign has been successful.

Even the most optimistic of pundits, however, is aware that these spectacular results won't last. As in the United States, response rates in the United Kingdom have declined as more nonprofits employ this method and donors have become increasingly used to it and increasingly resistant. Like most forms of fundraising its cost-effectiveness will probably continue to decline, so if you wish to use the telephone for reactivation—get cracking!

I Just Called to Say I Love You

The phone is also a useful way of thanking important donors or of personally communicating some important news or information. For years Guy Stringer at Oxfam used to ring larger donors (in the evening, at cheap calling rate) to thank them on the day that a particularly large gift had been received. This personal touch, he found, was widely appreciated and often brought in more, equally large donations. But one evening his call was answered by a particularly irascible-sounding gentleman. Guy asked for the lady of the house and the husband (for it was he) not surprisingly wanted to know who it was that was calling.

"Oh, I'm the director of Oxfam," breezed Guy, "and I wanted to thank your wife for her very generous donation of £200."

Well, it transpired that the good lady had been making these gifts without her husband's knowledge or approval, and Guy got the impression that he was a little annoyed about it. The telephone does have to be handled carefully, and Guy was in the perfect position to pour oil on troubled waters, to offer some tactful comfort and reassurance to mend matters, while remaining at a safe distance at the end of the line.

This experience taught Guy the first and most important lesson of telefundraising—always speak directly to the donor. He also found you have to say immediately who you are, you have to be patient and subtle, and you have to listen. Many donors welcome the chance to talk and will really open up to an interested caller, so the whole process can be taxing, if not exhausting. But Guy also found that those donors who were telephoned far exceeded those who were not in interest and involvement—and contributions to Oxfam.

News by Phone

Nonprofits live on news. They create it, they thrive on it. Fundraisers have access to newsworthy subjects in a way that is unthinkable for most commercial organizations. Nonprofits deal with big issues, life-and-death subjects. You just have to watch the TV news bulletins, listen to radio news, or look in your daily paper to see how effective fundraisers are at exploiting what's news.

Why not on the telephone? What better way to bring hot news personally to the really important people in your organization or to those people who can respond to the news with positive financial contributions?

If a disaster occurs overseas, you wouldn't think of writing to inform key field staff, whose response you hope will be to get to the disaster scene as quickly as possible. You'd telephone them to tell them immediately and avoid any possibility of delay. (You could now use e-mail, but the personal contact of the phone is better.)

So it should be with donors, whose response can be to provide the funds that you need to make your emergency operation possible. Most donors would appreciate that call more than anything else you can do. We all like to be needed. Donors particularly like to see what their contribution can achieve. So if it's warranted, call them. You can hardly get closer, and their involvement can only increase.

The Power of the Lobby

Unity is strength and power. Many nonprofits realized years ago that the combined voice of their supporters could be an irresistible force for change. Supporters' opinion can influence politicians and so alter legislation or create new laws. Often described as nonprofit politicking, it is usually independent of any party politics and is simply a visible demonstration of a nonprofit's potential to make the world a better place. Nonprofits almost invariably lobby against injustice and oppression and for a better lot for mankind.

Both warm and cold direct mail have long been used to find potential dissidents, giving recipients who agree with the nonprofit the chance to lobby either their own legislators or other figures of influence, usually by signing and sending preprinted postcards to targeted individuals. Greenpeace has used direct mail to encourage supporters to lobby governments that have transgressed the rules of the International Whaling Commission; Amnesty International has used it to lobby countries with particularly bad records of human rights violation; in Britain the Royal Society for the Prevention of Cruelty to Animals (RSPCA) has used it to encourage supporters to press for national dog registration.

Now the telephone and e-mail offer campaigning nonprofits much more effective, immediate, and accessible means of encouraging committed supporters to take direct lobbying action. The RSPCA has used the telephone to dramatic effect to support a parliamentary bill against the tethering of sows (female pigs). They called just over six thousand people who had helped in a previous lobby to persuade them to call or write and ask their local MP to be sure to attend Parliament when the bill would be voted on. Almost everyone telephoned agreed to do so.

Then, as a parting request, the nonprofit asked for a small donation to cover the cost of the campaign. The results were staggering. The RSPCA raised almost enough money to cover the entire cost of the campaign but, more important, the sow tethering bill was easily passed. In fact, one government minister told Gavin Grant, then RSPCA's director of public relations, that never before had he heard of so many calls generated on a single subject. To give some idea of the scale of this success, it happened in exactly the same week as the deadline given to Saddam Hussein of Iraq to get out of occupied Kuwait or face war, yet this same government minister reported that British MPs had received five to ten times as many letters and phone calls on the subject of sow tethering as they did on whether or not Britain should go to war.

Other valuable uses of outbound telefundraising include helping upgrade current donors by explaining schemes such as direct debit and electronic funds transfer, getting introductions to potential new donors from existing supporters, and discussing other methods of helping with non-donors where an already established relationship exists—for example, petition signers, catalogue customers, and so on. One fundraising sector that is making particularly good use of the telephone is education. What better way of approaching alumni than person-to-person, via the phone?

Just a Call Away

Inbound telefundraising is not likely to be nearly as contentious as outbound, but it is just as challenging and offers as many possibilities for the relationship fundraiser. Although they may not know it, most nonprofits are using inbound telefundraising already. Inbound telefundraising includes the use of a telephone number in a poster campaign, the "1-800" or other free number that appears at the end of a TV commercial or in the credits of a television program (if you are lucky), and increasingly the press advertisement that has a phone number on the coupon.

You can encourage people either to call in to your switchboard, to call a dedicated number that is staffed at certain times, to call in to a prerecorded message, or to call a professional outside call-handling agency. Inbound telefundraising also includes your "helpline" service or your customer service number that you advertise to encourage donors to phone you to discuss concerns, raise issues, or even to complain.

For general customer service and answering complaints I recommend you try to secure the resources to do the job properly in-house. When you are using the phone as a response vehicle you are actually talking directly to your customers, your donors. I wouldn't feel comfortable about leaving that responsibility in the hands of an anonymous outside operator. If an agency was involved it would have to be one that I could closely oversee and that I knew to have first-class experience of fundraising and the donor-nonprofit relationship. There's not too many of those at present.

In off-the-page advertising it is relatively easy to test the value (and the cost) of including a telephone number. The advantages are that your skilled and trained telefundraiser can refer callers to the benefits of nonprofit status and to the convenience of credit card donations (where gift averages are almost always higher), and to discuss any other relevant scheme, as well as the follow-up material that the callers will receive.

The telefundraiser must be a skilled and highly trained operative, carefully prepared with a good, imaginative script that can be departed from whenever necessary and will never be spotted by the caller. As in every fundraising use of the phone, the basic approach has to be customer care, not pressure.

The Call of the Wild

The telephone, with follow-up, is the best method of handling complaints. Then the complaint is immediately and personally acknowledged. Convincing donors that their complaint is taken seriously is the most important component of complaint handling. According to some research in America only 5 percent of dissatisfied customers actually complain. In my experience of talking to donors that's not an underestimate. In fact it may be much less for fundraisers because, by and large, donors really don't like to complain. So at least 95 percent of the people who think you are awful won't actually let you know what they are thinking, but, according to this same research, they will each go out and tell between ten and twelve other people how horrible you are—friends are like that.

That's bad news. You need to stop that. You need to increase the percentage of dissatisfied customers who call you—sounds weird, doesn't it? But think about it. Fundraisers don't want dissatisfied donors out there in the cold. You want them on the inside, where you can work on them and change their minds. Remember that research has shown that the most loyal of donors is the one who has complained and been responded to appropriately.

How many people stop buying a product because they've had a problem with it that the manufacturer could have fixed very easily—but never knew about it? The phone is quicker than the mail for handling complaints and may be just as cheap. And it's more effective and you can be sure your customer is satisfied. E-mail has some of these advantages and is much cheaper, so where it makes sense you should weave it into your customer service strategy too. As yet few nonprofits make good use of e-mail for handling complaints, or even gather e-mail addresses. This seems like a real opportunity to me.

Customer service is another area where first-class training is paramount. Operatives need to be trained in how to use the phone (there's far more to it than just knowing which end to speak into), how to answer questions, how to handle objections, the techniques of telephone sales, and the use of scripts. It's just as important as training them in what your nonprofit does. And really good people should be encouraged to depart from their script and do their own thing (within reason). Part of that training has to be to keep exemplary records of all phone calls and to record details of complaining donors, as they will be useful for further research.

When nonprofits get round to establishing dedicated customer service departments, a donor service line will be an essential component. Of course not all calls will be complaints. Many will be from satisfied donors ringing in for a chat. Encourage your donors to talk to you. Promote your helpline vigorously. The number to call should be clearly displayed on annual reports, on appeal reply forms, on everything you print and distribute to donors and potential donors.

Donors may prefer to call in the evening, after six P.M. You should therefore be there for them then. If appropriate, you could offer an answering service that is always on hand to help—twenty-four hours a day, seven days a week. Some of the larger nonprofits may be able to do this. Smaller organizations will find it is forgivable to offer an answering machine that promises a human response within twenty-four hours, so it has to be checked daily.

You might find that potential new donors will ring in also. You should encourage them. The telephone then would have a sales function. Report back regularly to donors on how the phone-in service is being used. Describe its benefits and successes. Make a big thing of it. You'll soon wonder how you ever managed to fundraise without it.

Even Closer Encounters

The closest you can get to your donors within the bounds of decency is to visit them in person. Clearly nonprofits already do this on quite a large scale, particularly in big gift fundraising or at a regional level. With the exception of some of these campaigns, however, not many have planned the visiting of donors into their marketing strategy, have worked out cost-benefit equations for visiting, or have established individual annual targets for visits.

Meeting donors is inevitably an expensive and time-consuming activity, yet it has unique value in many areas of fundraising. Whereas a few years ago most face-to-face fundraising in Britain was for small change, this has now changed, with many fundraisers regularly meeting larger donors and the growth in face-to-face fundraising that is evident in almost every busy high street (main street, in U.S. terms). Many of those who have pioneered one-to-one fundraising have built massive files of new committed donors and have banked seriously large amounts of money. An area that has yet to successfully exploit personal visits on a large scale is bequest marketing, perhaps for understandable reasons (see Chapter Twelve). But fundraisers are visiting donors at home to promote bequest giving, and the practice will surely grow in popularity, because it is very effective.

The potential for meeting donors face to face is considerable. Once fundraisers start thinking seriously about their donors' needs, a range of fundraising products will follow that can best be promoted in person, such as investments, insurance, and other individual propositions.

And, of course, we mustn't forget the potentially enormous benefits of encouraging donors to come and visit us. Again many nonprofits are already doing this, but few are doing it in any planned or structured way.

The benefits of face-to-face contact are considerable and largely obvious. I learned this in my first few days as a fundraiser, when my predecessor at the nonprofit I worked for, who was showing me the ropes, was invited to a well-known seaside town on England's South Coast to meet two elderly single ladies who had given the organization substantial support in the past. I went along too.

In anticipation of further large gifts we had prepared a shopping list of goodies because, like most donors, these women liked to be able to see where their money was going and to be able to imagine what it would achieve. Not surprisingly all our tangible products and propositions involved funding projects in our overseas programs, but I had discovered on my arrival that the nonprofit's real and immediate need then was for unearmarked general funds. So more in hope than in anticipation I had added a general fund project to our sheaf of overseas ones—I wanted to persuade these two donors to pay some of our press advertising costs.

We drove down to the South Coast and enjoyed a very civilized if rather formal afternoon tea with the ladies, who were pleased to see us, happy to learn of the success of past work they had supported, and quite prepared to hear of our further needs.

Over a toasted muffin and between sips of tea, I had the chance to explain my rather unusual proposition: that a gift of the cost of an advertisement could repay itself many times over, as the donors who would be recruited as a result would pay in far more over the years, for direct use overseas. Furthermore, if we could add a panel to our advertisement to explain that all costs of the advertisement had been donated by a generous supporter, that would generate further increased response. I had worked the whole thing out, including the cost of the ad and the likely response and likely donation level. I could show that every pound they gave for advertising could be turned into three pounds for the nonprofit's overseas work. It was a complicated and novel proposition. I doubt if I could have made it by letter or even by phone. The two ladies nevertheless held back from showing their generosity there and then, so we left our proposals with them. Later we received a check for £15,000, including £6,000 to pay for advertising in two national magazines.

Unfortunately at that time the nonprofit had no strategy for dealing with larger donors and I quickly became so absorbed in our general marketing that in my time there I failed to implement one. I regret to say that I never visited those two ladies again. Long-term gain sacrificed to short-term objectives, I confess. However, I believe the fundraiser who accompanied me, Ian Kerr, did keep up with the idea. Ian went on to become a very effective independent fundraiser and then was neither as young nor as foolish as I. He was also considerably more skilled and experienced at visiting donors.

A few years later I visited the nonprofit's program in Burundi, in central Africa, and was driven around that impenetrable country in an enormous Chevrolet truck—one of our shopping list items that had also been bought with the donation from our two ladies. If I had been a good relationship fundraiser I would have taken pictures of it and on return used that reason for another visit to the South Coast to show my donors the direct results of their generosity. They would have benefited and so would I. Oh, lost opportunities. . . .

Television

Television is the instant medium. It is the reality substitute that sits in the corner of the living room of every prospect you'll ever want to reach. Almost without fail it is used and listened to and watched every day of the week.

How can anyone ignore television? Most fundraisers have managed to—consistently. Many of those who have treated it rather more seriously since regulations in Britain were relaxed to allow nonprofits to advertise on television are now regretting their interest. They have learned the expensive and rather painful lesson that television comes nowhere near likely to cover its costs when used as a fundraising medium in the same way as Unilever uses it to sell detergent or Kellogg's to sell cornflakes. Nonprofits haven't begun to invest the necessary millions to build brand image by television and there's a good chance now that they never will.

In any event that seems to me to be the least interesting aspect of television for fundraisers. It was never likely to turn out to be a practical fundraising medium, certainly not for commercials of under two minutes' duration. Anything as long as that, of course, was equally doomed as prohibitively expensive. Some nonprofits have experienced direct payback from their TV ads, however, when they have used a direct marketing agency with fundraising experience to produce the ads rather than the head-in-the-clouds types who usually do these things.

From time to time one still hears of some nonprofit or other who, briefly, manages to get direct response TV to cover its costs, or just about. Yet I still believe that direct response fundraising is likely to be the least successful use you can make of television—but television nonetheless can be used for other purposes that are very important to fundraisers. Some of these other purposes require sophisticated backup such as banks of telephone operators, response and information packs, or retailer networks because, however powerful it is, television is one of the most transient of media. It is intangible. It is not a good medium for direct response.

John Hambley, formerly of Euston Films, London, says that television can create for you an informed and emotionally prepared audience, but you need to use methods other than television to turn the information into action and the emotion into giving. From fundraisers television demands advertising that seeks to inform rather than to persuade. It should make fundraising easier from a mass audience. It is fundamentally awareness advertising and it will only work if it can be sustained on a scale that is outside the reach of almost all fundraisers.

To get worthwhile exposure on television fundraisers have to take advantage of the program makers' increasing need for good material. What interests the viewing public—drama, human interest, emotion, tales of advantage out of adversity, courage against the odds? What have fundraisers got if not access to all these things?

The fundraiser's skill is to seek sensible opportunities to promote the nonprofit's concerns and issues as usable material for the program makers. This can often be done with great success, particularly by campaigning organizations. The Sympathetic Hearing Scheme, a consortium of nonprofits promoting care for the deaf, managed to place a sticker displaying their distinctive "ear" logo on the door of Alf Roberts's shop in Granada Television's *Coronation Street,* one of Britain's longest-running and most famous soap operas. This lasted for years and was seen by nearly 18 million viewers three times each week. Not a bad bit of free publicity.

(I have another use for *Coronation Street*'s famous corner shop. I hope someone will persuade the show's scriptwriters to weave the subject of will-making into their plots so that, among other things, when whoever happens to be running the shop at the time makes his will, along with taking care of his family and friends, he'll include a bequest to the Grocers' Benevolent Fund; see Chapter Twelve.)

ITV's *Telethon,* BBC's *Children in Need, Comic Relief (Red Nose Day),* Jerry Lewis's famous telethon in the United States, and so forth are other worthwhile uses of television that simply couldn't take place anywhere else. They show direct fundraising action to a huge audience made up mostly of people fundraisers could never hope to reach. For a brief time millions of people are unavoidably involved in doing something for the needs of others, which has to be a better use than television normally enjoys. But this is hardly relationship fundraising, so I give it no more space here.

The fact is large numbers of people do respond to telethons often just because it's the thing to do, so are unlikely to become long-term donors. The British Red Cross Society, on the other hand, has successfully used outbound telefundraising to solicit worthwhile further donations from a large part of the audience that initially responded via TV to one of their emergency appeals. So TV donors tend to be somewhat unpredictable.

Radio

Most of what I've said about television also applies to radio. Fundraisers should be targeting local and national radio for editorial purposes because local stations frequently need more good, relevant editorial matter. Radio's advertising possibilities are also largely unexploited by nonprofits and some, such as nonprofits helping blind people, have particularly appropriate messages for radio. Watch this space. I predict radio will feature strongly in future in many nonprofits' marketing plans. Radio reaches our donors in volume. We shouldn't neglect it.

Video

One Christmas my sister Jane (who, like me, is a fundraiser and has an unusual sense of humor) gave my father part of an elephant. But this wasn't any old part of any old elephant. It was part of Taru, an orphaned baby elephant in Kenya that had been rescued by an organization called Care for the Wild.

My father became part sponsor of Taru, and with his commemorative certificate to record this event came a twenty-minute video that showed Taru at play with his other little elefriends and told his history and explained his needs. Father proudly showed this video to me, as he showed it to many other visitors. I'd never sought to have an elephant as half-brother, but this endearing film brought the concept alive and gave Taru a personality and a reality that I would otherwise have missed.

That is the power of video. Dad would have been in real trouble had he failed to renew his sponsorship. The following year he received another video to show him how Taru had developed and to introduce the triumphs and trials of rearing orphaned elephants for return to the wild. Our entire extended family became hooked on Taru. And as each new visitor to our house ran the risk of meeting our recently acquired relative too, Care for the Wild must have been kept busy just in answering inquiries from the Scottish Highlands.

Videos can also be widely used for other relationship-building purposes, particularly in explaining new and complex situations and in making the organization's work come alive. A very high percentage of donors have a video cassette recorder. Fundraisers can send videos to donors that they can keep for a small fee or can return after viewing. The fundraiser can then record over the returned tape for subsequent use.

But the days of video publications are not here yet. In real terms video production costs have been dropping compared to print, but the perceived higher cost still remains. When videos appear regularly in the bookstands, that's when nonprofits should consider the possibilities again. It won't be long. Meanwhile, there is always the video party (see Chapter Nine). Or why not use video as Care for the Wild has done?

Getting It All Together

Many other ways of reaching donors are still impractical now but may work well in the future—cable and satellite television, cinema, door-to-door, media cards, piggybacks, joint communications, and so on. All are potentially useful ways of reaching donors and fund-raisers must be constantly vigilant to ensure no worthwhile avenues are overlooked. The Internet and face-to-face fundraising, new developments since this book first appeared, are covered in Chapter Thirteen.

No single method of communication should be seen in isolation from the others. No single contact should be considered without considering all the other contacts that have gone before or will follow. The secret of donor communication is to operate an integrated total communication strategy—total relationship fundraising. This involves seeing your contacts with the donor entirely from the donor's point of view and resisting the temptation to divide your marketing into neat little parcels, allocating one function to one department and the next function to another, with no contact between them. If your communications are integrated the donor will receive relevant, coordinated, and continued communication and will be informed, involved, and motivated without being inundated or irritated.

An example of integrated communication is Legacy Leadership, a program that is being pioneered by Rich Fox and Associates in the United States, and is achieving great results. This program combines opt-out direct mail, the telephone, and face-to-face visits in a very soft approach to find people on donor or member lists who might consider leaving a bequest, and gently move them in that direction. The opt-out pre-call letter gives the donor the opportunity to decide whether or not to receive the call (and someone who'd rather not be called can still give through the mail). Once the calling nonprofit has identified those who either have left a legacy or indicate a willingness to do so, or might consider doing so, then either a personal visit or a telephone call can be used to draw donors out to discuss their situation. What can result from this is not only larger bequests but also the possibility of outright major gifts from some people who otherwise would have fallen well below the major donor radar screen.

If genuinely integrated communication is happening, with all donor contact emanating from one central point, then true segmentation can begin to be practiced. Some donors will hear from you only once or twice a year. Others will hear from you every month. Some will hear on only one or two subjects, others will know about every aspect of your work. Some will get letter copy A, others will get letter copy B, and the rest will get one of the other twenty-four letters you now send to your superbly segmented donor file.

No longer will everyone get the same mailing, in the fundraiser's version of grapeshot. Some will hear by e-mail only, because that's what they prefer. Others will ask just to receive traditional hard-copy letters. Most will be happy to hear as appropriate through a selection of coordinated media that will add richness and variety to their contacts with you. In the future, each communication from you to them will be finely targeted and precisely timed. With its subject, content, and tone of voice just right. Because that's what you both want. That's relationship fundraising.

Action Points

▲ Beware of vague concepts in promotion, such as awareness. Always seek ways to measure your results.

▲ See how donors react when they receive their mail. Subject all your communications to "the mailbox test."

▲ Make sure all your letters have AICDA.

▲ Test, test, and test again. Never give up testing.

▲ Don't always ask for money. Look for opportunities to give your donors something in return.

▲ Don't talk about appeals and mailings. Call them letters or messages.

▲ Always send a letter with your publications. And include a reply device too.

▲ Give your donors only interesting material. It will pay in the long run.

▲ Check your reply forms and coupons. Replace those that don't have all the essentials.

▲ Make better use of the phone, both inbound and outbound.

▲ Promote your helpline vigorously on all your printed materials, even your letterhead.

▲ Prepare an individual, appropriate, and variable thank you letter. See if you can give it some of the functions of a welcome pack.

▲ Train your telefundraising staff well. Don't leave any aspect to amateurs, any more than you would assign a new recruit to manage your direct mail.

▲ Keep good telefundraising records.

▲ Encourage complaints. Use any device you can. Set up a donor complaints facility.

▲ Don't forget to build e-mail and your Web site into your customer service strategy.

▲ Plan donor visits into your annual strategy. Establish targets and costs per visit.

▲ Encourage donors to come and visit you. Invite them to special occasions at your office.

▲ Exploit radio and television's increasing demand for good news stories.

▲ Consider how your organization can make appropriate use of video.

▲ Integrate all your donor communications through one central point—your donor service department.

Donor Profile: Ian Dunlop

Ian is thirty-four and very active. If he had been born fifteen years earlier he would definitely have been a hippie or even a beatnik, but the establishment at his school simply consider him a scruff.

He is untidy. Ian drives an old VW van and belongs to a club of similarly scruffy people who go scuba diving and caving on weekends. During the week Ian is a teacher of geography—and a very good one. Popular with his pupils if not with his headmaster, Ian has single-handedly started just about every conceivable type of spare-time activity in the school, from boating and mountaineering clubs to the local chapters of Greenpeace and Amnesty International.

Ian believes in education for change. He sees the organizations he supports as resources for him and his students, sources of information, display material, and campaign ideas. They also give him a channel for action that Ian *knows* will work.

Ian is no passive armchair supporter. He has campaigned for recycling facilities from the local authority, lobbied Parliament over the development aid budget, written dozens of letters to prisoners of conscience, and pedaled sixty miles for parrots, raising money and publicity for the campaign against the live import of exotic birds. In each of these endeavors, and more, Ian is supported by an enthusiastic and growing group of young pupils from his school who have been encouraged to see that support for nonprofits is only truly effective if backed by positive political action.

The promotional materials and education packs produced by the nonprofits to support these campaigns are a great help to Ian. He has papered the walls of the staff room with posters and slogans, and now instead of objecting or muttering under their breath many of his colleagues come up and ask him about the campaigns and sometimes make more positive gestures of support.

Ian is now planning two major initiatives that he wants to introduce to his school when the moment is right. The first will involve bringing one of the major environmental nonprofits into the classroom on a formal basis to provide tuition on specialist environmental themes contained in the new school curriculum. That's not controversial. The second idea may take more selling to the headmaster. Ian wants the whole school to join in an official walk against whaling, culminating in a candlelit vigil outside a certain Scandinavian embassy.

Ian's not optimistic, but he is going to give it a try. He has a fallback option if it doesn't work—a full-scale sponsored walk within the school. Ian is banking on the fact that his headmaster hates sponsored walks so much that the alternative may even seem appealing.

Chapter Eleven

Creative Approaches to Relationship Building

I was seldom able to see an opportunity until it had ceased to be one.
MARK TWAIN, *PUDD'NHEAD WILSON*

Fundraising is all about opportunities. Recognizing opportunities, discovering opportunities, creating opportunities, developing opportunities, seizing opportunities, turning ideas into opportunities. Mark Twain would have been a lousy fundraiser.

Despite recession, despite greatly increased competition, despite the pace and scale of recent developments, there have never been more opportunities for relationship fundraisers than now.

Some of these opportunities have been covered in earlier chapters: creative use of the telephone, meeting donors, a thank you and welcome policy, repeated reactivation campaigns, setting up a complaints line, establishing central service facilities, and so on. The most important opportunity of all, bequest marketing, is so substantial and remarkable in the potential it offers fundraisers that I feel it deserves a chapter all on its own (see Chapter Twelve). But other opportunities abound and I'd like to review a few of these here.

The Non-Event

Very often opportunity arises out of adversity and that is usually when the best ideas are formed. The non-event is just such a marvelous idea; it involves almost no work and gives people an unchallengable excuse to do just what they most want to do—nothing!

In the United States now fundraising events have reached the saturation point in some areas. There are just too many big-ticket events. For some people (presumably those strange individuals who just can't say no) nonprofit events are a real problem because they never have a free night in their social calendar to stay home and watch TV. For the organizers, market saturation has meant diminishing returns and, of course, the ever-present danger with big events—failure to cover costs. Enter the non-event.

"Send us your $500 and stay at home."

That was the offer. You won't have to rent a tuxedo, hire a limo, come out on a rainy night, or make small talk with all those vacant glitterati. Just stay at home and feel good.

The non-event organizers went even further. They sent "participants" (I use the term loosely) a bottle of rather nice champagne to help them enjoy the evening, snug in the knowledge that by taking part in this statewide non-event they were helping to raise huge amounts of money for the cause. And it works very well. Some nonprofits now claim that the non-event is their most cost-effective method of raising funds. How long it will work? Who knows? How long before John Q. Public and his wife start complaining that they've got just too many non-events to go to and there just aren't enough evenings in the week? Who knows? Who cares? Grab the opportunity while you can.

Getting the Best Out of People

Too often we approach fundraising activities as if they were a matter of technique, that all we have to do is mechanically follow procedures and all will be well. This definitely isn't so. The greatest opportunities of all arise from the fundraiser's ability to get the best out of people. Fundraising is a people business, not a procedures business.

> If anything goes bad then I did it. If anything goes semi-good then we did it. If anything goes real good then you did it.
>
> That's all it takes to get people to win football games for you!

That quote is from American football coach Paul Bryant, but it applies just as well to fundraising. In fact, I found it in James Gregory Lord's book *The Raising of Money*.

Donors don't like it when fundraisers take credit for their successes. So you should always take due care to remain in the background, like the football coach, taking complaints and criticisms but never the credit. To come between the donor and the footlights is bad manners.

Provide Involvement

Lord also tells his readers that the way to raise real money is to provide real involvement. Obviously there are countless different ways of providing involvement but the key word here is not involvement, it is *real*. Fundraisers have to differentiate between tricks and gimmicks—so-called *involvement devices*—and real, sincere involvement. Bernie Cornfeld, the insurance swindler who ran Investors Overseas Services, had a favorite question of all potential recruits to his organization; at first glance, it seemed to provide an obvious answer. He asked, "Do you sincerely want to be rich?" Naturally all the eager young people who came knocking on his door answered affirmatively, but Cornfeld wasn't just asking if they wanted to be rich. Obviously everyone would answer yes to that. The key word was "sincerely." "Do you *sincerely* want to be rich?" To Cornfeld this meant that chasing riches took precedence over *everything* else. Applicants had to be sincere enough to work all hours, doing whatever they were asked, sacrificing friends, family, and all other interests.

Real involvement, of course, needn't go that far. But it has to be real, not illusory. Donors have a right to be involved in your nonprofit, just as shareholders have a right to be involved in the companies they partly own. As investors both the donor and the shareholder are entitled to influence and active involvement.

Major Gifts

Providing selected donors with the opportunity for real involvement gives the fundraiser a ready means of setting up a major gift campaign. This is one of the most challenging opportunities available the strategic fundraiser, so it's worth at least a mention here even though it's too involved a topic for detailed coverage. As with so many other areas of fundraising, success in big gift fundraising depends on the development of effective donor relationships.

There is no minimum or maximum gift size that qualifies a campaign to be termed "big gift." The common characteristic is that all gifts in a big gift campaign are solicited face to face or over the phone and the amounts given tend to reflect that personal approach.

For many campaigns, particularly specific or tangible appeals such as a new hospital wing or a university chair where general public appeal is limited, the most likely route to success is via a major gift campaign, carefully planned and targeted toward those rare individuals who can make substantial donations. In these campaigns often a small group of people can be so focused and cultivated that less than a hundred donors are needed to take a multimillion-pound appeal over its target. On average, half of the targeted figure will come from just ten or twelve donors. The keys to big gift fundraising are careful planning and unhurried assembly of all the crucial components. The fundraiser's skills are in motivating a carefully selected group of donors to do the asking and enabling them to ask their peers for the *right* amount of money at the *right* time.

The really difficult part in big gift fundraising is not in getting people to give money, it is in getting people to ask. For no fundraiser will make any headway by attempting to solicit big gifts directly. That is a job for other people—other donors. It is the perfect example of active involvement from donors, but it is not easy.

Most people in Britain seem to have great difficulty in asking. It's a national failing. We want to ask and we know we should, but just at the crucial moment we stumble, we apologize, and our palms begin to sweat. No matter how carefully and diligently you have built up to this moment, if this happens, the asking is usually diluted or fudged and loses its impact. Unfortunately, in Britain even many paid fundraisers don't like to ask for money either, so would-be volunteers often find little inspiration from the professionals.

Shyness when it comes to asking is not unique to Britain. Many other countries don't have any significant culture of asking for money so it becomes a rather abnormal and frightening thing to do. The French seem to abhor it. There's something in the Gallic character that rises up against the need, or even the very suggestion of the need, to ask for money for a cause.

Not so in America. The American people have been reared on fundraising. It's part of every community, every neighborhood, every childhood. Asking for money is as natural to Americans as watching television.

One way to make asking easier is to ensure that the asker has already made a very big gift (even the lead gift) personally. This makes the request almost irresistible to members of the asker's peer group, who after all are not going to be outdone by one of their own.

If you subscribe to the Robin Hood view of fundraising (see Chapter One), where the fundraiser's role is considered to be redistributing wealth from the rich to the deserving poor, then there's something very pleasing about the big gift concept, where one of the rich's own leaders actually does your stick-ups for you.

Big gift campaigns are essentially volunteer programs where the volunteers are usually local eminent individuals or captains of industry and commerce, what is often termed "the great and the good." They are volunteers for your cause, just like the people who stand behind the counter of your charity shop, sipping tea and looking as if they own the shop. Volunteers work best if they feel a sense of ownership of their project. In big gift fundraising this is essential. They are the heroes. The professional fundraiser's task is to treat them well, to keep their sights high, and never to let them feel anything other than vitally needed. Good relationships are paramount.

If a committee is necessary, and most big gift campaigners seem to believe it is (I can't quite understand why committees are still seen as important to the human condition—as advertising guru David Oglivy was fond of saying, "search your parks in all your cities, you'll find no statues of committees"), then it is essential that the volunteers themselves elect it and choose its leader. Let them think of it as the campaign cabinet if they wish and encourage them to have whatever fun they can while raising your funds.

However, the forming of the committee is not an opportunity to add a lot of illustrious names. This is real involvement; there must be no token attenders or committee servers. Chuck them off. All potential members must believe it is a privilege to serve on this group and to help the cause in such a vital way. They have to earn their place all the time, work hard, and be the most generous and regular of donors. Their role must be to ask identified persons for prearranged specific sums. If they feel ownership of the appeal, they will do it. In return you have to work out with them a finite time scale, a finite number of hours they have to give, and to provide them with a written list of their responsibilities. Then you can be quite certain that their contribution is defined and understood. In the politest possible way you can ask them to account for it later just to emphasize that their responsibility is real and not a token.

These are the fundamentals of big gift fundraising:

- A succinct, clear, and persuasive case
- Accurate identification of the donor constituency
- Good leadership from sound and committed volunteers
- Immaculate direction from the fundraiser

With the escalation of capital appeals in recent years it seems likely that those potential donors who will do the asking, the most important cornerstones of every big gift campaign, will soon be in short supply. Meanwhile, fundraisers are establishing big gift campaigns for all they are worth and are achieving some noteworthy successes. If the competition for good donor-askers does become tougher, then my bet is that those relationship fundraisers who have cultivated their donor-askers over some years will still be able to mount big gift campaigns, come what may, because the donor-askers will stick with them.

Pricing and Propositions

I have already mentioned price in Chapter Eight in terms of its importance in any fundraiser's marketing plan. It seems to me that strategic pricing represents some worthwhile opportunities for fundraisers, because in the past so little thought has been given to the price of fundraising propositions, and fundraisers have often failed to let market forces naturally fix their price levels.

The addition of prompt boxes to reply forms and coupons was one moderately successful way of attempting to influence price for general charitable donations, although it has to be said that many donors don't like these. The average giving level, however, is still too low. When the proposition is general it seems very difficult to persuade the average donor to raise the ante. It is a curious imbalance but when confronted with a tragedy on the scale of, say, the famine and starvation that faced millions in Ethiopia, the typical member of the public responds with a gift of around $15 or $20. Of course, the public is constantly being asked to respond generously and does. But $15 or $20 against such a large need is a drop in the ocean and the public knows it. However, $45 can buy a plough with which an Ethiopian family can double the yield from their tiny plot of land, not only enabling them to feed themselves but also to have a small surplus for sale in the local market.

In this example the donor can see where the money might go and what it might achieve. Many donors would prefer to give $45 to an identifiable, comprehensible goal than to give $10 to a general appeal. This technique is well understood by the international aid agencies in whose programs small amounts of cash can achieve great things: $5 can immunize a child against five killer diseases, £10 can make a blind man see, and so on.

But is it used enough? And can some home-based nonprofits not make better use of it than they do? We know the public likes it. The Ryton Gardens appeal mailing, which could be recycled as seed pots, was hugely successful in financial terms, but was its success due to its intriguing format, its "big idea," or because it got the pricing right? Ryton invited donors to sponsor their work at different levels—an ordinary sponsor at 50p a week, a seedsman sponsor at £1 a week, a cultivator sponsor at £2 a week, and a gardener sponsor at £5 a week. Appropriate benefits were offered at each level. People did indeed come forward and sign on as gardener sponsors, paying £260 a year. For them, the price was right. They could make the choice themselves. If they hadn't been given the chance, they might just as easily have given £10 only and the Ryton Gardens appeal would not have been nearly so successful.

This, of course, is as much a question of identifying the proposition as deciding the price. The two are inextricably linked. But consider again the $5 that immunizes and protects a child. What a proposition! People would flock to send their $5 checks. But because the unit cost is so low, it might not be worth the nonprofit's while to process them or, to put it another way, perhaps the price could be increased without affecting overall response.

Basically there are two principal ways of fixing price: by considering the unit cost of production and adding a percentage for profit and contingencies, or by considering how much the market might bear. (There is a third option, which is to base your price on your competitor's charge.) Fundraisers use all these methods—but in my experience, whatever they choose they often aim too low. Perhaps this is because fundraisers have always been badly paid, so they overestimate the value of money. Of course, for the donor price relates to benefits and so $5 to protect against five killer diseases and £10 to make a blind man see represent almost unbelievable value for money. The price is so low I expect it puts many people off, because they find it simply incredible and they can't relate the enormous impact of the action—saving a life or saving someone's sight—to such a small amount. Price testing—offering the same product at two different prices—is not permitted in Britain but it would be interesting to split-run these offers against doubled or even trebled amounts to see what the difference in response would be (see later in this chapter).

Donors' ability to pay, however, depends to a large extent on their perceived disposable income. As fundraisers are usually offering intangible products or propositions it makes sense to offer them across a range of prices, such as the Ryton Gardens example, so the donors can choose. Where the product or service is tangible, however, as it is with child sponsorship, the fundraiser has to find an optimum pricing level above the cost of providing the service but below the point where too many people will drop out because they can't afford it. A fundraising "product" such as child sponsorship can justifiably be priced high as the cost of recruitment and administration is high and demand is not noticeably price-sensitive. Even if demand does fall as the price increases, the fundraiser may still find this a preferable situation as fewer donors will now be paying the same or even more money, and the costs of administration will be less.

The downside is that, in theory at least, fewer children will be able to enjoy the benefits of sponsorship. But child sponsorship remains one of fundraising's most appealing and effective products from the donor's point of view. It has enabled nonprofits to present a $250-a-year proposition that is bought by people from all walks of life, from the residents of mansions to those who live in low-income housing.

Sponsorship schemes clearly show the advantages of "thinking monthly" when structuring product prices. Donors on monthly subscription give a lot more, with less thought and concern. It makes sense. Most people are paid once or twice each month. And $500 seems a lot of money to give in one go, but $50 a month appears much more manageable to most donors (and, of course, it results in an extra $100 each year for the cause).

At the other end of the scale, membership cost for an organization that supports the victims of a disabling disease might need to be priced toward the lower end of the spectrum because the organization does not wish to deter people who should be benefiting from membership purely on the basis of cost. However, the price should not be so low that the scheme becomes a drain on the organization rather than a benefit. That's why different price levels are so important.

The first thing an organization must decide in developing a pricing strategy is what it wants to achieve. If you are seeking to build a large database for future development there is no value in setting the price of entry too high. Fundraisers often find a conflict between maximizing their surplus (that is, making a profit) and maximizing their market share. This is why pricing policy is so important and why nonprofit managements or boards of governors must understand what the objectives of your policy are. For example, the objective of cold direct mail is to build a donor list. It is regrettable that this process will cost rather than raise money, but it is now a fact of economic life.

Raising the price would almost inevitably lower the response, so fundraisers—and their boards—have to accept this as an instance where they must speculate to accumulate, where it will take a long time, perhaps many years, before that investment is repaid. They also have to find acceptable ways to explain and justify this to their donors.

When you have decided on your pricing objective you can then consider whether your pricing strategy should be cost-oriented, based on market tolerance, or led by your competitors. Whichever you choose, price is a potent and effective tool. You can lower it to stimulate demand, or raise it to take advantage of high demand or donor indifference to price. You can use price to promote a particular proposition such as group membership, which might attract a lower price, or to introduce supporters to a new project, which might attract a higher price to cover start-up costs. But whatever you do, don't overlook price. That would be to miss a worthwhile opportunity.

Creative Targeting

While discussing price it is also worthwhile considering the negative and positive influences of targets. Fundraisers frequently publicize huge financial targets and often the effect of this is to demotivate rather than impress. Many donors are deterred by an appeal for millions. "Against such a huge target," they think, "what difference will my $15 or $20 make?"

Setting the right level of target can have a major influence on your appeal. Two examples from Britain's NSPCC illustrate this point. In a split mailing test some years ago the NSPCC selected three identical segments of its donor file and sent each group letters that were also identical but for one tiny change. The letter to the first group mentioned an appeal target of £1 million, the second group's letter mentioned a target of £100,000 and the third's just £10,000. The response was good at £1 million, but better at £100,000 and best of all at £10,000, probably because donors felt encouraged that that amount was attainable and their contribution would make a difference.

Targets can also be strategic. At the planning phase of the NSPCC's Centenary Appeal some of the organization's committee members suggested a target of £5 million. They felt that was certainly achievable and it would be good publicity for the appeal to succeed. The NSPCC's appeals director argued for a much higher target of £12 million on the basis that they might fail and only raise £8 million, but an £8 million failure was better than a £5 million success. The director's argument won the day and the appeal went on to raise £16 million.

Sponsorship of Publications

One of the features of successfully grasped opportunities is that they often involve recognizing when a situation has changed and taking advantage of it before anyone else has realized what's happening. I have said more than once in this book that fundraisers are surrounded by change. This leads to many opportunities.

One visible and easily demonstrable change in the United Kingdom in recent years has been the quantum leap in the quality of fundraising publications. All fundraising organizations are prolific publishers: annual reports, reviews, newsletters, magazines, leaflets, posters, and more. Every fundraiser relies on the printed word to communicate a variety of messages to large and varied audiences wherever they may be.

Good publications cost money, although, it has to be said, not as much as bad publications do. They are a very tangible and potentially attractive part of any fundraising program. So they can be sponsored. Of course, a little while ago no sane donor would have wished to sponsor the kind of publication produced by a British nonprofit, or college, or medical center. There were some exceptions, but not many.

In the past the dismal affairs most fundraisers used to send out deterred corporate sponsors. The melancholy drabness that once characterized British nonprofits has no appeal for their corporate counterparts. But all that has now changed. Fundraising organizations of all kinds are now making efforts to present themselves in better light. Commerce and industry, surely, can be persuaded to support these efforts and to direct their largesse toward financing such obvious evidence of a good cause.

This kind of support is most likely to appeal to corporate donors who might welcome in return the opportunity to display their generosity through some kind of credit, such as their logo, and some words of thanks discreetly placed on the back page. Some companies already sponsor nonprofit publications and one or two can clearly be seen to prefer this way of helping. But fundraisers have not sold the opportunity very well so far.

Corporate sponsors need to see what they are supporting. They need physical evidence that you intend to produce something far superior to their established notion of nonprofit promotion. They will need to know who will get the brochure, how it will be distributed, and what purposes it will serve. If you have already produced a new-style report they may feel you don't need the money. If you have not, they may need convincing by a detailed plan of your proposed contents and structure for the publication, accompanied by well-presented design visuals to show how it will look. And when you make your pitch, don't forget to include your prospective sponsor's logo in some reasonably prominent place.

Commercial Partnerships

Numerous other opportunities exist within the general area of corporate fundraising, many in areas so complex and even risky as to render their description beyond the scope of this publication. A major component of corporate fundraising or joint ventures with commerce is that both parties must benefit in recognizable ways. If they do, the venture will almost certainly be a success. Here some cooperation between nonprofits (and other appropriate causes) would certainly be worthwhile. Commerce needs to take nonprofits seriously, to see them as valuable partners and to include them automatically when drawing up plans.

For fundraisers the most important opportunity is in establishing and developing partnerships with selected appropriate commercial organizations. These can be short-term—for example, a nonprofit's selection as "Charity of the Year" for a high-profile organization—or they can be longer-term, often lasting for many years. Fundraisers need to build the kind of relationships with companies that will make more such partnerships possible. The advent of cause-related marketing concepts has prompted many corporations to reconsider their relationships with nonprofits, but according to *Giving USA 2001,* the corporate sector in the United States still gives only a pathetic 1.2 percent of pretax income to charitable causes, and the percentage is much less in other countries. Opportunities to expand this should be considerable.

A central service agency promoting fundraising opportunities to possible commercial partners would seem to me to have practical value. Such an agency might considerably enhance fundraisers' opportunities to link with big business. In practice this central agency might operate along similar lines to what the Direct Mail Sales and Service Bureau used to do in the United Kingdom—it centrally promoted the medium of direct mail to every kind of business and also acted as a clearinghouse to unite interested companies with a host of relevant suppliers from which the customer can choose (a bit like a marriage bureau).

Such a bureau would be invaluable for fundraisers in a number of areas: locating customers for corporate entertainment and hospitality at events, finding sales promotion partners, stimulating companies interested in employee fundraising, developing affinity marketing opportunities, and so on. It could also sort out impractical approaches and issue warnings about industries looking to use charitable partners in undesirable ways, such as to upgrade their tarnished image.

I am not advocating an exclusive system where the central service agency would take over the fundraising and relationship-building role of the individual organizations; far from it. That didn't happen with the Direct Mail Sales and Service Bureau and it wouldn't happen with fundraising. But it might help fundraising's interactions with the commercial world to work a bit better than they do now.

Employee Fundraising

Many companies can boost their staff's morale and self-esteem, raise the company's profile and standing in the community, develop customer relationships, *and* improve profits by running employee fundraising schemes.

A suitable high-profile, basic-need cause is selected (it could be your organization) and made the subject of a high-visibility appeal. Targets are set within a specific time frame. The company's management can even chip in a matching fund so that for every £1 or $1 raised an equivalent sum will be put in by the company up to a fixed amount. The PR department is brought in. Notices and posters appear all round the workplace. Departments vie to outdo each other in yet more innovative and involving ways to reach their individual target. People have a lot of fun and feel good when they reach or exceed their targets. Meanwhile, your nonprofit raises a lot of money and builds a relationship with a corporate partner that will become a lifelong friend.

Payroll giving is, in theory at least, the easiest, simplest way of ensuring ongoing employee involvement. Small amounts given regularly down the years can add up to big income. At the time of writing payroll giving has not achieved its full potential for British fundraisers but it might yet, as the government is keen on it and has revised the British tax system to encourage it. Payroll giving is very big in some countries such as the United States and Singapore. In the United States, it's rarely done on behalf of individual nonprofits; they go through an organization like the United Way, which collects the donations and divvies up the pot.

Volunteers

I briefly alluded to volunteers in the opening chapter of this book. Voluntary organizations could encourage many more people to find a way to contribute to society by volunteering. It is something *everyone* can do. It is not the prerogative of one privileged sector, such as the middle-class, middle-aged, predominantly white, predominantly female ghetto whence most donors come.

If fundraisers could offer the public useful, productive, accessible volunteer activity and present and deliver these opportunities in customer-oriented packages, particularly those targeted toward young people, the potential benefits for our total society would be huge. A big task—but nevertheless a big opportunity and one many voluntary organizations have yet to address.

Inform Your Ambassadors

Imagine you are interested in a range of merchandise and you visit the local supplier, hoping to resolve some queries before finalizing your purchase. What would you think if a complete portfolio describing that range was not available, or if the salespeople did not have, at their fingertips, all the benefits, reasons to buy, and competitive advantages.

You'd be unimpressed. It wouldn't matter if the sales staff didn't know every answer at once, but you would expect them to find out quickly by referring to a file or catalogue, or by ringing the head office, or some other immediate way of answering your query.

Despite their regular and universal contact with the public through regional organizations, shops, events, local groups, volunteers, and other networks, few representatives of fundraising organizations are anything like so well equipped. Many regional organizers and branch volunteers aren't even given a copy of their employer's annual report, far less trained in its use. Too many simply don't know what their nonprofit does.

Fundraisers are missing a useful opportunity if they fail to equip their public sales force with the basic tools they need to do their job. Looseleaf sheets produced on a word processor are simple to update and relatively inexpensive. They'll be appreciated and will help isolated field staff feel more involved. A little training can also be inexpensive and won't go amiss. "Voluntary" shouldn't equate with "incompetent." In too many people's minds, it does.

The RFM Route to Upgrading Donors

RFM stands for recency, frequency, and monetary value. It is a system of awarding points for these three characteristics and it is (or was) used in America to evaluate mail order customers. Advances in technology over the last decade have no doubt rendered this system passé but it still seems to me to be a simple way of illustrating the principle of RFM.

The purpose of RFM monitoring is to enable you to award a standard point value to every donor on your list and then to watch their progress as you try various methods of upgrading. The following example is to illustrate the system only. Points and values can be varied to suit each individual organization, so long as they are always consistent within that organization. It works like this:

Recency

- Award eight points to a donor who last donated within the last six months.
- Award four points to a donor who last donated between six and twelve months ago.
- Award two points to a donor who last donated between twelve and twenty-four months ago.
- Award one point to a donor who last donated more than two years ago.

Frequency

- Take the number of donations and multiply by four points.

Monetary Value

- Award one point for every £25 value to a maximum of forty points. (Anyone giving above this level deserves individual treatment.)

So a donor who last gave £100 two months ago and has given three other gifts, bringing the total including the last gift to £250, would be given an RFM value of thirty-four points.

The fundraiser's objectives then are to increase the donors' individual point values, the average point value, and the total point values. The principles of relationship fundraising will make this possible.

Targets and objectives are always valuable. It seems likely to me that if such a system could be implemented to monitor the results of upgrading it would add a new purpose and vigor to every fundraiser's efforts.

Although the calculations themselves are relatively simple, donor values would be constantly changing up and down with the passage of time, so your computer might need a nifty bit of programming. I'm sure there are other and probably more sophisticated systems for monitoring RFM. John Rodd (the computer expert mentioned in Chapter Four) tells me, however, that RFM isn't yet built into many packages and you may have to build your own. Those organizations who have done so have a hugely valuable tool, particularly if it can be built into the database rather than having to be run each time as a special report. If you know of any other system for monitoring donors' individual performance over time, please let me know—apart from your organization's bank statement; I already know of that one.

Thank You, Thank You, and Welcome

The game show host's standard words of introduction always make me think of one of the direct mail fundraiser's biggest hurdles, converting the one-time responder into a true donor—getting the vital second gift that indicates that, perhaps, here is a real friend.

I've said all I want to say about thank you letters. An example of a thank you letter that is almost a welcome pack in itself is described in Chapter Ten. But the welcome package is an underused tool for fundraisers. It can provide the opportunity to convert your responders into real donors.

The welcome pack has to be appropriate. It must not be extravagant but neither should it be cheap and nasty. Above all it has to be welcoming. Some back issues of your newsletter and a photocopied sheet are not good enough. A special welcome issue of your newsletter is a worthwhile idea. Make it bright, readable, busy, visual. Explain to readers what it means to be a donor. Start at the beginning and show what their help is achieving. Assume no prior knowledge of your work but don't overburden your readers with details. Be short, dramatic, and newsy. And display details of your phone service, who to call, and so on. Think about the kind of welcome newsletter you'd like to receive and make it just like that.

In the United Kingdom, Greenpeace produced a welcome pack that was simply an A3 (double width) sheet folded over to letter size. One side was laser-personalized in several places, not just with the new supporter's name but with membership details too. The reverse side was printed with glue. Recipients could easily cut out various labels for their address book and diary. A window sticker was even included for them to display if they wished. A reply form was also included so by removing and affixing some more stickers the new supporter could easily tell Greenpeace the kind of help the organization could expect in the future.

All Greenpeace's current campaigns were summarized too. The package was very action-oriented, which suits Greenpeace as it wants supporters to realize that they are joining an organization committed to action—and their action is expected too. For another example, see the description of a brilliant welcome pack from WWF Canada in my book *Friends for Life*, listed in the Bibliography.

New Products and New Product Development

Innovation in the design and development of new products has always been venerated. Industry and commerce depend on it and spend large amounts of time and money in researching and testing new ideas and new propositions. Some work, some don't. That's the name of the game. The essence of progress is never to stand still.

Research and development is a very strange subject for a fundraising organization to consider. Nonprofits are almost devoid of any risk capital and many board members find the concept almost impossible to grasp. It just doesn't fit their notion of what a nonprofit is.

But if their organizations are to thrive and develop, fundraisers must find effective new products. Otherwise their organizations will be overtaken, wither, and die. Just like commercial organizations, fundraising organizations need to know when to introduce new products and when to drop, or play down, old products. An example of a new product that works well, after time, is the affinity credit card. It is run in association with an established credit card issuer and is just like any other credit card except the nonprofit's name is printed on it and the nonprofit gets a benefit each time the card is used. Most nonprofits have found this an easy product to launch and promote to their existing membership. It works for me. I've never liked the exorbitant charges levied by credit card companies but it is somewhat more bearable when I know a nonprofit will benefit even by a little bit. On the other hand, an example of a product in decline, it seems to me, is street collections, perhaps because the public no longer has sympathy for them.

But launching a new product can be hazardous and sometimes requires considerable investment, as well as skill and know-how. This is particularly true for products that apply to all nonprofits, such as payroll giving plans.

Successful launch of a product is a highly specialized business and in the fundraising area, certainly in Europe, that specialty is very rare indeed. Until nonprofits learn to treat new product launches less casually and accept the inevitable investment of money and skills that they demand, we can't be surprised that the launch of some fundraising products will be disappointing. In future nonprofits will have to invest more in researching and developing new products and propositions. If they don't they will be left behind.

Planned Giving

Bequests (or legacies) account for by far the largest part of what is sometimes referred to as planned giving—the arrangement of a donor's affairs in advance to provide affordable and tax-efficient ways of helping favored causes.

Planned giving is well developed in the United States, where philanthropy is well understood and widely aspired to. Donors can choose among a wide range of insurance, health, and investment-linked schemes and are encouraged to view substantial gifts to nonprofits as part of their planning for retirement. Fundraisers in other countries now have the opportunity to introduce similar products to their home markets. This seems to me to be an area rich in opportunity, both for joint partnerships with appropriate financial services organizations and for developing worthwhile products that would provide value to donors during their lifetime and income for their chosen nonprofit after their death. The fundraiser who consults donors, finds out what they want, and involves them in designing the planned giving product will be more likely to see success than the fundraiser who presents donors with a fait accompli.

Central Promotion

The idea of centralized promotion on behalf of nonprofits is very attractive, but fundraisers should be cautious before diving in. Rather than a treasure ship, they may land on a shark.

Certainly fundraisers could and should cooperate on certain subjects to cut out duplication and to present one strong central message, which might be well beyond the means or resources of any individual organization. One such area is bequest marketing. Obviously each individual nonprofit must promote its own interest, but the basic idea—the notion of leaving a bequest to a worthwhile cause—can be more effectively promoted centrally using the combined resources of all nonprofits, than by the diffuse energies of each one, all trying to do the same thing.

I hope nonprofits can get together—without excluding anyone—to do it. They have much to gain. This concept was quite radical in Britain ten years ago but after years of debate now seems about to happen—see the section on the Legacy Campaign in Chapter Twelve.

As for the central promotion of the generic concept of giving, that seems to me a much harder task, much more difficult to do effectively. I am prepared to be proved wrong, but it seems to me that giving is an abstract and meaningless concept if it is taken away from the subject of the gift—the worthy cause. Why on earth would people want to give per se?

Despite my skepticism several countries and states have in the past few years developed ambitious campaigns designed to encourage their publics toward a more positive view of the nonprofit sector, a more philanthropic approach toward giving, and a better understanding of giving mechanisms and incentives. Some, notably Canada with its "Imagine" campaign, have been quite creative and have reported worthwhile successes, although how long these might last is open to conjecture. But I shouldn't be a cynic. As I write an ambitious British endeavor in this direction has been launched, backed by funding and encouragement from leading nonprofits and the government of the day, and led by many eminent figures both from the voluntary sector and the world of commerce. It's called "The Giving Campaign," and I very much hope it works, for all our sakes. At least it will provide visible evidence of fundraisers working together. Donors will certainly welcome that.

What's in a Name?

I mention in Chapter Nine the opportunities that will arise from an integrated donor service department. The fundraiser of the future will go even further. Not only will terms such as "mailings" and "packs" disappear, so too will job titles such as direct mail manager and head of appeals. In their place will come much more friendly titles and terminology to reflect the much more friendly departments they manage. Goodbye head of direct mail, welcome donor development manager.

Change Brings Opportunities

Despite seemingly eternal pressures from nonprofit boards to play safe and not take risks, fundraisers must be constantly alert for new opportunities and chances to be "fifteen minutes ahead." There is no doubt that we fundraisers work in a naturally conservative area, the nonprofit sector, and that the forces of caution and conservatism combine to make many fundraisers instinctively risk averse. This really has to change, because the urgency of our missions and the scale of problems and suffering we exist to address should not permit any stone to be left unturned if it might advance our cause. So there is no excuse for timidity and no justification for the status quo. We have a duty to take advantage of each of the many opportunities that come our way, and that means we must be prepared to invest in change and to make mistakes. As compensation we can expect the rewards that come to pioneers and innovators.

Action Points

▲ Fundraising is all about opportunity, so be prepared to grasp yours while you can, before someone else does.

▲ Try a non-event. It could be just what your expense ratio needs.

▲ Offer real involvement. See your donors as investors who are entitled to have influence *and* active involvement in your work.

▲ Look after your donor-askers. Put them near the top of your relationship fundraising priorities.

▲ Review your pricing policy and strategy. Use price to stimulate and control demand.

▲ Think monthly when pricing propositions.

▲ Set targets carefully to benefit from maximum motivation.

▲ Prepare a portfolio of your publications suitable for sponsorship so you can sell the idea to corporate donors.

▲ See if other fundraisers respond to the idea of setting up a central agency to facilitate links with corporate donors.

▲ Try to interest local employers in employee fundraising schemes.

▲ Look for opportunities to encourage volunteers.

▲ Equip your sales team (your staff and volunteers) well with information and basic training.

▲ Use the RFM method to measure your donors' support and to monitor the success of your upgrading activities.

▲ Reconsider how your organization welcomes new supporters. Could your welcome package be improved?

▲ Invest in research and development. Keep innovating to avoid stagnation.

▲ Encourage and support *appropriate* central promotion.

▲ Consider restructuring and retitling job descriptions to reflect your new donor orientation and eliminate purely functional descriptions.

Donor Profile: Eric Levine

Eric Levine was only six years old when he arrived at the Port of Liverpool in 1914, a refugee from the Austro-Hungarian Empire. With him were his father, mother, grandmother, two sisters, and all they could carry: two bundles, some carrier bags, and an old, battered suitcase. The family settled in two rooms in a Manchester tenement block round the corner from the basement where Eric's father made a kind of living mending shoes, clocks, and sometimes watches.

Eric didn't mix with other children, just as his family didn't mix much with other families on their street. Eric's schooling was sporadic, to say the least. At twelve he got a job as a delivery boy for a large department store. He learned the retail trade from the bottom, training that stood him in good stead later on.

As he grew Eric realized that he had a talent for just two things: he knew how to sell and he knew how to buy. Using capital scraped together over years from any source he could find, Eric Levine went into business buying derelict, run-down sites in areas with potential and turning them into general stores and corner shops. He started a down-market jewelry shop that became a national chain. By the time he was thirty Eric had made himself a millionaire from each of his business areas—jewelry, property, and shops. Nobody knew how much he was worth, not even Eric.

He never married. His home was in a depressed part of central Manchester and there he stayed. He lived simply with few interests other than work. As he grew older Eric's obsession changed from his work to his health. He began to worry that he smoked too much and took little exercise. Concern for his physical well-being developed into a kind of hypochondria and his general practitioner began to regard him as something of a nuisance.

Just before his sixty-fifth birthday Eric suffered a mild heart attack. By then he had sold all his business interests so his preoccupation with his health had the opportunity to become a full-time neurosis. He took to writing to and visiting every noteworthy authority on any aspect of personal health, particularly the heart. He assiduously collected any published information he could—booklets, posters, leaflets. His daily visits to the local outpatient clinic were treated with kindly tolerance.

In the end it was a bout of influenza that killed Eric Levine at the age of seventy-five. After his death his estate was valued at more than £23 million. He left almost all of it to medical and research nonprofits, including £1.5 million to develop a new heart unit at his local hospital. Some of the causes he chose as beneficiaries were quite surprising, having little or nothing to do with any ailment he was known to have. Yet two of the larger heart research organizations received nothing at all.

They never found out why, because no one could connect the down-at-heel, aggressive little man who rang and wrote and constantly questioned them with the fabulously wealthy Mr. Eric Levine.

Chapter Twelve

Bequest Marketing
The Last Great Fundraising Opportunity

You'll have more fun and success when you stop trying to get what you want and start helping other people get what they want.
DALE CARNEGIE

Bequest marketing is, I believe, the largest and most important area of all for fundraisers. Amazingly enough it is a comparatively new area. Its potential has been virtually neglected until quite recently. That means it is still largely unexplored territory with all sorts of interesting opportunities for people like you and me. It's also an area where all the principles of relationship fundraising apply.

Let me first of all ask a question of you, the reader. Have you made a will? If you have, good. You've shown commendable foresight, but you are in the minority. If you haven't, I'll bet you have thought about it, you have no strong reservations or objections to making a will, and you haven't done it yet simply because you haven't got round to it.

That's why most people don't make a will—good old inertia, the most consistent public response to the really important things of life. As a result, each year tens of thousands of people die *intestate*—without ever having made a will. In Britain they leave behind a sum approaching £4,000 million, and the worldwide total is staggering. Because they failed to make a will the law decides for them who gets what from their estate. They are, well and truly, out of it.

In most cases, death prevents this inertia from ever being overcome. Many others, however, do decide to make a will dangerously late in life (will-making is probably more popular than religion when it comes to death-bed conversions). While seven out of ten adults have *not* made a will, by the time of death the figure has dropped to just less than half. (These statistics have kindly been provided for me by Tom Smith of Smee and Ford Limited, a unique company whose staff tirelessly read every will that is proved in England and Wales and record, analyze, digest, and distribute this priceless data to any nonprofit that is really serious about preserving and developing its bequest income.)

Here are some more basics of bequest marketing, again courtesy of Smee and Ford. These are based on data collected in the United Kingdom. Although comparable statistics for other countries are hard to find, it is reasonable to assume that the situation will be similar in countries where the charitable bequest enjoys the same social status that it does in Britain.

- Nonprofits depend on bequest income. It accounts for about one-third of all voluntary income and is bigger than both government grants and donations from grant-making foundations *combined.*
- Bequests to nonprofits in England and Wales total nearly £1.4 thousand million per annum—a great deal of money. There is little evidence that this is growing in real terms, although the individual share of some nonprofits is increasing (those that are good at bequest marketing) and clearly there is enormous potential for growth.
- The value of all estates in England, Scotland, and Wales totals more than £25 thousand million per annum. So nonprofits get only around 5 percent of the total, which is not a very large share, if you think about it. An increase of just 0.5 percent would mean a lot of new money for nonprofits—around £140 million!
- Only one in eight wills (12 percent) mention a nonprofit. That's just 6 percent of the population who will support their favorite causes in this most substantial and least painful of ways.

- Of the 280,000 estates that each year pass through the British probate system, 50,000 will be intestate; disposal of the remaining 230,000 estates will be determined by the contents of a valid will. A total of 600,000 British people die each year, but just over half of the resulting estates are too small to merit going through probate, and the majority of these will be intestate.
- Collectively it's the poorer half of the population that dies intestate.
- The average age on death of someone who leaves a bequest to a nonprofit is eighty-one years. By a 60:40 ratio, women lead in leaving bequests to nonprofits, and they also leave more residuary bequests—that is, rather than a specific gift, the nonprofit gets the whole or a share of the remainder of the estate after other bequests have been made. Residuary bequests are worth, generally, at least ten times the value of pecuniary (cash) bequests.
- The average age of a final will that includes a bequest to a nonprofit is less than five years (25 percent are less than one year old). Therefore bequest marketing is not nearly as long term as some people suppose. This is easily proved: several nonprofits my company started working with in bequest promotion in recent years have already seen substantial direct returns from their investment.
- Following on from that, it is now quite clear that bequest income can be influenced. It can even be predicted. Potential legators can be identified by their shaky handwriting, by their length of membership, by the fact that they live in a retirement area. They can be recruited from your own donor base and from the public at large. And they can be specifically targeted through the specialist press and specialist lists, and through their special interests and where they live.

All this points to a comfortably agreeable thought for the nonprofit marketer—a clearly identifiable need exists, we know that many donors are only too happy to leave something of their estate to a favored cause, a huge market is available for the proposition, and there are many affordable ways of reaching that market. What could be better? It all adds up to a quite fantastic opportunity for fundraisers.

Statistics show that the average value of estates that include a charitable bequest is about 40 percent higher than the average value of those that don't. And the average age on death of women leaving a charitable bequest is eighty-three, while for men it is seventy-nine, whereas the average age on death of women who *don't* leave a charitable bequest is eighty-one, and for men seventy-six. However, unfortunately and despite initial appearances, this doesn't constitute conclusive proof that generosity to nonprofits in your will will ensure either longevity or greater riches in this world, any more than it will ensure greater contentment through all eternity in the next. But it might help.

Fundraisers should be aware that large bequests are not easily or quickly to be gained. Bequests are the ultimate reward of a lifetime of relationship fundraising. But up until now they have probably just as often been the product of pure chance.

Through leaving a bequest anyone and everyone can become a major donor. The average amount left to a nonprofit in England and Wales is £3,000 for a pecuniary bequest and £34,000 for a residuary bequest. Very few bequests are for small amounts.

Different Strokes for Different Folks

Different people prefer to leave money in different ways. Following on from the observation that residuary bequests are vastly more lucrative than pecuniary, it may appear sensible for fundraisers to promote the former strongly. This may be so, but like everything else in bequest promotion it has to be done with great care.

Many nonprofits find that a very common form of bequest, if not the most common, is what is known as a reversionary bequest. This is when a named person has access to the value of the estate, which only reverts to the nonprofit on the death of that person. For instance, the original will states that a friend or partner is allowed to live in the legator's house until their death, when it will revert to the nonprofit.

Fundraisers don't like this practice because it invariably means they have to wait for their money. Therefore they rarely mention it. However, donors clearly like it very much, so fundraisers would perhaps be advised to promote reversionary bequests more strongly, along with any other schemes they can devise that will have public appeal.

The Cost of Bad Relations

Bequest marketing is not wholly about response. Many factors can influence the decision whether or not to leave a bequest. For example, your intrusive, badly targeted, and overtly commercial direct mail might easily put off a large number of donors. Your dull, uninformative publications might deter quite a few. Your impenetrable accounts and your deceptive financial charts will unquestionably see you left out by many of your more financially astute donors. And the interminable delay before that stroppy person on the switchboard managed to come up with some inaccurate half-answers to incoming questions about the your organization's use of funds will have had many of your best prospects scuttling off to their solicitors to cut you off without a penny, leaving the lot to the local dogs' home. It's amusing to imagine, but I have no doubt that some versions of these scenarios do happen just about every day.

That's why I say bequest marketing is the ultimate pinnacle of relationship fundraising, the collection of a just reward for a lifetime of carefully developing and maintaining the right kind of relationship with the right kind of people. Simon Turner, until recently director of the United Kingdom's Legacy Campaign, tells of a woman who had pledged a bequest to a nonprofit and was later invited by the nonprofit to an open day at their offices. To get to this meeting she had had to cross the nonprofit's car park, where she was struck by the number of BMWs and Mercedes parked therein. This bequest pledger never got to the meeting; instead she turned round, went home, and wrote the nonprofit out of her will because she didn't want her precious bequest to go to an organization of fat cats. It didn't matter that the parked cars might not have belonged to nonprofit employees. It's perceptions that count.

A New Language

One aspect of wills, bequests, and legacies that nonprofits can influence for the better is the terminology. It's an area full of arcane words and phrases such as legator, residuary, codicil, executor, and so on. We have even contributed by introducing terms of our own such as pledging, which isn't a very user-friendly concept or at least doesn't sound as if it is. (Would you want to live next door to someone who was a lapsed pledger?) If fundraisers are to promote bequests widely, perhaps we should reexamine the language we use to make it more appropriate to what donors want to hear.

A Collective Chance

Adjusting the language is just one step we can take. I don't see bequest marketing just as a chance for each individual organization to increase its own income from bequests. It is a chance for all fundraisers to work together to fundamentally alter the public's perception of the concept of leaving some money to a favored cause. If we can change the public's attitude to charitable bequests, enormous benefits will follow not just for nonprofits but for universities, hospitals, arts companies, and a whole list of other worthwhile organizations and causes.

Leaving a bequest to a nonprofit must become part of our culture, as fashionable as independent pensions, retirement homes, holidays by the sea, and fish and chips are in Britain, and their equivalents are around the world. Donors must be persuaded that they can afford to leave a bequest, that it will cost them nothing in their lifetime, and that it is an extremely satisfying and effective way to help their favorite causes. The concept, the idea of leaving bequests to do good work after you have gone, has to be widely promoted *as an idea itself.* So far this hasn't been done.

The commitment and compulsion that some people feel must be felt by everyone. At least they must be the norm rather than the exception. The satisfaction, sense of purpose, and fulfillment felt by some must be available to everyone. There should be nothing elite about leaving a living legacy.

We'll know we've succeeded when we get it written into the script of a popular television drama. It may sound daft but this could be one of the most constructive uses of television for fundraisers as few things are as effective at getting a subject into the public's consciousness as getting it onto the box. Editorial exposure on television is just what bequest marketers need. See Chapter Ten for my suggestion.

Bequests already form the biggest single source of voluntary charitable giving, and yet we are getting all this money, with hardly any effort, from only 5 percent of the population. That is what I mean about a fantastic opportunity. So far, charitable bequests have only begun to scratch the surface of their potential, because the idea is not often properly presented—yet.

Tread Softly

Inevitably the subject of bequests is a delicate one. Any marketing initiatives have to be appropriate and extraordinarily sensitive, otherwise the opposite of the desired effect will result. It is easy to get things wrong in bequest promotion. Mostly that just means the promotion is wasted, but it is possible to create offense where really none is intended.

A few years ago a major nonprofit sent out a bequest mailing in an envelope with the challenging message, "Do you believe in life after death?" boldly emblazoned on it. Many complaints were received, but the most devastating retort I saw was a returned envelope marked simply "deceased" across its front. It's funny, I know, but in bequest marketing, this kind of insensitivity can be thought of as suicide.

I saw a similar mistake from an American nonprofit, in one of their "lost friend" (a term I much prefer to the standard British "lapsed donor") reactivation mailings. It had splashed across the envelope "lost friend, please come back"—underneath which was handwritten, "Harry would love to but he died last fall."

To be successful, bequest marketing has to be subtle and sensitive, which is hardly surprising. Handle bequest marketing with care as well as flair.

Donors' communications, particularly from obviously very elderly supporters, should also be treated with considerable care and a policy should be established to cope with almost any situation that will arise. A nonprofit I work with received a letter from an obviously frail elderly woman, who complained that she was too old and infirm to appreciate the publication they sent and would they please stop sending it. Her irritation was clear, the nonprofit was obviously doing something wrong and needed to put it right. How a nonprofit responds to the writer of such a letter could be very important. She was no doubt treated carefully and courteously, which is just as well, for she may be a bequest prospect. Every non-profit should be prepared to deal sensitively with situations like this.

What Bequest Marketing Means in Practice

I must tell you about a visit I made some time back to my mother at her home in the Scottish Highlands. My mum is now in her mid-eighties, and not nearly such an active charity supporter as she used to be (she lives on a fixed income and inflation has hit her hard). Through no fault of her own, she can't now help the orga-nizations she supported all her life—the animal charities and the children's home that still mean a tremendous amount to her.

During her long years supporting a range of worthwhile causes, my mum unfortunately got herself onto quite a few mailing lists. Whenever she received a letter calling on her for help my mum took it very seriously. She's from a generation that takes these kind of things at face value, trusting organizations that do so much good to be sincere, honest, and worth listening to. She believed in them. But, of course, they were marketing to her. To them, she was just a name on a list. She was a statistic. A target.

Now, I don't think she believes as much as she once did in the national nonprofits she's supported all her life. I discovered this when I noticed a pile of unopened mail on the table in her hall-way. On examination it turned out to be several appeal mailings, from various nonprofits. Well, my mum's not stupid, and because the formulas of fundraising direct marketing are so transparent and obvious, it seems it wasn't long before she began to realize what they were doing.

That's why the mail in her hallway was languishing unopened. She uses phrases like "I just get too many of these appeals," or "I can't support them all, you know." But really she has stopped tak-ing them seriously. She has stopped believing in them, even to the point of not even bothering to hear what they have to say. I sus-pect there are tens of thousands like her—people who for natural reasons have paused in their giving. People fundraisers think of as lapsed donors and bombard with appeals. My mother's disdain for the flood of charitable appeals she receives has colored my own view of nonprofit direct mail. Surely we fundraisers could be more distinctive and original—and so more welcomed—when we write.

What's this got to do with bequests? Well, I guess my mother is now at a time of life when she won't be a regular donor, for purely practical reasons. But as she owns her own home and her children have all gone their own ways and done reasonably well for themselves, it could be in her best interest to plan to include a bequest in her will for two or three favorite nonprofits. Of course you'd have to put that idea to her in the right way, so she could consider all the options fully and make the decision confidently, for herself. Probably it would have been easier for her to have considered these options some time back—you can't start these things too early.

Only I don't think the fundraisers who have her in their sights have cottoned on to that, or even see things through her eyes at all. Their loss. And a substantial loss also for the causes they exist to support.

More Rigorous Strategy

Many nonprofits in recent years have begun to take bequest marketing seriously and, although this is far from universal, several have adopted a more sensible, strategic approach. The strategic directions followed by one major British nonprofit, the Royal National Lifeboat Institution, shows how detailed this can be, and serves as an example any organization can adapt to its own needs. Here is a somewhat generalized version of the RNLI list:

- Constantly reinforce bequest message to existing supporters.
- Promote benefits of leaving a bequest.
- Encourage and monitor pledges.
- Integrate bequest message with all fundraising and publicity messages.
- Research the bequest area. That is, analyze your own records and consult sources for data on other nonprofits—both competitors and bedfellows. (*Bedfellows* are other major nonprofits with whom your organization frequently finds itself sharing a charitable estate.)
- Send a simple letter to supporters.
- Prepare an integrated set of materials: take-one, booklet, video.
- Train regional staff.

- Appoint one senior staff member to build relationships with pledgers.
- Set up "bequest help desk" for inquiries and requests.
- Place bequest messages and advertisements in all of the organization's media.
- Issue appropriate press releases.
- Organize a direct mail campaign to selected audiences.
- Communicate regularly with people who assist potential donors (lawyers, financial advisers, and the like), including free annual calendar.
- Stage a major media launch of campaign using video and message geared to importance of bequests to the organization.

It's perhaps not surprising that the RNLI is one of Britain's most successful nonprofits at developing bequest income.

Some New Approaches

Until the late 1980s Britain's nonprofits had done remarkably little to encourage bequest income, tending to treat whatever landed on their plates as just that—a windfall. The only form of promotion before that time was a very limited type of largely unmeasurable advertising. By this I mean the allocation of a small but significant part of a nonprofit's promotional budget to buying space in the various yearbooks and journals directed toward solicitors. Hundreds of nonprofits squander their meager resources year after year in this way, placing irrelevant ads in ill-designed compendiums that are hardly ever read by solicitors, or indeed by anybody else.

The usual response to these ads is a resounding zilch. Yet nonprofits continue the folly year after year because, "Well, you never know, old boy. . . . " Even the apparently serious-minded try to explain this phenomenon away by stating "bequest advertising is indirect and long term" and "well, you can't expect to know where bequests come from."

Piffle! Spend half an hour or more with a collection of these publications and you'll soon find out why people avoid them. The ones I refer to are not much more than loose collections of badly designed advertisements that show limited imagination and even less individuality. I believe they have done little to promote the cause of leaving money to a nonprofit. These ads frequently feature headlines such as "Fight cancer with a will," or "Where there's a will, there's heart research," and so forth. I am sure most nonprofits have better things to do with their money. Thankfully there are fewer of these useless publications around now than there were.

In the late 1980s two national nonprofits in the United Kingdom, seemingly independently of each other, began to try a new approach. Instead of asking for a bequest, these nonprofits decided to offer information. Their objectives were to be helpful, to encourage more people generally to make wills, and to build a database of individuals known to be interested in either making or changing their will. This database, these far-sighted nonprofits realized, might be enormously valuable one day quite soon.

Inevitably the first nonprofits doing this were innovating in what was an unknown area. However, now they have been doing it for a few years and have experience of what works and what doesn't. Here are the key points of this kind of bequest marketing campaign:

- Prepare a strategy and brief your field staff and local groups.
- Reinvest a percentage of current bequest income in future promotion.
- Talk about bequests with your supporters. Give examples in your newsletter and in your annual report. This is the most neglected area. Everyone wants to dig in the street without digging their own back garden first.
- Research your supporters—know your strengths and weaknesses.
- Prepare relevant, helpful information on how to make or change a will.
- Offer it as widely as possible to your key targets.
- Prepare a flyer leaflet for general use

    - By people who ask for information
    - With the annual report
    - In the membership pack
    - Everywhere

- Prepare a campaign to assist professional advisers.
- Offer incentives, if practical and appropriate, and test their value.
- Keep excellent records.

This kind of campaign is a very indirect soft sell. There are many now who can say categorically from their own bequest income that it works, but equally there are others who feel it is wasteful and only helps freeloaders who for their own selfish ends want to get their hands on freebies that nonprofits can ill afford to dish out willy-nilly (odd people, I feel, but they might exist). There is certainly little evidence yet that fundraisers have enlarged the total number of charitable bequests in this way, although many enthusiasts claim it has helped them secure a greater market share. And just a few years ago many were predicting that the numbers of bequests would fall dramatically as donors were living longer in an increasingly uncertain world, and so were holding on to their money. That hasn't happened noticeably, so perhaps this approach has helped to stem a decline.

Creativity in Bequest Marketing

Having criticized the advertisements many nonprofits prepare for the legal press, perhaps I should now describe what I believe is creative in bequest marketing. As evidence of the extent of some nonprofits' neglect of bequest marketing, many nonprofits have not got round to reinvesting a percentage of their current bequest income in future promotion. This is extraordinarily shortsighted. Competition for bequests is increasing. Those large corporate nonprofits that collect such vast unsolicited bequest income need to look to their laurels. Without doubt it makes sense for any nonprofit to invest in developing new sources of bequest income. The expense ratio inevitably will be infinitesimally small when compared with most other sources of fundraised income. What follows is an array of different opportunities for creative bequest marketing.

Plagiarize!

Learning from others, borrowing what works for them, is the most sincere form of flattery. It is also the least expensive road to success, so in my view it must be creative—if it is well done. Poor imitation, on the other hand, is an insult. It's like misquoting someone, or like borrowing a friend's car and returning it dented. None of us can protect our ideas once published, so lie back and accept plagiarism without complaint. If your ideas are good, it'll happen anyway, and if they're not worth plagiarizing, well. . . .

Creative Targeting

If fifty people left you a bequest last year it would be really creative to find another hundred or more just like them, each and every year. The key is research. Who leaves you bequests? What are their previous connections with your organization? Where do they live? What characteristics do they have in common?

The easiest target to reach, of course, is in your own back garden. Talk to your existing supporters first. They're the most likely group to react favorably to your bequest proposition. Identify those who live in known retirement areas, those who have been on your list for many years, and those whose handwriting is a bit shaky. Flag your donor base with details of these prospects and keep a record of their activity. Treat them well, and drop gentle suggestions about looking to the future.

Then go outside your own list to target people with special interests or hobbies, who belong to clubs specially for older people or whose lifestyle indicates that they are likely to be elderly. Target readers of the "gray" press, such as *Retirement Age, Saga* magazine, and *Modern Maturity*. Target people on certain commercial mailing lists, for instance gardeners, particularly those who live in the known retirement areas. In this way you can cut out the traditional donor pyramid and talk directly to people who might be bequest prospects, most of whom may have had no previous contact with your cause. If resources are limited, prioritize your targets.

Creativity in Approach

The "new approach" already described involves the nonprofit's positioning itself as a helpful source of information. Its aim is to encourage more people to make a will and its objective is to build a database of people that it knows were considering either making or changing their will at the time when they were recruited on to that database. From this point, the key to this approach is in successfully developing a relationship with these inquirers that will, in time, become mutually beneficial.

But this is only one possible approach. Fundraisers have to demonstrate their ingenuity, to develop and test many others.

Creativity in Strategy and Objectives

Any organization undertaking bequest marketing needs to be clear about its proposition and its objectives in making it. You need to be very sure about what you want to achieve and you need to know all you can about your organization and its supporters. Any bequest marketing initiative must include sufficient resources for research into donors and bequesters.

Next, your strategy has to take account of your available staff and deploy them wisely. Similarly with volunteers and local groups. If you have a regional network you will be able to use them to spread the bequest message through the ripple effect, but you will need straightforward, easy-to-use training materials to ensure that people know what they are doing and why. Full briefing is essential preparation for anyone involved in bequest marketing.

Preparing the right materials is important. One national nonprofit that has been very successful in generating new pledges for bequest income has developed organized training sessions for its field staff and volunteers. Among other things it has prepared a visually appealing computerized presentation summarizing the potential and importance of bequest income, the strategy of the campaign, the benefits for donors, the materials available, and the backup help the organization can provide to stimulate discussion, particularly among groups of donors at home. A short video has been prepared, featuring the key points about making a will and the benefits of the nonprofit's helpful information. Combined with special leaflets and a detailed booklet describing how to make or change a will, this equips the nonprofit's regional staff and volunteers with all they need to go out and talk to their supporters about bequests.

Sometimes an incentive helps to encourage local groups to promote bequests. Usually it is quite a simple piece of internal accounting to credit them with a percentage of bequests received from their area. When they see how increased bequest income can transform their figures, they won't need to be told twice to go forth and evangelize for the cause of making a will.

Creativity in Language

Like most fundraising communications, simple, direct, everyday language is what is needed in all bequest promotional materials. Avoid any complex descriptions, solid paragraphs, weighty text, and long words. The late Harold Sumption, father of U.K. nonprofit marketing and the man who taught me much of what I know about it, had a phrase I've never forgotten. "Talk to people where they are, not where you want them to be." This sums up the task for the copywriter perfectly. Know your readers. Make your copy relevant to them. Make it accessible, make it interesting. Tell them what they want to know, not what you want to say.

Simplicity always works, and this also relates to image. Show homelike, familiar situations using real people that the average older donor can relate to—not bewigged lords, millionaires, or young trendies.

I mention lords in their wigs and robes because a bequest advertisement that frequently springs to mind is one that featured the United Kingdom's former Lord Chancellor, the late Lord Hailsham, and was run by I forget which organization. This was, I believe, ill-advised and an inappropriate use of his high office but I'm not oblivious to the power and impact that such senior and imposing figures can have. I will digress a little here to relate an anecdote about the said lord, which confirms my point.

One day Neil Kinnock, at that time leader of the U.K.'s Labour Party, was showing a group of his constituents around the imposing halls of Westminster, Britain's Houses of Parliament. En route the party happened to meet the then Lord Chancellor thundering along the corridor in full robes and regalia.

"Neil!" boomed the eminent statesman in friendly greeting— and meekly half of Kinnock's constituents dropped to their knees in obeisance. Like most political tales it may not be entirely true, but I hope it is.

Creativity in Using Media

If you have a promotional budget for bequest marketing, most of it will probably be spent in press advertising. Media costs are so high that even the bravest have to be very careful. One shortcut is to go for free publicity. There is tremendous editorial interest in matters financial and that includes will-making and bequests. Most newspapers and many magazines have a money section, which from time to time will focus on the needs of older readers and advise them on issues relating to their financial health. Your initiative on will-making, therefore, might well be considered newsworthy, particularly by local papers or radio if you can bring in a local angle or get the piece placed personally by your local group secretary. Sometimes you may need to link an advertisement to the article to secure the kind of coverage you need. Using a celebrity to introduce the campaign will be particularly useful in ensuring you get the free column inches. And the new electronic media and proliferation of broadcast channels all add to this opportunity, because all need relevant editorial matter.

This is not pie in the sky. At one time I was simultaneously working on five major bequest campaigns and all the organizations involved had gained valuable free publicity. Eventually, of course, they all had to pay for advertising space to generate the volume of queries they required and to build that all-important database. Here the key word is *negotiate*. Cost per reply is the crucial equation in bequest marketing and nothing improves that so much as your ability to pay only 40 or 50 percent of standard rates for your advertising space. Successful space negotiation will have a far more immediate and beneficial effect on your cost per reply than any number of clever headlines in your advertisements. If your current agency doesn't get you similar discounts, change your agency.

Off-the-page advertising in the quality general and specialist press has proved extraordinarily cost-effective for new-approach bequest campaigns. But all media should be tested and rigorous records of each insertion kept in your campaign guard book—the binder where you keep samples of every advertisement and letter. Direct mail has frequently been tested against press advertising for this kind of bequest marketing but generally it works less well because of the higher unit cost per reader. Magazine inserts too can be used. One nonprofit I know has tested bequest ads on the radio (it is a nonprofit that helps blind people so there's some logic here) and fundraisers also continue to use the telephone very successfully as part of integrated bequest campaigns.

Creativity in Offer

The cornerstone of many bequest campaigns is the offer of an informative and helpful bequest information booklet, of which the key ingredient is simple and straightforward text covering why and how to make a will. The booklet will describe the benefits of making a will so that people can ensure that their money goes to those they really care about (including, of course, their favorite nonprofits) and how to set about it—choosing a solicitor or lawyer, gauging net worth, appointing executors, and selecting types of bequest—and the advantages of reducing the gross value of an estate to avoid tax on it. But it is a matter of opinion as to how much this publication should be an ostentatious promotion of your organization. Some feel it will be more used and valued if the advice appears independent and unbiased. I recommend that your nonprofit's involvement should take quite a low profile, at this stage at least.

In the back of the booklet you should accompany your information with several loose inserts, either to be filled in by the recipient, such as a list of personal assets and liabilities that will save time when visiting a solicitor or lawyer, forms of codicil and so on, or information that needs to be updated frequently, such as estate tax levels and the like. This latter document naturally gives the nonprofit a perfect excuse to write again to all bequest booklet inquirers every time the estate tax thresholds are changed.

The final loose inserts are of course the inevitable reply envelope and the detailed pledge form (reply card) so that supporters can confirm that they have included the nonprofit in their will and indicate the kind and size of bequest planned.

Many supporters will be quite happy to do this, but most will prefer not to. Some will think it is none of your or your employer's business. Others will feel that to tell of a planned bequest might be interpreted as boasting. But if you explain your reasons for wanting to know and what you will do with the information, a surprisingly high percentage will be happy to tell you. And without this information, how will you measure the success of your bequest marketing?

Some nonprofits have included incentives to encourage return of the pledge form—for instance, tie-pins or free books—but there is little evidence that these tokens increase response. What does seem to have an effect, although it is difficult to quantify, is the prospect of a kind of immortality that is offered by such devices as the "book of remembrance," a permanent inscription of your name in a leather-bound record, or the "tree of life" when a metal leaf inscribed with your name is added to a symbolic tree, probably attached to the nonprofit's boardroom wall. One nonprofit I know has several such trees as over the years the branches have filled up with leaves. Perhaps eventually they'll have to have a forest of remembrance. (By then they'll be able to afford it!) Some fundraisers may feel uncomfortable with these ideas but it is a matter of choice and I doubt if the existence of such a device would put many people off. Clearly it can turn some people on.

From the simplest helpful booklet to the most elaborate tree of life—all these form part of the offer to potential bequest donors. Recently a consortium of Third World development nonprofits called WillAid came up with an additional offer that worked remarkably well.

The WillAid scheme simply involved the commendable participation of a large number of solicitors from around the U.K. Its objective was to encourage more people to make a will and its means was to promote a special discount of £25 off the cost of drawing up a will, that sum to go to the nonprofits that make up WillAid. The scheme was a success and proved to be an excellent example of creativity that worked in five different ways:

- It got substantial publicity nationwide.
- It gave solicitors a useful PR boost.
- It encouraged lots of people to make a will.
- It raised lots of money for the member nonprofits.
- Ninety percent of solicitors said they would do it again.

These are only the immediate benefits. Of the new wills made through WillAid, how many do you think will contain a bequest to a nonprofit?

Some years ago the British nonprofit Royal National Institute for the Blind (RNIB) launched a new approach bequest campaign and successfully linked it with its URG (unique reason to give, see Chapter Eight). The nonprofit had a splendid opportunity to change the offer relevantly because its bequest marketing materials were largely directed toward older people and, its development personnel reasoned, as people get older they often start to experience eyesight problems; many have difficulty reading and some lose their sight altogether. So RNIB produced the bequest information booklet in four different formats: standard print, large print, tape, and Braille. Readers could choose whichever format suited them. No one was denied access to the information because of a visual impairment, which suited RNIB very much, and interestingly one out of every five requests specified a preference for large print, tape, or Braille.

Such a relevant offer would also have done RNIB's image no harm at all. The large majority of readers of the advertisement will not respond to the ads simply because at the time they are not in the market for bequest information, but the message will certainly create a good impression with many current and potential supporters. If the ads create a positive image with this large group then the nonprofit will receive a further significant benefit from its new approach bequest promotion. This is an example of the importance of communicating with those who *don't* respond, which I mentioned in Chapter Seven—the impression your advertising has on nonresponders.

Creative Advertisements

Position, media used, the offer, competition from other sources: these are all more important, in terms of their effect on response, than the so-called creative content of the advertisement. This is a terrible admission for a copywriter to make, but it is true. However, the appearance and wording of the advertisement can have a negative effect if badly executed. Again the watchwords must be simplicity, clarity, and ease of reply.

RNIB press advertisements featured celebrity actress Joan Hickson, well known in Britain as Agatha Christie's Miss Marple from the popular TV series of that name, and the ads were headlined "Solve the mystery of making a will." The response was very much higher than expected, partly I believe because of the positive reaction to the offer of different formats and partly because of the fortuitous choice of celebrity to introduce the proposition.

Coupons in particular must be clear and easy to complete. An advertisement from the YMCA worked particularly well not just because it was one of the first of its kind but also its offer was absolutely clear, reader oriented, and unambiguous. And the YMCA made a good choice of the celebrity used to front the campaign, the wartime songstress Dame Vera Lynn. The child-care nonprofit NSPCC made a similarly good choice when its national bequest campaign was fronted by comedian Sir Harry Secombe. Celebrities should be of the right age group, well known and well liked by all your audience, inoffensive—don't include any politicians—and cheerful. These are still early days for bequest fundraising and doubtless fresh creative ideas are even now in preparation.

Creative Communications

As in every other aspect of fundraising, the quality and consistency of your ongoing communication with bequest pledgers will undoubtedly be crucial. Many nonprofits now have dedicated staff to serve this important group of major donors; most have developed specially targeted newsletters and mail and phone programs designed to deliver the right quality of information in the right volume at the right time—and of course, to offer donors choices in how they wish to be communicated with. Many older donors, of course, will be quite comfortable with the Internet and will probably be interested to know of your e-communication strategy (a good reason, perhaps, for you to think about having one). Communicating with bequest prospects and pledgers is no easy task, but a very rewarding one for the committed fundraiser.

Creative Response and Follow-Up

You might now consider launching a more individual campaign aimed at the advisory sector, particularly solicitors or lawyers. Explain the thinking behind your current public campaign and your purpose of encouraging more people to make a will. If more people make a will solicitors or lawyers get more business so present your campaign as good news for them. You can also offer quantities of your helpful information for them to pass to their clients. That's good for both them and you. Get them on your side. If you can, make sure your network of volunteers is trained to visit their local law offices to make sure they are well stocked with the latest materials from your organization. You may be able to use retired solicitors or lawyers for this purpose who will find it much easier to make contact at peer level. Oxfam did this some years ago, recruiting a team of retired solicitors who were known internally as "the death squad."

Recruiting names and addresses for a bequest database is just the start. Some research, both initially and ongoing, is paramount. What do these people want? What is their profile? What do they think of the work you do? Research should enable you to sort out the serious prospects from the rest. After that the keynote is involvement. The list should be mailed regularly, whenever a practical and valid reason presents itself. The most obvious is the need to keep these potential supporters informed of any fiscal changes that might alter or affect the information you sent them earlier.

Your objective is to build a relationship with these people. All the techniques and practices of relationship fundraising apply. Perhaps you can develop a twice-yearly newsletter. You might wish to invite them to a special open house, or set up a bequest planning event (to complement the donor recognition events you were planning). At some stage, as the relationship develops, you may wish to telephone or visit them or to offer a telephone call or a personal visit from one of your tax or legal specialists. This is a sales operation, of course, but it has to be a very soft sell. Bequest solicitation will have to be regulated and guidelines should be prepared as the potential for abuse is obvious. In the United Kingdom the professional association for fundraisers, Institute of Fundraising, has done so, as have fundraisers' organizations in other countries. (To obtain a copy of its code of practice on bequests see enquiries@theinstituteoffundraising.org.uk, and click on "Information" on the home page.)

The risk of abuse in bequest marketing must be minimized and considered against the potential benefits. The opportunities for bequest marketing are almost limitless, once nonprofits—and that includes universities, hospitals, and arts organizations—realize that they can naturally and easily occupy the position of helpful counselor and source of information on everything to do with estate planning. In this way nonprofits will begin to change the public's attitudes to and perceptions of charitable bequests—and there will be no looking back.

Nonprofits really do need to campaign to change the *culture* of society to alter people's attitudes to making a bequest. Too many people still believe a bequest to a nonprofit is only for the very well-off, or that they have done enough during their lifetime, or that their responsibility to their family and friends precludes a charitable bequest. The current status of a nonprofit bequest is too low. We need to raise its desirability, to give it a cachet that is all but irresistible.

No single fundraising organization will achieve this on its own. It will require collaboration, careful strategy, perseverance, and substantial investment. But it *is* possible to radically alter the public's perception of charitable bequests, just as the insurance industry did for personal pension schemes about thirty years ago. And the possible benefits for nonprofits are simply staggering. By comparison, Aladdin's cave would look like Mother Hubbard's cupboard. There is no greater challenge or opportunity for fundraisers today.

The Legacy Campaign

The United Kingdom's Legacy Campaign was initiated in 2001 by a group of British fundraisers to concentrate the best fundraising experience, brains, and resources on the central promotion of the charitable bequest as a concept—to make it as British a notion as complaining about the weather. Similar initiatives seem to be taking root in other countries too—I know of one happening now in Canada and another in New Zealand.

Lots of British nonprofits have eagerly rushed to fund the Legacy Campaign. The RNLI's David Brann was its guiding light in its early stages and a very bright and determined acting director (Simon Turner, formerly with Burnett Associates) was seconded until the campaign could recruit its own full-time staff. A vast opportunity is before them, to transform charitable giving as we know it. I await their achievements with bated breath.

The Will-Making Clinic

I was hosting a session on bequest marketing at an Institute of Fundraising seminar once and someone in the audience came up with the idea of organizing a series of local clinics on making a will, using his nonprofit's local office—there's one in almost every town—and inviting people in for free advice and a cup of tea (and a short presentation from the nonprofit). Hand-outs would be made available. I am sure that if it followed up the idea, this organization could build its bequest base more quickly and at less cost than most others.

The One-Percent Club

"I'm on umpteen nonprofit mailing lists," said a friend of mine one day, "but no one has ever written to me and asked for a bequest." My friend also happens to be quite well-off. He went on to say that of the myriad requests for money he gets from nonprofits, sometimes for quite large amounts, not one fundraiser had ever suggested that he give them a small percentage—say 1 percent—of the residue of his estate.

"I wouldn't miss it, because I'd be dead," said my friend. "And frankly neither would my estate. I think a lot of my friends would agree with that."

Put in these terms, it really doesn't seem a lot. Who could refuse such a moderate proposition? But my goodness, it would soon mount up! Does that sound like a crazy idea to you? To me it sounds like a potential gold mine for someone. Imagine if every nonprofit could successfully encourage its supporters to leave it just 1 percent of their estate.

Action Points

▲ Read this chapter again (this really is the most important subject in this book).

▲ Make a will.

▲ Make sure no other promotional activity is jeopardizing your bequest income.

▲ Prepare a strategy for recognizing and dealing with obviously elderly people.

▲ Take care not to waste money in unproductive bequest advertising.

▲ Invest a percentage of your current bequest income in initiatives to develop new sources.

▲ Adopt new approaches to bequest marketing.

▲ Start to build a bequest database.

▲ Learn from others. Copy their successes and avoid their mistakes.

▲ Research your bequesters. Ask your donors what they feel about bequests and whether they intend to include your cause in their will.

▲ Encourage bequesters to leave money to your cause in ways that are most suitable to them, rather than in ways convenient to you.

▲ Target new potential bequesters already on your donor file.

▲ Write down a concise description of your objectives and your offer. Train and equip your staff and volunteers. Provide them with practical incentives to promote bequests.

▲ Use simple, direct, everyday language.

▲ Talk to people where they are, not where you want them to be.

▲ Negotiate hard for discounts on press space.

▲ Test different media. Keep a guard book of results.

▲ See if you can introduce an offer or adaptation of offer that is unique to you and valuable to donors.

▲ Test any relevant incentives.

▲ Consider a suitable celebrity to introduce your campaign.

▲ Include a bequest message on your stationery, and in all your publications.

▲ Launch a campaign to cultivate solicitors or lawyers and other advisers.

▲ Research your new bequest database.

▲ Plan an ongoing involvement campaign, possibly including a special newsletter.

▲ Consider running bequest clinics if you can. Test them first.

▲ Start a one-percent club.

▲ Support the central legacy or bequest campaign in your country—or get one going if there isn't one already!

Donor Profile: Alice Jenks

"Drat!"

The peacefulness of Alice Jenks's Friday afternoon reading by the fireside had been sharply interrupted by the front gate banging. It had startled her and caused her to drop her glasses on the floor. "Drat!" she exclaimed again.

Alice could hear her granddaughters shouting and laughing as they came running up the drive. She felt around her chair for the lost glasses. There was no way she could make it to the front door without them. The shouting and general melee at the door increased, punctuated by the occasional anxious call through the mail slot from her daughter Geraldine, who was mildly attempting to establish order on the doorstep.

"Got them!" Triumph mixed with relief as Alice's fingers felt the familiar frames. With the loudest voice she could summon she implored her guests to wait—she was just coming.

Geraldine's worried face met Alice at the door. "How ghastly you look," they both thought as Geraldine brushed past her mother to flap and fuss on the inside. The girls stampeded upstairs to make even more noise on the landing. Alice flopped back into her easy chair. Eventually Geraldine calmed down enough to make Alice a cup of tea and that worked wonders. Geraldine remembered why she had come. "I've got you that booklet you wanted— you know, the one on how to make a will."

"Thank you, my dear," said Alice, taking it and putting it to one side without a glance. She'd read it later when her tiresome daughter and equally tiresome grandchildren had gone.

If she had known what was in her mother's mind perhaps the dutiful daughter wouldn't have been so helpful. Alice had decided she wanted to do some good in the world. That meant doing something more useful with all her worldly goods than leaving everything to Geraldine and her family, who were dependents no longer. They were well established and, Alice reasoned, would be quite unable to appreciate the benefits of granny Alice's estate.

So Alice was going to make some changes. All sorts of things were possible, she now realized, if she were to change her will. . . .

Chapter Thirteen

Keeping Up with Change

*Change used to be something that happened every 10 years
or so. Now it seems it's always with us, always different
and not always what we'd like.*
CHARLES HANDY, *INSIDE ORGANISATIONS*

Although many people don't like it, change seems to be a constant
in our lives these days, particularly at work. This makes it worthwhile to consider some of the more important changes that have
happened recently or are happening now in fundraising.

Changing Ideas About Boards and Governance

Shortly after the publication of the first edition of this book, someone whose opinion I respect said to me that I'd been a touch harsh
in it about boards and their members. He was referring to Chapter
Fourteen, wherein I say many fundraisers consider their board to
be an obstacle rather than an asset. This I'm sure is still much too
often true, but he assured me it was not accurate in the case of his
board, which is really effective. Now I myself knew there were some
good or even great boards in the United Kingdom, the United
States, and elsewhere, though I suspected these would be the exception rather than the rule. So I set about learning more about
boards and what they should be doing. Having served on the boards
of two smallish organizations I was then elected to the board of my
former employer ActionAid, one of Britain's top nonprofits, and
eventually became its chairman. Apart from being one of the most
fulfilling episodes of my professional career, that experience taught

me a lot and gave me a new crusade in life, to help boards wherever I can to be as effective as possible.

A good board really can make a world of difference, particularly in the area of fundraising. Or maybe it would be more accurate to say a bad board can really make the fundraiser's mission impossible.

There's still lots of room for improvement, but clearly from being almost entirely ignored governance has become a hot topic over the last few years; thinking has changed dramatically for the better, and the subject is getting the attention it deserves in many quarters, so it's worth saying a little more about governance in this edition. An effective board has a fundamental impact on an organization's approach to fundraising and its effectiveness in raising funds, so I don't believe there is any aspect of governance that isn't of importance to fundraisers. Here are the main things I've learned from nearly ten years' experience on three nonprofit boards.

- Boards govern. Management manages. It is vital that everyone appreciates the difference.
- The main criteria for board membership are time, talent, and commitment.
- A good board is a balanced board. Equal representation from men and women, young(ish) as well as older, and representatives from all key constituencies too. A board that is just made up of the great and the good rarely works well.
- Board members should be generalists as well as specialists. But when they work outside the board they should do so as respected volunteers and not as elite board members.
- All boards should have clear governance procedures and published guidelines. A handbook for board members is a good idea.
- Fixed terms of service are advisable. At ActionAid board members are elected for a three-year term after which, all being well, they will be reelected for a further three years. Thereafter they must stand down and cannot be reelected for at least a year.
- Every board should reserve for itself the right to make exceptions to its own rules if that is in the interests of the nonprofit. It should exercise this right sparingly.

- Identification, recruitment, and development of new board members is a key and ongoing task for the chair. Ideally there should be several suitable candidates for each vacant place.
- A formal induction program is worth having.
- Boards can easily be too large or too small. At ActionAid we believe fifteen members is ideal. However, we are contemplating increasing this as the organization's increasing complexity has caused us to consider meeting more than four times each year and the difficulties some board members have in attending all meetings means we sometimes risk not having a quorum.
- All boards should be regularly assessed (excellent guides for doing this include the National Center for Nonprofit Boards's *Evaluation of the Nonprofit Board* and Holland and Blackmon's *Measuring Board Effectiveness*).

Anyone can see from this list that managing a nonprofit board is no easy matter, given its voluntary nature, the likely eminence and individuality of its members, the infrequency of its meetings, the diversity of its makeup, and the complexity of its role. With withering perception someone once described the chair's role as being a bit like herding cats. If only it were that easy. . . .

Mergers and Acquisitions

A new development in the nonprofit sector that I think donors and the public at large will enthusiastically applaud is the current fashion for mergers between nonprofits. There's a whole raft of these in progress in Britain as I write. The two huge and dominant nonprofits in the cancer research field—Imperial Cancer Research Fund and the Cancer Research Campaign—have united to become Cancer Research UK, and the Terrence Higgins Trust recently merged with four smaller AIDS nonprofits, although plans to merge Shelter and Crisis, two admirable organizations for the homeless, were recently called off at a quite advanced stage, showing that merging isn't always appropriate.

Perhaps the new interest in governance provides a better environment for encouraging sensible rationalization. It used to be assumed that mergers between causes were a rarity because boards were unlikely to vote themselves out of existence. If that's changed then perhaps there is hope for the world, after all.

As I say, the public I'm sure will undoubtedly view nonprofit mergers as a good thing, although I'm equally sure that for the organizations concerned the process will not be easy. I think they are to be saluted for trying. That so many appear to be successful is something of an achievement.

One plus one does not necessarily make two in the nonprofit merger business. I know of two children's organizations that merged on the assumption that donors common to both would continue to give to the united organization at the combined level of their previous gifts to the individual constituents. They didn't. In fact this new organization found that one plus one made only one and a quarter— income after the merger added up to a little more than half of the combined incomes the partners had enjoyed when single.

Nonprofits contemplating merger have to ask whether what's happening is not in reality an acquisition. Mergers rarely involve the integrating of equal halves; the bigger "half" usually consumes the smaller. This is not necessarily a bad thing, but it has to be recognized. Perhaps if the smaller of the two nonprofits is the stronger brand, however, it might make sense for the lesser party to play the dominant role in the new organization. For "branding" the new entity is certain to be a key consideration. Merger and acquisition can negate years of expensive brand building unless there's careful management of both brands, particularly the dominant one. If a new brand has to emerge from the termination of two old brands, the cost of this has to be recognized, for this factor alone may outweigh whatever economies are envisaged to justify the union.

But the public would surely agree that if rationalization of administrations, cost reductions, and economies of scale do genuinely arise from mergers and acquisitions then these are to be encouraged. They may also help to reduce the bewildering choice that so often seems to confound the non-donor.

Entrepreneurial Donors and the New Rich

One interesting demographic change recently has been the emergence and growth of the new rich. Most evident perhaps in North America but widespread elsewhere too, this is the "self-made" slice from the top layer of our ever more egalitarian societies, where what used to be referred to as the nouveau riche are now so numerous as to be almost commonplace. But no one sneers at them any more.

I mentioned the entrepreneurial donor in Chapter Six. Taken together, these groups provide some really interesting new challenges and opportunities for fundraisers. There are more seriously wealthy people around than ever before. In the United States at the turn of the millennium there were 350,000 households with a net worth of over $10 million apiece, and six million millionaires (which tends to support what I've said elsewhere about it not being such a big deal to be a millionaire these days). *Forbes* magazine has revealed that there are 267 Americans worth $1 billion or more (which is a big deal).

According to Harvey McKinnon, author of *Hidden Gold* and other texts and widely regarded in the Western world as the leading exponent of monthly giving, the new rich are business executives, consultants, high-tech workers, venture capitalists, athletes, film stars, media owners, authors, dry cleaners, and car dealers. The concept of "the millionaire next door" is now widely appreciated.

Harvey believes that whereas with traditional donors you might send in a proposal then wait six months, with these new donors you might have lunch and walk away with a six-figure check. These new donors, he asserts, will be more open to funding operating and infrastructure costs than the traditional donor. They want to be part of a long-term solution, want measurable results and accountability. They like to be involved, so are less likely just to give you the money and let you get on with it. They can be impatient and intrusive, but properly managed are worth it. So fundraisers will have to get used to dealing face to face with what is perhaps a new breed of donor.

Venture Philanthropy

The new rich are likely to come at philanthropy in a variety of ways, one of the most exciting of which is the appearance of the venture philanthropist. An example of this that's just been launched in the United Kingdom is the setting up of Charity Technology Trust. CTT was founded to increase the efficiency of U.K. nonprofits' use of technology to create new revenue streams and attract new donors.

Started by a former investment banker, thirty-one-year-old Peter Sweatman, CTT enjoys the support and financial encouragement of a group of successful businessmen who have capitalized CTT with initial donations. Their role in Peter's enterprise is perhaps best described as that of venture philanthropists, in that they (together with four technology business partner companies) provided not only £640,000 in funding along with resources and technical equipment to get the idea off the ground, but as board members of this new nonprofit they also provide their skills and business experience to guide the venture.

CTT, itself a registered nonprofit, offers its technological services to other nonprofits, saving them the cost of having to develop high-tech solutions in a number of crucial areas. The Trust operates as a catalyst, with a portfolio of technology initiatives that will be managed on commercial principles to deliver services to nonprofits that they would be unable to afford or develop successfully themselves.

CTT's first initiative, CTT Raffles, provides on-line raffling technology for the first time to U.K. nonprofits. The Trust predicts that by hosting nonprofit raffles on-line, U.K. nonprofits will save significantly on raffle production and accrue more than £34 million in additional funds to be distributed to good causes over the next six years. Major U.K. nonprofits, including Oxfam, the National Trust, Barnardo's, and Guide Dogs for the Blind, were pilots for CTT's simple-to-use and very appealing new technology, designed, they hope, to end the days of paper-based raffles and take the £100 million–plus nonprofit raffle business on-line, reducing nonprofits' costs from the present 50+ percent to around 20 percent.

Venture philanthropists, it seems, do exist although whether they think of themselves as such is another question. In reality the concept of venture philanthropy may be nothing more than wishful thinking from nonprofits combined with entrepreneurial packaging of a new opportunity and donor involvement in good, old-fashioned gifts in kind—donating skills as well as money. Perhaps the key to turning this wish into something tangible will be if nonprofit entrepreneurs from inside and outside the sector can present opportunities in ways that will appeal to the modern "new rich" donor.

What's New in Customer Relationship Management

Although fundraisers have been enthusiasts for customer relationship management (CRM) for more than a decade I'm not sure if we are the cutting edge of thinking or practice in this fast-changing field. To try to get a perspective on this I sought advice from two leading practitioners, the heads of two British direct marketing agencies that work with major commercial clients committed to getting the most from their relationships with customers.

Terry and Tesco

My first contact was Terry Hunt, a former colleague from my direct marketing agency days who is now chairman of one of the United Kingdom's leading direct marketing agencies, EHS Brann, with a client roster including such giants as retail chain Tesco, British Gas, and Microsoft. Curiously Terry's early inspiration in CRM wasn't any of the great multinationals, it was Maurice Denham, his brother's accountant. Maurice runs a one-man practice—but from the service he gives, his clients could all easily imagine themselves to be Maurice's only customer. Maurice knows all about the financial affairs of Terry's brother, Barry, of course, but he also knows the names of Barry's wife and children and when the next birthday is coming up. Maurice and Barry watch cricket together. Maurice's network of contacts has opened many doors for Barry. Whenever there's a relevant financial development Barry gets a note explaining in simple terms what it means to him. At Christmas Maurice always sends a card and at other times too. Terry's brother not only relies on Maurice, he likes him. He wouldn't ever think of leaving him for someone else.

Inspired by Maurice, Terry now works for organizations who are really serious about customer relationships and have invested the time, people, and resources necessary to capitalize on these to the full. Terry's agency believes in active customer relationship management, and makes a strong distinction between this and the management of relationships with customers. They put the customer first, believing that otherwise business convenience will override customer needs and corporate strategies will drive the agenda rather than customer priorities. His philosophy is that if the relationship can work for the customer it will work for the business.

Relationships, Terry says, are with people—not processes. Customer is the first word. The first principle of CRM is that you should strive to make customers happier; that's what will make your business richer. Perfection isn't essential. It's better to do one thing well than ten things badly—but make it the one thing that really makes a difference for your customers.

A quote from Tim Mason, Group Marketing Director at Terry's client Tesco, sums up the attitude. He says, "The future of our brand lies in the strength of relationship we build with individual customers. The Tesco brand should be like a mirror in which the customer sees herself. We have to talk directly to her in whatever ways we can."

Making customers happier (and Tesco richer) involves joining up the critical contact points with customers to create a consistent experience and an integrated, enjoyable customer journey. It means one brand, one set of values, one customer relationship. It means marketing with a memory and always striving for relevance—the right offer and service at the right time. Terry and Tesco reason that this customer focus is necessary to deliver improved customer value, profitability, satisfaction, and retention—which will lead to the primacy of their brand, lower selling costs, and increased growth.

In other words it's a committed relationship, not a quick fling.

Tesco leaders set themselves ambitious and challenging targets when they introduced their on-line shopping and delivery service under the slogan "from mouse to house."

In developing an integrated contact strategy to retain and acquire customers they wanted to achieve one million registrations, convert 60 percent of these to real sales, double sales volume—to £400 million—and reduce the number of lapsing customers to an annual 10 percent. They did this using the established vehicle of the Tesco *Clubcard* loyalty program, integrating all media—Web sites, stores, database, publications, and all on- and offline media—to ensure the right message in the right medium at the right time.

Working with clients such as Tesco has enabled EHS Brann to develop an integrated approach to CRM that they refer to as "me-commerce" (interview with Terry Hunt, Aug. 1, 2001). Me-commerce has four key platforms: reach me, recognize me, remember me, and reward me (see Exhibit 13.1).

Exhibit 13.1. The Me-Commerce Platform.

REACH ME

The customer says

- Talk to me in a way that suits me.
- Don't waste my time and energy.
- Don't clutter my life with irrelevance.
- Make me a good offer.
- Make it easy to reach you 24/7.

The business says

- Integrate our media to give best service and access.
- Build customer's relationship with the brand.
- Reduce waste through better targeting.
- Prioritize best prospects.
- Open for business 24/7.

RECOGNIZE ME

The customer says

- Know me.
- Acknowledge me as a good customer.
- Make me feel valued.
- Understand my individual needs.
- Don't waste my time if I've contacted you before.

The business says

- Personalize our offer.
- Integrate our systems to make service seamless.
- Prioritize cross-selling opportunities.
- Make exclusive and premium price offers.
- Improve satisfaction levels.

REMEMBER ME

The customer says

- Don't make me repeat information.
- Remember that I called, wrote, sent e-mail before.
- Recall what I like and dislike.
- Remind me of valuable offers that might interest me.

The business says

- Integrate our customer service.
- Use customer knowledge to gain new sales.
- Segment the database for marketing efficiency.
- Use customer events and life cycle as sales opportunities.

REWARD ME

The customer says

- Make it worth my while to prefer you to other brands.
- Make it worth my while to buy more, more often, and wider.
- Make it *my* brand.

The business says

- Invest in customers with the most sales potential.
- Reward the behavior we seek.
- Invest in valuable customer information.
- Practice joined-up marketing.

Tesco had the commitment, resources, and vision to implement this approach and the results are spectacular. The chain's 10 million active customer records are updated daily with details of 200 million different items purchased every day. Not only does Tesco constantly and quickly know who its customers are and where they live, it also updates their demographic and lifestyle data with details of how much they spend and how often, what they buy and when they buy it. This vast program of data collection and analysis is the engine that drives all of Tesco's customer communication.

It's hugely impressive, of course, even if it does contain vague overtones of Big Brother. But then I guess, if we want to, we can always confound the marketers by buying nappies (diapers) even if we have no kids, or denture fixative even if we still have all our teeth, dog biscuits even if we hate animals, and so on (just to ensure they don't know everything about us).

Knowing a lot about your customers really works. In something as fundamental to life for all of us as buying our daily provisions, it ensures relevance, convenience, and value. Tesco can now offer its customers "four Christmases each year." Each quarter the chain's highly targeted direct mail program rewards 10 million customers (employing 7.2 million letter or coupon variations) with money-off vouchers worth £40 million that are redeemed at 90 percent. Each mailing generates around 3 percent sales growth, which on Tesco's turnover is massive.

Despite such volumes Tesco has learned that every little bit helps. There's a special category of loyal customers known as "can't stay aways," who on average shop at twelve out of Tesco's sixteen departments. Tesco has calculated that if this already enthusiastic group could be encouraged to shop just once in the other four, they'd generate an extra £1.8 thousand million in revenue!

Tesco is now the United Kingdom's number one food retailer, with a market share of 26.4 percent, 10 million active shoppers, and a *Clubcard* in 45 percent of U.K. households. Via *Clubcard* Tesco has launched a bank, a mother and baby club, and a wine club. And Tesco.com is now the world's largest on-line grocery business. Maurice, I think, would approve.

Chris and "Experience Marketing"

Chris Barraclough is chairman of London-based direct marketing agency Proximity London Limited and coincidentally, like Terry Hunt, is also a former workmate of mine. Chris's agency client list is studded with household names including Lever Brothers, Volkswagen, BT (British Telecom), Pedigree Petfoods, and Alliance & Leicester Building Society, and the agency has also worked with some major nonprofits, including the British Red Cross and Worldwide Fund for Nature (WWF).

Chris is inclined to be somewhat cynical about customer relationship management, particularly the way it has been hyped as a panacea for all clients, the solution to everyone's marketing ills.

"Rather obviously relationship marketing isn't for everyone, or at least shouldn't be practiced uniformly" says Chris. "Conceivably I just might want to have a relationship with my car, or rather, with my car's dealership, or even direct with the manufacturer. But do I really want a relationship with my toothpaste? I don't think so. This isn't just me or even men. Most women really don't think of their toothpaste in terms of having a relationship. So it's not realistic for some product managers to imagine that they are in the business of building relationships."

Chris's view is not dissimilar to opinions expressed widely both within the nonprofit sector and in marketing generally. Perhaps it's something to do with the generic use of the word "relationship," which means different things to different people. Customer relationship management is certainly not synonymous with being customer-focused. Many marketers would claim to be that, while not aspiring to manage or attempt to form relationships.

Volkswagen UK may be a case in point. It has developed a complex and very focused communications program that builds rapport and understanding not with customers but with people who've never owned a VW, but might. The purpose is to "surprise and delight" these prospects (through brilliant use of data, personalization, a real understanding of the audience, appropriate incentives, and a program of amusing and involving mailings), to lead them to take a test drive with their nearest dealer—who is fully prepared to receive them. Response rates and subsequent sales are impressive.

Now this sounds a lot like relationship marketing to me, even though Volkswagen refers to it as a "nurture" program. It certainly is creative use of research, data, appropriate branding and positioning, and enticing offers, all of which are presented with technical and creative excellence. Plus, it works. Which is good enough for me, whatever it's called. Nonprofit marketing is undoubtedly different from such commercial applications of our craft, and may be more relationship-oriented. But we would be foolish indeed to ignore the lessons we can learn from how others apply similar communications objectives and techniques.

But even I might draw a line at the concept of relationship marketing for a detergent. Persil and its agency don't approach customer relationship management in the same way as Volkswagen, but they certainly have a customer-focused approach. This is where Chris showed me how, despite appearances, marketing can be a reasonable occupation for grown-up people, and introduced me to a concept that I think could have massive application for fundraisers—"experience" marketing.

Proximity's client Lever Brothers owns the brand Persil, which is the United Kingdom's leading laundry detergent. It seems almost sacrilege to refer to Persil in such basic terms, as we all know the resources and creativity that go into distinguishing the leading brands in this category. But if you didn't know better, you could say one detergent is much like another. Not Persil, though. The team at Lever's came up with a spectacular way of distinguishing Persil from the pack and elevating the brand to "must have" status in households up, down, and across the country. They created the Persil "love your skin" campaign and so lifted what once was merely a powder for washing clothes to an entirely new experience.

The idea behind "love your skin" is bold—but not daft. Its ambition was to persuade women to view their laundry detergent as part of their skin-care routine. Chris's agency was briefed to produce creative concepts that worked with public relations and promotional activity to take the focus away from washing and talk to consumers about skin care (a subject they knew, through data selection, to be important to their target group). By associating non-biological Persil with skin care, they sought to create consumer understanding that a laundry detergent can complement a skin-care routine. I won't go into the exquisite mailings, leaflets, and promotional materials they produced to convey this concept or the sophisticated data management they employed (except to say how I wish my nonprofit clients had even a fraction of their budgets), but will just reiterate that we fundraisers have a lot to learn even from apparently humble consumer products.

While discussing such matters Chris alluded to what he called "the new fashion for experience marketing" particularly among the makers of high-image products. He told me of a certain manufacturer of designer drinks (the wine coolers and other so-called alcopop mixtures that seem more like high-priced fashion accessories than liquid refreshment) that was so into "experience marketing" it was paying out-of-work male models to position themselves in fashionable bars and watering holes during prime sales hours, where they would be prominently visible, drinking the product the manufacturer was seeking to promote. Now these models have to be of a certain age group (I know because Chris dissuaded me from applying for what has to be my ideal job), dressed in the fashions of the moment, and with Palm Pilot and Nokia mobile phone clearly in view. All these accessories complete the "experience" the manufacturer is trying to create and to associate with its product, *pour encourager les autres*. Silly, isn't it? The shocking thing is, it probably works.

But pause for a minute to consider this approach from a nonprofit's point of view. Is not the "experience" part of experience marketing exactly what we should be trying to convey? Imagine how powerful it would be if nonprofit communicators could impart the essence of what it is like, say, to live in a refugee camp, or to survive a flood or hurricane, or to be on the brink of a breakthrough in the treatment of a killer disease, or to be called out to launch a lifeboat in a force-nine gale. . . .

Of course depictions of experiences such as these are what fundraising is really all about, but too few fundraisers see themselves as being in the business of communicating experiences to their donors. Perhaps we'd change our approach if we did. We'd have to use styles and approaches different from the ones that work for the makers of designer drinks, of course. But that's nothing new.

Maybe the man standing next to you at your local bar and looking anxiously at his watch is less concerned about whether he's been stood up by his date than when it's time for him to clock off. If designer drinks can be this committed to conveying the experience they offer to their customers, so can we.

Disenchantment with Relationship Marketing

There are, of course, quite a lot of negative views about customer relationship management, particularly as (with some possible exceptions noted earlier) by and large it hasn't delivered the riches it promised for commercial marketers. But there are enough success stories around to confirm my view that much of this disenchantment stems from companies not practicing what they preach, usually because they haven't committed themselves fully to it. They aren't sincere about it. They see CRM as a route to greater profits rather than something they should be doing anyway.

These are the same organizations, of course, who are spending huge sums to find new customers while failing to develop their existing relationships. They probably also have voice mail systems instead of real people to answer their phones as well as inappropriate databases and company-focused rather than customer-focused segmentation. So they probably don't provide useful or relevant information to their customers at the right times, don't live up to the promises they make, and have no practical ways of listening to their customers or implementing their views.

Still they will complain that customer relationship management doesn't work, because for them, rather unsurprisingly, it hasn't. And no doubt this in time will become accepted wisdom for many. You should be glad relationship marketing isn't working for them. It gives you yet another chance to be fifteen minutes ahead.

Face-to-Face Fundraising

Face-to-face fundraising has been around in various guises for donkey's years. It's of course crucial in big gift fundraising, ActionAid was recruiting new sponsors house-to-house as long ago as the 1970s and face-to-face recruitment of supporters to payroll giving has been around in the United Kingdom since at least the early nineties. In fact in the Middle Ages the building of many a European cathedral was financed by a form of face-to-face solicitation (sometimes combined with the threat of boiling in oil, or similar inducements). But use of this most basic of techniques for large-scale solicitation had been overlooked by most fundraisers until the late 1990s when Greenpeace developed its now famous direct dialogue, where passers-by in busy shopping areas are solicited by specially trained young people distinguished by their "tabard" style tops (prominently displaying the nonprofit's name and logo) and signed up on the spot to regular committed giving. Such was Greenpeace's success at this in various European countries (the idea originated in Austria) that before long many major nonprofits, particularly in Britain, were jumping on this latest of donor recruitment bandwagons. I think this new fundraising phenomenon represents both a considerable challenge and one of the biggest fundraising opportunities to come our way for decades.

Some fundraisers have qualms about the technique but as innovative fundraising it's not to be sneered at. Having got ahead of the game Greenpeace quickly rolled the concept out in fundraising offices around the world and by early 2001 could claim more than 300,000 new regular donors recruited face to face. After several years of decline using more traditional recruitment methods, member numbers and income are both on the rise just about everywhere.

According to Neil Sloggie of Australian consultancy Fundraising Solutions International Pty, who worked as Asia Pacific Region fundraising manager for Greenpeace during the major roll-out of direct dialogue in that region, this is traditional fundraising, one person asking another to give directly to a cause. It is fundraising in its simplest form. I asked Neil to brief me on his experience of this technique, which he did with typical Scottish thoroughness and enthusiasm, so I'll paraphrase liberally from his report here.

Being an asker on the street or at a venue is a hard job. It requires lengthy hours and askers have to face considerable amounts of rejection and sometimes abuse by passers-by. Askers therefore need to be highly trained, well-managed, and exceptionally motivated individuals. Most organizations seem to find that only professionals can make it work.

Because it has to be done by professionals the cost is high—and therefore, to get an acceptable return on investment, donors with a high lifetime value are needed. Most organizations seem to achieve this by accepting only those donors who give by an automatic payment mechanism (direct debit, EFT, or ongoing credit card authorization), with a minimum donation. This policy, which precludes accepting cash, is also seen to minimize potential for fraud.

This is the basic concept then, professional askers signing up people to automatic payment donations, and asking for a high minimum donation so as to produce an acceptable return. There are many additional variables. Average gift varies, sign-ups per hour, in-house versus agency sales teams, sales locations, staff training, materials used, monthly, quarterly, or annual automatic payments, and so on. But to ensure an acceptable return the fundamental principles described in this section seem to underpin most operations.

A Successful Innovation

Direct dialogue has spread rapidly across Europe, and is now a central fundraising tool for many nonprofits. One reason for the rapid spread has been the high levels of innovation and professionalism in Europe's fundraising markets, another has been the promotion of the concept by specialist direct dialogue agencies. Direct dialogue has even been tested in the United States, and although as yet it's early days there's no reason why it should not be equally successful there.

Annie Moreton was Greenpeace UK's marketing director when they took the plunge on face-to-face in 1997. It was Annie who made the decision, and she appointed an external agency to develop the concept and do most of the work. But she recognized early on that Greenpeace's own staff too would have a substantial role to play and, inevitably, this would involve their doing a lot of new work themselves. For face-to-face a different set of skills was needed from Greenpeace's usual direct marketing expertise. Annie explains:

> It became obvious after a while that even with an agency doing
> most of the work, we needed a staff member to work just on
> this—the skill-set needed was different from the direct marketing
> expertise of our recruitment fundraiser. We managed the testing
> and early roll-out through a combination of myself managing the

financial and top level management (dealing with negative press coverage, planning volume, price, etc.), and two fundraisers managing the operational side.

We then recruited someone part time to do induction training, site visits and spot checks, liaison with operations, admin and accounts. This includes mundane stuff like ensuring canvassers wear the right clothes and have the right materials, through to such things as dealing with managing complaints from the public or traders, or the fact of a recruiter having a bag full of materials, including direct debit forms, stolen off the street. This part-timer also had to keep check on performance against target and ensure the quality of form completion and data entry was up to scratch.

This was an interesting addition, as it brought a person into the team who was out of the office a great deal, but needed to be right up to the minute on what was happening in the world of Greenpeace in order to do briefings. She needed good presentation and people skills and had to enjoy getting out there and being on the street with teams—we expected her to go through recruitment training and actually do some face-to-face fundraising herself.

Unlike direct mail or press ads, the face-to-face method was literally "in people's faces" and there were early concerns about the public getting sick of seeing Greenpeace on the street. As part of a thorough checking process Greenpeace campaigners and other staff walked past recruiters at least once a week, "mystery shopping" to see how things were really going. This enabled them to sort out concerns on an individual basis, and also to bring in positive reports on recruiters who proved to be pleasant, well informed, and not high pressure.

Once the system was up and running Annie was able to leave it in the hands of Greenpeace UK's direct marketing manager (at the time, Jan Chisholm) with direct involvement of just one full- and one part-time staff member. The first test in 1997 recruited about two thousand people at a cost of US$60 each, with an average gift that indicated they would break even on these donors in just over a year. But now they had a group of donors much younger than the traditional direct-mail-recruited Greenpeace supporter, and less likely to respond to traditional letter-based communications.

Annie stresses that the lessons Greenpeace UK learned included the need for really good systems to record and monitor these donors and to communicate promptly and properly with them, particularly in the early stages. It also needs senior, committed management.

Greenpeace launched direct dialogue in Australia, New Zealand, and Hong Kong late in 1999. Each program has been highly successful. Greenpeace's South East Asia office tested direct dialogue in Bangkok (it was in its first weeks of testing when this was written, but early indications looked good).

For some three years Greenpeace was the only nonprofit using this approach in Australia. However, in late 2000 several other nonprofits adopted it, and face-to-face now looks like it is developing rapidly as a central fundraising tool for Australian nonprofits.

Jan Chisholm worked with Annie Moreton in the United Kingdom before transferring to head up Greenpeace's fundraising in Australia, where among other things she has responsibility for managing the face-to-face concept. From initial skepticism, Jan has become a staunch advocate of direct dialogue. She explains,

> This is not something to dabble in. It demands a commitment to a way of working that was, at first, hard for a seasoned direct marketer like myself. Getting so close to your supporters and investing so much in your recruiters can be hard for an organization (and its fundraisers!) to get used to. There's no hiding behind your computer with direct dialogue.
>
> It is high-energy recruitment and it demands high-energy retention strategies. I don't see direct dialogue as an easy way to grow your supporter base.
>
> For me the shock was finding that we were often recruiting people who weren't giving to any other nonprofits. They didn't know "the rules." They had no idea they were supposed to respond to our fantastically smooth-running and cost-effective direct mail program once they'd joined. So they didn't. We had to talk to them and find out what it was *they* wanted from us. This, of course, is good relationship fundraising, and it was a useful reminder to me that smooth-running programs need to be looked at afresh every now and then!

As for concerns about being "mugged" as you walk down the street, some face-to-face fundraisers now have signs that they put out on the street saying "in 100 meters you'll meet nonprofit X." I think this is a fantastic idea. We shouldn't be ashamed of being out there on the street, we should be proud of it and selling the fact that the public have a chance to meet us. It also gives people who might not want to meet us time to cross the road and therefore avoid annoyance!

Jan points out another fact about Greenpeace's experience of face-to-face fundraising in Australia. "In 1999 Greenpeace's regular 'health-check' survey found that 9 percent of the sample (representative of the Australian population) had heard about Greenpeace from talking to fundraisers on the street. Our 2001 survey, just carried out, has that figure at 23 percent." As she says, "Managed well, how much good for the environment and our campaigning efforts can come from so many opportunities to get our message out?"

The Future for Face-to-Face

Although many people, particularly in the United Kingdom, think this form of fundraising will have a limited life span, Neil Sloggie, Jan Chisholm, and Annie Moreton are not so sure. Neil accepts that if expansion goes ahead unchecked it has the potential to become a nuisance and be limited by legislation, but remains optimistic that self-regulation by nonprofits will achieve some limitation of the nuisance effect. And because face-to-face works so very well Neil feels it would be difficult to envisage nonprofits giving the method up without a considerable fight.

The constant controversy surrounding this fundraising method in Britain has had more to do with whether the fundraisers should be paid rather than any issues of public acceptability or resistance. There is some concern among the public that these fundraisers are paid, particularly that they are paid on a commission basis. While we have to understand and listen to the public's concerns, what seems important to me is which is more efficient and effective. I accept what all the organizers of face-to-face seem agreed on: that paid fundraisers do a better job, are much more controllable than volunteers, and so are worth the cost.

The issues of acceptability and tolerance seem much more important to me. So far, relatively few organizations are able to mount these campaigns on any scale. But it's easy to imagine a rapid decline in public tolerance if, rather than be left behind, dozens or even hundreds of different fundraisers all feel obliged to embrace face-to-face and so end up vying with each other to secure the best available sites from which to confront most regularly the largest number of potential donors.

Given the limited effectiveness of self-regulation in the past and the prospect of being ambushed by fundraisers whenever I go out for a walk, I'm sitting on the fence on this one. I have to say that the young people I have encountered on the street (almost invariably when I'm running late for something or other) have always been very nice and polite. And I confess that on more than one occasion I have seen face-to-face recruiters and members of the public clearly enjoying their encounter. But I've also seen people cross the road to avoid a canvasser. This tends to suggest that it's not the method itself but how it is conducted and perceived that will ultimately decide the public's verdict on this new fundraising method. Time will tell, and as usual we ourselves have some control over the outcome. It'll be interesting to see what fundraisers make of it.

The following story from Tim Longfoot of the U.K. marketing and fundraising agency Bluefrog gives me hope. Tim's agency works with top charity clients and a specialist face-to-face fundraising agency, called Gift, to develop individual, effective, and appropriate uses of this controversial fundraising method. Their client Sense helps children who are deaf and blind. It's a tough cause and quite difficult to put across in print. Tim believes face-to-face is ideal for it. "Imagine the isolated world of a deaf and blind child," he says. "Yet the most amazing things can be done to reach these children with Sense's help. Our fundraisers are trained to show this to potential donors in the most dramatic and involving way."

When a passer-by is prepared to stop and listen, then and there on the sidewalk, the fundraiser creates for that person the imaginary silent world of a deaf and blind child. In one hand, the fundraiser holds a length of chain and in the other a piece of cloth. "Touch is crucial communication for a deaf and blind child," explains Tim. "We ask our potential donors to close their eyes and grasp the chain in their hand. They imagine the chain is from a child's swing and can see immediately the pleasure of a child who is holding such a simple gift and how it reaches into the child's silent world. The piece of cloth symbolizes the mother's sleeve as she adopts the open-arm greeting that for these children symbolizes love. In this simple and involving way, people on the street are able to touch and feel what it means to be a child without sight and vision. They are touched by this experience, and many willingly agree to help."

This is inspirational experience fundraising in practice. Apply that kind of thinking to face-to-face fundraising, and the public may not so often be crossing the street to avoid us.

Tim believes the face-to-face askers can and must believe passionately in the causes they are promoting. Because it is primarily young people who do this work, they are recruiting mostly people like themselves. But there's no reason to believe that older fundraisers and others might not be just as effective if they are imaginatively and carefully trained.

Louder Than Words

The spread of in-your-face fundraising around the globe, of course, will give rise to some amusing and potentially embarrassing situations for us as professional fundraisers—we'll now have to add international body language to our repertoire of skills. Aside from speech, the language of hand gestures, facial expressions, body postures, and movements all can vary hugely from country to country. For example, the OK sign, where the hand makes a ring shape with the thumb and forefinger, is in some countries used to signify nought, or zero, that is, worthless. A V-sign means victory in some cultures, but "go away" (or similar sentiments) in others. In northern Europe people beckon "come here" with palm held up, whereas in parts of southern Europe they beckon with the palm down, so what means "come on" in Cardiff may mean "go back" in Calabria. And notions of invading private space vary greatly too. The British feel threatened by anything less than an arm's length between them and the person they are interacting with. In certain Arab countries anything more than half an arm's length is deemed rude. One can imagine scenes around the globe where a British-trained fundraiser retreats to a safe distance while the Arab prospect, feeling rejected, advances again, so the pair cut a swathe through the throng of shoppers until one pins the other against a wall or lamppost before finally realizing the approach was for nothing more exciting than monthly committed giving.

The Revolution on Our Desktops

A decade ago fundraisers barely knew of the Internet but now they all seem to think of little else, many persisting in the belief that it will provide the solution to all their ills. This is wishful thinking, driven I'm sure by the belief that it's the sexy "now" medium. Such romanticism, of course, baffles an old Luddite such as yours truly, who can't get excited about it at all. I know that the Internet now means that all human knowledge is searchable, which is great and I do use it to buy books, airline tickets, and other things that never really excited me when I bought them in other, perhaps less convenient ways—and still don't. But I find the Internet tedious to use—it is of course far from slow by comparison to most old ways of looking things up—and unutterably boring, whereas before I accepted I just didn't know something, and so could go for long walks with my dogs instead. E-mail is certainly wonderful in that it's quick and cheap, but the downside is I have to spend half my day dealing with dozens of messages when I could be playing with my kids. I consider my mobile phone an intrusion and leave it off most of the time, which is hardly the social norm these days, so I accept that I'm a bit odd.

To spite my technophobia, many fundraisers now claim spectacular successes on the Internet and via e-mail. The American Red Cross apparently raised $27 million on the Internet in 2000. Greenpeace International receives $60,000 per month on-line—with $10,000 in unsolicited gifts, presumably what used to be called "white mail." In 1999 Greenpeace International raised around $8,000 on-line; in 2001 this total will be in excess of $200,000. UNHCR raised over $100,000 in the first fourteen days after the

2001 Afghan refugee crisis unfolded, just by putting a banner linking to the donation form on their own Web site (www.unhcr.ch). Post September 11, the LibertyUnites.org site raised over $100 million in a month.

Most fundraising communications companies nowadays will have a division devoted to "new media" (Internet and e-mail) where earnest and committed young people talk wide-eyed of fabulous fundraising returns that once would have seemed pure fiction but now are happening regularly thanks to this wizard new development. Faced with this kind of success, I embrace it wholeheartedly.

Despite the initial euphoria, however, most people who know what they're about now believe that fundraising via the Internet does not work at its optimum as a stand-alone function. According to California-based fundraising guru Mal Warwick it works best when combined with other proven media, particularly direct mail. This is undoubtedly right and makes a powerful case for what I hope will be the hot topic for fundraisers in the coming decade, integrated communication (see "Getting It All Together" in Chapter Ten). The Internet will be a key component of that integration. I believe integrated communications are a prerequisite for relationship fundraising, but sadly both are more difficult in practice than in theory so implementation of both will be patchy and they will both probably fall out of favor before long.

But even as I write, events have shown yet again just how quickly things can change. In the aftermath of the September 11, 2001, terrorist attacks in the United States, for the first time the Internet showed itself to be the ideal fundraising vehicle for nonprofits. In just a few weeks nonprofits collected hundreds of millions of dollars on-line. At the same time these nonprofits also compiled what must be among the largest databases of donor information ever. How useful these spontaneous responders will be for future fundraising and support remains to be seen.

Nevertheless, on that tragic day, Internet fundraising came into its own, dispelling any lingering doubts as to the medium's potential. According to Stephanie Balzer, writing in the *Phoenix Business Journal,* since then nonprofits locally and nationally have been scrambling to ensure their Web sites can process the necessary floods of credit card and donor data. E-philanthropy has turned a corner.

The Internet, E-Mail, and the Phone

One of the biggest problems with telephone fundraising is that, over time, fulfillment percentages on pledges have dropped. This is for several reasons, one of which is that people are more often saying yes when they don't mean it just to get off the call. Even people who mean to fulfill a pledge often don't do so. Other things intervene between the time they make the pledge and the time they would write out and send in their payment—they overlook the pledge pack, change their mind, or run into other bills, or their spouse disagrees about the pledge.

So it has become more and more important to get the pledge fulfilled as soon as possible, and preferably while the donor is still on the phone. This is most often accomplished by getting a credit card payment over the phone. But because there are more and more telephone frauds being perpetrated, donors are rightly becoming increasingly concerned about giving out credit card numbers when they receive a telemarketing call. (When the donor calls the nonprofit, this is not a problem as the donor can be confident of talking to the real intended recipient.)

One way around this is to direct the donor to the nonprofit's Web site to make the gift in the secure part of the site. If the nonprofit has regularly made donors aware of the site's address, they will have confidence that they are indeed giving their information to the nonprofit. If donors have separate access to the Internet other than via the telephone line on which they are speaking, the caller can even walk them through the Web site as they make the gift. And if the databases are linked, the caller can even tell the donor that the gift has been received.

Other tie-ins between the Internet and the phone include asking the donor for an e-mail address and for permission to e-mail certain things to them. An e-mail address now is, apparently, worth £6 (US$9) to a fundraiser. This can be asked for as part of another call as a last request, and therefore at little or no additional cost.

If a donor who does make a pledge gives an e-mail address, the caller can immediately e-mail them to thank them again and to tell them to look out for the pledge pack that is already in the mail. Similarly if someone is considering a gift and gives an e-mail address, you can thank them and tell them to look out for further information that you'll put in the mail (or you can provide them with information via e-mail and send them to the Web site where they would not only find information but also have the chance to make their gift). Opt-out pre-call letters can be sent to people at little cost, which can help build relationships and raise more money.

The Internet can also be used in conjunction with inbound telemarketing in that the Web site can offer a toll-free number to communicate by phone should the donor wish. You can also set up automatic billing to those who do not want to use direct debit (EFT) or banker's orders. If people agree on the phone to monthly giving and give you their e-mail address you can bill them each month with a link back to the Web site for immediate payment.

One thing is for sure: the Internet has changed, and will change forever, how people communicate. And there are far more new developments to come than we can even guess at now. So far, we've just skimmed the surface of Internet potential. We will probably look back on how the Internet has been used over the past decade or so in much the same way that we now look back at television in the 1950s. This is an area ripe for entrepreneurial fundraising pioneers.

Screening Out Fundraisers

As part of my job I travel to various corners of the globe giving talks and seminars to fundraisers. Inevitably I am asked to make predictions about the future of fundraising. For some years now I've been predicting that electronic communication and donors' dislike of our modern marketing methods might lead to increasing attempts to find ways of screening fundraisers out of donors' lives entirely. It's not a particularly gifted observation and it saddens me that this prediction is increasingly coming true. Yet for a time at least, fundraisers can find ways round these attempts. Whether they should or not is another issue.

Now, more and more, people have answering devices that they often use to screen out telemarketers. As the hopefully not entirely unwelcome fundraiser, of course, if this happens you can leave a message saying you tried to reach the donor and couldn't so you will be sending a letter that you would like them to look out for. Or you can send them to your Web site. Or leave a toll-free number.

Fundraisers can now do whole campaigns by message. You can ask people in the message to call a toll-free number. Now technology can automatically place millions of such calls in a day with personally recorded messages that are identical or different for different segments. The call can be from the membership director or the head of fundraising or some other credible person. Fundraisers in the United States have used celebrities to front this kind of campaign, but that doesn't always work as it is often not credible—most donors realize that Bill Clinton would be unlikely to have tried to call them personally. But a message from the nonprofit's CEO might be listened to. These calls cost very little to place (less than 5 cents each in the United States for big enough volumes). This technique can be used for campaigning to government, to generate calls to an MP or congressman, or to bring out a crowd to a demonstration. It can also be used for special event support.

Message campaigns might best be used for cultivation. You can place these calls during the daytime when people are less likely to be home and thank them, or welcome them, or tell them about an upcoming TV show of interest, or ask if they received the gift you sent them, or ask if they have any concerns you can help with, or anything else that might draw them into communicating with you. Already this technique has been abused in America, particularly in political fundraising. Doubtless it will be elsewhere too.

Call Monitoring Devices

There are other ways that new technologies are being used to avoid telemarketers. Caller ID (a system that alerts the recipient as to who's calling) can be used to screen out calls from people the recipient doesn't know, as can using an answering machine and monitoring before picking up.

Telemarketers generally block their number from caller ID so they don't get called back and so that people don't see that they are getting calls for different things from the same phones. So many telephone service providers (in the United States, of course) now offer people the ability to stop all calls coming to them from blocked numbers. There's also something called a personal privacy manager. Rather than stopping all blocked calls this device asks anyone with a blocked number to say their name. The person being called hears the caller say their name and decides whether or not to pick up the phone.

As a result of all of this, telemarketers are finding their penetration percentages are going down considerably. Where they used to be able to penetrate 67 to 70 percent of a given list, now they are hard-pressed to do higher than 55 percent. I tell you, it's war out there for commercial telemarketers, and a lot of well-meaning and otherwise welcome nonprofit fundraisers are getting caught in the cross-fire.

Greenpeace and Visitor Relationship Management

Taking the principles of relationship fundraising—allowing choice and providing exceptional service to donors—and applying them on-line can be very cost-effective. Greenpeace, an organization that early on built an on-line donor base, is not surprisingly moving to the next level, which is really taking care of these donors and understanding the value this will bring.

Greenpeace believes that the Internet is similar in many ways to other fundraising channels in that there are costs, response percentages, average gifts, and other measurable features. So—as with any other promotional activity—for the Internet Greenpeace sets measurable benchmarks and goals, defines what is to be measured, sets controlled tests, and measures success in the usual way. The organization's visitor relationship management project set out to establish whether a more personalized, individual electronic relationship would produce supporters who are more satisfied, more loyal, and more profitable to Greenpeace than those developed via other methods—and at a lower cost to service and support.

Greenpeace reasoned that, whereas there is plenty of evidence that personalization enhances donor relationships, the cost of detailed personalization often outweighs its benefits offline. But that cost would be substantially lower and therefore well worthwhile online. Indeed it might be both possible and beneficial to personalize not just appeals but e-newsletters and Web pages too. Participants would be asked at every opportunity for appropriate information that could be used later to improve the depth of personalization and increase the feeling of an individual experience.

This process, known rather unappealingly as drip marketing, has in theory at least the potential for securing loyalty because after a while so much information is built into the system on individual visitors that they each find it just too much bother to go elsewhere.

Initially this test is being carried out by the international office with the intention to roll out the learning to offices around the world. Various test cells are being recruited as this is being written (committed givers, single givers, cyberactivists, and so on), directing them to a new microsite. Communications programs have been developed to ensure that supporters would be recruited to the microsite and then communicated with appropriately. Among other things, special features on the site include a "call me" button, a live chat facility, and an enhanced e-mail communication program delivered by an outsourced contact center.

Recruitment could even be made selective by use of a very simple pop-up questionnaire on the feeder sites. Based on their responses to these questionnaires visitors would be allowed into the test matrix, or thanked for their contribution but not let in.

At the time of writing these tests are ongoing so no results are available. But it will be reasonably straightforward for Greenpeace to compare the monetary value of test cells with more traditional offline recruitment and development, to measure the number of interactions the system generates, and to quantify potential cost savings. Satisfaction levels too can be surveyed at the beginning and end of the test periods and by monitoring communications over time to see their impact on satisfaction levels. In addition all data gathered on these supporters can be stored and used to create profiles of on-line supporters for future marketing use.

How Ethical Are We?

I remember some years ago interviewing the director of a wildlife organization. It had just received a substantial donation from a chemical company that had been accused of polluting an area of wetlands that the organization owned. When I questioned his wisdom in accepting this donation he said, "There's no such thing as tainted money. There just ain't enough of it!" Apparently it's a famous phrase, trotted out by academics and fundraisers whenever a donor's motives for giving are open to question. We laughed, but

I remember thinking that if this was an example of his ethical stance I wouldn't give his organization any of my money!

Ethical considerations have always been of high importance for fundraisers but, perhaps understandably, study of the subject was largely put on hold during the heady "churn and burn" days of the fundraising marketing revolution in the 1980s and early 1990s. Now ethics is again emerging as a favorite topic for conferences and workshops.

The confusing thing about ethics for fundraisers at this turn of the century is that nobody seems entirely sure what the questions are. We all like to believe we are essentially ethical in what we think and do, and that we wouldn't dream of setting about our fundraising jobs clad in anything less than a top-to-toe cloak of ethical certainty. More than in most jobs, the public expects fundraisers to think and act ethically. But are we really ethical and in an ethical profession? Do we make our decisions on the basis of ethics or expediency? Or is it a bit of both? And how ethical is that? And when confronted with ethical issues, just how do we decide between what's right and what's wrong?

As never before, these days ethical dilemmas confront us all in our daily lives. Absolute certainty is rare nowadays. Moral uncertainty surrounds us. We all have to choose between right and wrong in a variety of complex issues and situations. In this uncertain world, there's little moral certainty to guide us. Here are just a few of those issues:

- Is freedom of the individual more important than the rules of society?
- Does the right to abortion trump the right to life?
- Do we prolong or extinguish a life of suffering?
- Do we allow genetic modification or follow nature's way?
- Do investment returns counterbalance unethical business behavior?
- Are shareholder and employee interests more important than the welfare of our planet?
- Should we fight terrorism with war or peace?

And so on. There's equal uncertainty around ethical issues in fundraising. Ethics for fundraisers is a huge, complex, and diverse subject with no easy answers. The ethical dilemmas facing fundraisers seem to grow daily and we sometimes seem in danger of losing our moral bearings in fundraising. Here are a few dilemmas specially for fundraisers:

- Do we emphasize short-term gains or the long-term interests of our organizations and the wider society in which we operate?
- Should we meet today's targets at the expense of donor comfort, trust, and confidence?
- How effective can we get at legacy marketing without running into issues of undue influence?
- Is direct mail justified when all of a donor's gift goes to pay mailing costs?
- How much personal data is it ethical to keep on our prospects?
- How do we balance intrusion against effectiveness?
- How do we use relationships without exploiting them?
- How do we respond to donor influence and motives for making a gift?

Our choices are tough. But luckily for us we can draw on some useful resources when considering ethical dilemmas.

- Our own knowledge, understanding of, and respect for the subject, the issues, and the people we serve (either directly or by providing an avenue for supporting our cause)
- Our skill and judgment in applying our "triple agent" responsibility to our donors, our employer, and our cause
- Our stewardship of the donor's charitable intent
- Our individual and organizational values
- Our codes of practice—individual and industry-wide
- Our professional associations
- The many good books available, including Albert Anderson's appropriately named *Ethics for Fundraisers*
- The law
- The whole range of new courses and training for fundraisers now being offered in ethical issues and how to deal with them

I think this subject is important because it is essential for the future of fundraising and the nonprofit sector generally that our publics should view fundraisers as members of a supremely ethical profession. The object of a wide understanding among fundraisers of ethical issues, choices, and how we make those choices is to preserve and promote trust and confidence among our key constituencies (see Chapter Six). So I welcome a new enthusiasm among fundraisers for the study and understanding of ethical issues and how to deal with them.

I should have been able to offer more than just conspiratorial laughter to my friend the director of that wildlife trust, all those years ago.

Some Thoughts on Future Change

Daryl Upsall, for almost eight years international fundraising and marketing director for Greenpeace International and responsible for building one of the word's most successful international fundraising organizations, recently found himself dared to predict the future of fundraising for a seminar he gave in Switzerland. As he asked me for my input to this I requested in return his permission to quote here from the many interesting things he said. Here are some of his views:

- Fundraisers of the future will have to move in new social circles and have face-to-face meetings with potential megadonors, a major new source of revenue.
- You will no longer own your donors on your database, they will own you. They will want to have access to all the information you hold on them, change it, and set the nature of their relationship with you. Your donors will decide when to donate— and it won't necessarily be when you want them to.
- Corporate "charity giving" will be history. Social marketing will be the norm and nonprofits will need to cut win-win-win deals.
- Corporations will choose the nonprofits they will form partnerships with on the strength of their brand value in the global market.
- Commercial organizations will start to fill the role of nonprofits. As an example Daryl noted that the Russian military can fly food aid quicker and cheaper to disasters than nongovernmental organizations (NGOs) can—for a fee.

- It will be harder for the public in future to distinguish ethical business from nonprofit efforts.
- Our past thinking about raising funds in the North to give as aid to the South may change. Southern NGOs are now out there raising funds. What has ceased to work here may work there. New fundraising techniques will emerge from the South from which we can learn.
- We can expect a whole new generation and culture of giving to emerge as countries such as China expand their philanthropy from Hong Kong to the rest of the nation. Direct mail is already working in China. Face-to-face is most successful for Greenpeace in Hong Kong (average gift US$18 per month) and there is huge major donor potential there. And in India, where 200 million people live at the same standard as the "middle class" of the North, there is an established culture of giving and a rapidly developing, expanding fundraising industry with perhaps the highest potential for growth in the world.

Like all prophets, Daryl may or may not always be right, but a lot of these ideas make sense to me. The one sure thing about the future, of course, is that it will be different. Change is constant. The last decade showed that fairly conclusively, as did each decade before. It seems to me that we fundraisers are required to be very adaptable people. We have to be resilient too, for some change will certainly not be in our favor. But at least we need never be dull.

Action Points

▲ Don't forget that some things in fundraising never change. Remind yourself regularly about the fundamentals of fundraising.

▲ If standards of governance are not up to scratch in your organization, try to make reform a priority. Research all appropriate sources of guidance and best practice.

▲ Check if your employer is a good candidate for a merger or acquisition.

▲ Be sure you are communicating sensibly with entrepreneurial donors and the new rich.

▲ Practice "me-commerce."

▲ Consider being one of the first fundraisers to really develop the potential of "experience fundraising."

▲ Check out face-to-face fundraising in your market. If you're not there already you could be too late, in some countries.

▲ Make sure you read the right books and go to the right classes to learn the secrets of fundraising in the electronic age.

▲ Ensure your behavior and your codes of practice will be of such a high standard that you at least won't be screened out of communicating with your donors as soon as they get the necessary technology.

▲ Become an expert on the ethical rights and wrongs for all fundraising situations. That way your employer will always want you around.

▲ Consider testing a telephone message campaign.

▲ Remember change is a constant, and keep it constantly under review, both for problems and possibilities.

Donor Profile: Sophie Cairncross

Sophie surveyed the chaos that was her desk. Moments earlier she had been the proud owner of a clean, clear, and uncluttered workspace, the centerpiece of which was a large Victorian "partners" desk that had grafted to its right-hand side—but rather harmoniously and quite effectively—a separate workstation for her computer. Sophie took pride in her impressive desk and strove to keep it clean and clear. But this was the last Tuesday of the month, the day before the Trust's regular grants meeting. And Sam, the messenger, had just piled the usual sackload of last-minute applications onto Sophie's ample desktop, loading it to overflowing.

"For goodness sake," Sophie muttered under her breath, "won't they ever learn?" A stack of unsolicited mail slid down the mountain of envelopes on her desk and cascaded onto her feet.

It was like this before every board meeting. Hastily completed and even incomplete last-minute applications from aspiring grant-seekers seemed to outnumber well-thought-out, well-researched, and timely applications by about three to one. A staggering number of applications would be rejected simply because the fundraiser didn't show even a basic understanding of the organization's requirements. Sophie recognized letterheads from several nonprofits that she'd rejected before previous grants meetings, for similar reasons.

"Some people really never learn," Sophie repeated to herself again. With an air of quiet resignation she set about sorting the mail into three piles—those she could put forward, those she would have to go back to for further information and so hold until the next meeting, and those that would receive her standard letter of polite rejection. The first pile was very much smaller than the other two.

The phone at Sophie's elbow rang and she answered it with less trepidation than you'd expect, based on her sudden workload; she'd been expecting the call. "Hi, Johanna," she said cheerily, welcoming the call as a distraction from something unpleasant. An appropriate amount of personal pleasantries and chit-chat were exchanged. Anyone overhearing the conversation might assume Sophie was chatting to an old friend. But this was no ordinary or casual conversation. Johanna worked with one of the major non-profits that Sophie's foundation supported on a regular basis. The nonprofit had an application in for consideration at tomorrow's meeting, and Johanna was calling to check that there were no last-minute questions, that everything was there, and clear, so nothing unforeseen could cause this important proposal to be delayed or rejected.

Sophie liked talking to Johanna. Over the months they had developed a good rapport. She reflected how unusual it was for non-profits to take the trouble to establish personal relationships with her foundation, and decided that this was because its grants are usually around £10,000, so maybe most thought it wasn't worth it. After the call she went back to sorting her piles of unsuccessful applications, mentally noting that she must order some more copies of her standard letter of rejection.

Chapter Fourteen

Fundraising for the Twenty-First Century

Still thou art blessed compared wi' me
The present only toucheth thee
But och, I backward cast my e'e
On prospects drear
And forward, though I canna see
I guess, and fear.
ROBERT BURNS, "TO A MOUSE"

Crystal ball gazing is usually a futile exercise. Life seems to have a habit of proving all our predictions wrong, just for the hell of it. Most people, I suspect, would prefer not to know what's in store for them in this world, for if they did they'd just get even more depressed, rather like Burns's Ayrshire farmer. We humans are inclined to be naturally negative.

The exception to this inherent human condition, of course, is the relationship fundraiser—who has much to look forward to. It's a great time to be a fundraiser. Not only are we part of one of the greatest growth industries to be found anywhere, we are also part of this industry at a time of fundamental and very positive change. Fundraising, I believe, is definitely moving up.

But How High Is Up?

It pays to temper enthusiasm and optimism with some carefully balanced negatives. To consider just where this fundraising "up" might lead, I think it is worth examining some of the problems of crisis dimensions fundraisers now face. For although prospects for our profession remain good, the eventual outcome still depends on how these problems will be addressed. And that, I'm pleased to say, lies fairly, squarely, and entirely in the hands of fundraisers themselves.

Short-Term Thinking

"The bottom line matters most"—so says our commercial culture. Commercial organizations tend naturally to think and behave short term and nonprofits are no different. They are, after all, commercial organizations themselves and it is a mistake to think of them otherwise. They have objectives, targets, budgets, plans, and goals. As in other commercial organizations the people in charge are usually obsessed with meeting this month's target to the exclusion of all other concerns. So they neglect to lay the foundations for longer-term income, they neglect to sow the seeds that would bring them rich harvests in years to come. They'd rather eat the seeds now—and in eating their seed corn, ultimately, they destroy themselves.

Yet fundraising is unquestionably a long-term activity and relationship fundraising demands that at intervals throughout that long relationship the fundraising organization will be required to invest in the relationship with no immediate prospect of financial return. In the future fundraisers will require the vision to see the long term and the courage to resist the clamoring demands for short-term signs of gain. Perhaps in the future the people who surround fundraisers will also come to see that the organization's interests are best served by those prepared to wait.

Of course, I am not advocating that if your organization is about to go under from immediate lack of funds you should be investing resources you haven't got in a bequest marketing program. Fundraisers always have to keep their short-, medium-, and long-term aims in balance. Survival may be the only possible strategy in the short term, but after a while it becomes something of a strain.

Unfortunately nonprofits seem to me to have become more rather than less wedded to short-term thinking in recent years. Perhaps this is merely a symptom of the increasing transience of fundraisers, who seldom stay with their employers for long before moving on to climb the greasy pole more quickly somewhere else.

If you're only in a job for eighteen months you have to make a quick impact, not hang about to implement a program of relationship fundraising that maybe won't pay real dividends for its first few years.

Or perhaps blame for today's culture of short-termism can be laid at the door of nonprofit boards who can see no further than their cost ratios and don't wish to see their organization slip down the voluntary income league table.

Whatever the cause, short-term thinking could be contributing to the biggest threat of all to our fundraising future, as I shall try to describe in the final paragraphs of this chapter and this book. It will, I hope, make for a sobering and thought-provoking ending.

Consumerism

Central and even local government intervention in nonprofits' affairs, prompted no doubt by strongly held beliefs that consumers are in need of statutory protection from unscrupulous fundraisers or their agents, is now a fact of our lives. This current of consumer protectionism is found just about everywhere.

In many ways it is a good thing that accountability from nonprofits is a high public concern, and we should all welcome the spotlight and open our doors enthusiastically to whatever scrutiny the media or public wishes. Any sign of secrecy or defensiveness will not be welcomed by donors. Proactive accountability from nonprofits will be seen as a plus.

Consumers have a right to know the full story behind our use of their charitable donations. If they wish to know the precise background to any specific point, that information should not be withheld. But regulators can go too far. Consumers don't need to have every aspect of their transaction spelled out in detail every time: that sort of background technical minutia is hardly likely to enhance the emotional message so essential to any fundraising appeal and is unlikely to be either in the interest of the nonprofit or interesting to the donor.

Before externally imposed restrictions become intolerable and unworkable, fundraisers must show that, in general, the public has no need for protection from them and that specific offenders will be quickly dealt with *within the profession*. We have to be better self-regulators than we are at present.

Public attention is now on fundraisers. We have to react with both care and reassurance. If we show we can be trusted then all will be well. If not, the forces that would restrict our enterprises need only the slightest further encouragement to pounce, so we would be well advised to adopt positive policies of accountability, to actively show the world that our houses are in order.

How to Change Your Board

A further problem facing fundraisers is the increasingly important question of how to deal with the board. Now don't get me wrong. I wouldn't replace the volunteer-based governance system for nonprofits that's grown up in most Western countries. It has great advantages and we should be enormously proud of it and guard it jealously. But what is a superbly noble ideal often functions badly in practice.

This may not seem to be a legitimate aspect of relationship fundraising, and I have already commented in Chapter Thirteen on the recent growth of interest from nonprofits in all aspects of good governance, and I have given there some of my views on how to build a representative and effective board. But it would be silly to pretend that the fundraiser's relationship with the board isn't one of the most difficult and problematical areas for a very large number of people in fundraising today. The problem still consistently emerges at seminars, conferences, and workshops as one of the biggest of fundraisers' worries.

"This is a great idea," the fundraiser will say, "but how on earth can I get it past my board? They come in once every three months, they skim through their background briefing papers on their way to the meeting, then spend just two minutes specifically discussing our entire overseas programs and twenty minutes debating the most suitable location for the nonprofit's gift shop in some obscure town. They haven't a clue why we're here and what we do."

Another standard fundraiser's tale of woe concerns the board's premature panic in the early stages of a big gift or direct mail campaign, when money is flowing out to cover start-up costs but no money as yet is flowing in. However much fundraisers do to warn their boards that this is natural, even desirable, it seems almost inevitable that individually or collectively they will lose their nerve, just when they need it most.

These are familiar stories. Many nonprofits complain that the people in real need of training and developing are the board itself, and they're the very ones who either think they know it all already, haven't got the time, or haven't got the commitment. Of course, not all board members are like that and many nonprofits are fortunate enough to be served by truly exceptional individuals as board members. But generally these are the exceptions that prove the rule. The system of institutionalized trust that nonprofits are built upon has an in-built flaw. There is no system for ensuring the quality and ability of board members. The nonprofit board is, sadly, too often an incompetent group of highly competent people.

This has to change. As professionalism increases among fundraisers it becomes ever more apparent that nonprofit management is not the legitimate province of the well-intentioned amateur. It probably never was, but the increasing complexity and sophistication of the modern voluntary organization means that well-meaning incompetents can now do considerable harm as well as waste copious amounts of time and money.

Nonprofits don't want or need more names on the letterhead. They do need experienced, imaginative, and available senior practitioners who understand their role and are prepared to undertake the task of supporting and guiding the full-time salaried staff. But even if standards and codes of practice could be established for nonprofit boards, it is still hard to see how they could be implemented by any but the most brave or most foolish senior management teams. Unfortunately, boards appoint fundraisers—not the other way round.

The tragedy is that those board members who are aware of how much nonprofits have changed over past decades and of the implications and potential of that change are precisely the ones fundraisers *don't* need to convert. The rest remain in blissful ignorance—it's nothing to do with them.

"Never did like that computer thing, you know."

"My wife got some direct mail last week. Hates it, positively hates it."

"Yes, I think Cleethorpes would be a good place for a charity shop, you know. It's got a jolly good station hotel."

"I think our fundraising department is really quite adequate—two people and a secretary."

"What an appalling idea, that big gift thing. Next we know, you'll be asking me for money, what?!"

Similar phrases are familiar fare to fundraisers who've sat through successions of old-style board meetings that seem as interminable as they are unstructured and unproductive. As I've said, a wind of change has been blowing for boards for some time now, but it's not yet reached many organizations and in some others change isn't happening quickly enough.

If you have difficulty with your board, perhaps a useful starting point toward effecting change might be to give them a copy of this book. There is often a lot the fundraiser can do to bring relationship fundraising to the board. Involve them in planning your strategy, prepare special materials and presentations to keep them informed and involved, don't take them for granted. The best way to disarm an enemy is to make friends.

Persuade your board to meet donors, to visit projects, to go to workshops and seminars. And encourage them to learn from other organizations that have got their governance right.

The Technique Takeover

Most fundraisers are coming to realize there is a proper limit to technique. Technique can only take us so far. Yet some still rigidly adhere to the formulas that worked so well a few years ago but are now showing increasing signs of tiredness. They are the minority.

The old formulas are now being challenged. Fundraisers are becoming increasingly aware that donors are not sitting targets to be fooled into supporting any nonprofit that gets hold of them. What worked today won't necessarily work tomorrow. The future, as always, will belong to the innovator and those who are close behind.

The technique takeover is one crisis that I think is passing and indeed is almost past now. It is only a matter of time. We are not going to become an industry of soulless money-making machines. The embrace of the cutthroat world of commerce has left most fundraisers cold although the experience has not been entirely worthless. It has taught us quite a lot. Technique, thankfully, will not be taking over. It will perhaps be taking its rightful place, as a valued assistant.

An Absence of Innovation

Having just said that the future will belong to the innovator, it saddens me to see how cautious and conservative the majority of fundraisers have become. I alluded to this briefly in the conclusion to Chapter Eleven and feel strongly about it.

What has happened to the nonprofit entrepreneur? Where are the brave pioneers ready to take calculated risks and to court failure for the sake of advancing their cause, for the glory of invention, for the chance of gaining a lead?

There are some around, of course, still plugging away bravely. But the average fundraiser's approach to innovation can, I think, be summed up by a tale told me by a fellow lecturer on the fundraising seminar circuit, and he told this with such despair in his voice and pain in his heart I was genuinely moved. He said, "Recently I was asked by a client to come up with something innovative, something new, something no one had ever done before. When I did unveil for this organization a great new innovation, the client said, 'I want proof that this new idea of yours will work. What hard evidence can you show, by way of previous results?'"

Fundraisers seem at their most conservative and unadventurous when it comes to promoting the concept of charitable bequests. There are really alarmingly few new initiatives from fundraisers these days in the field of bequest promotion—in the prevailing atmosphere of caution and accountability few nonprofits seem willing to take even small or relatively safe risks. So where will the big breakthrough come from? Or indeed any breakthrough, come to that. We shouldn't forget that in bequest marketing particularly even small breakthroughs can lead to big income. So, it seems to me, fundraisers have a duty to be pioneers. After all, fortune favors the brave. No guts, no glory, and all that.

The Lack of Committed Talent

Another epic and persistent problem facing fundraisers worldwide is the need to attract new people, the right people, into this business. We also have to find ways to retain the good people we have got and to reverse the current disastrous trend of high staff turnover as people leave the fundraising business after a few short years because it simply doesn't offer enough to make staying worthwhile. We need talented, resourceful, energetic, well-qualified, and experienced personnel at all levels who really want to make a career in fundraising. Above all we need people who are committed, or are capable of becoming committed to the work they are going to do.

A Happy Ending?

One thing I am sure of is that Theodore Levitt (see Chapter Eight) was right. The future for marketing professionals will indeed be one of more and more intensified relationships with customers in every field, from car buyers to magazine readers, from ice-cream addicts to footwear fans, from holiday-makers to homeowners, from gardeners and golfers to givers to charitable causes. That gives me a great deal of cause for optimism. Because when it comes to relationship building, to developing and maximizing the potential benefits of a long-standing customer relationship, fundraisers have the edge on all other marketing areas. So if that is the future it seems to be going our way. Here are some of the good things I predict will happen for fundraisers in the near future and some of the not so good things that I confidently believe won't happen:

We will see . . .

- More and better research.
- Better training and recruitment resulting in a regular supply of "career" fundraisers.
- An enhanced image of our profession and improved understanding of what we do.
- Better leadership from board members.
- An end to the absurd notion of fixed cost:income ratios for nonprofits. How can a full-service child care nonprofit expect to run its organization on the same expense ratio as one that merely allocates grants? And why should they be judged on the same basis?

Instead, we will see better educating of donors as to what running a large voluntary organization really involves and what it costs. The emphasis then will clearly be on *value for money*, which will benefit both the donor and the cause.

We will not see . . .

- The decline of print as a key medium of communicating with donors—*whatever* technology may bring.
- The increasing commercialism of nonprofits as exemplified by sweepstake mailings, lotteries, and so forth. Nonprofits can sometimes ride piggyback on these devices but in the long run they only harm themselves if they take too dominant a part in this kind of promotion.
- The restriction of personal data to such an extent that we can't accurately target who *not* to send appeals to.
- The disappearance of donors as the baby boomers grow older and the "unimaginative" TV generation reaches maturity. I just don't believe these people will choose to resist a good fundraising appeal any more than their parents did.

After that, I'd like to indulge in some wishful thinking.

I'd really like to see . . .

- More imaginative and courageous communications from non-profits. After all, fundraisers have the most dramatic and moving stories in the world to tell.
- Better leadership and motivation for volunteers and for staff at all levels and a less haphazard approach to the development of people—fundraising's greatest asset.
- More collaboration between nonprofits, both on research and on promotion. If in some cases this leads to more mergers, fine.
- Fundraising become established in our schools and universities as a viable and rewarding career opportunity.
- A better image for fundraisers and nonprofits generally.
- Encouragement of a more positive view of donors among fundraising professionals. If we can elevate the status of donors we can promote giving generally.
- Real teeth for our professional associations in regulating and controlling junk marketing and other unprofessional conduct from fundraisers. This is already happening, with very positive results.
- Truly integrated communication across all functions—direct mail, press, bequest, major donor, Internet—so that whatever

the medium or proposition, the message is consistent and coordinated.

- Dedicated donor service departments set up to handle all contact with donors including all mail and telephone calls, making use of all the information donors provide so that donors can have one coordinated point of contact in one central place.
- A practical alternative to the standard salutation, "dear friend." That has all the sincerity and warmth of "have a nice day"—yet we seem to be stuck with it.
- A better word or phrase to describe the sector in society that fundraisers operate within.

Expanding on that last point, our sphere is called the voluntary sector, or the charity sector, or even the nonprofit sector, yet none of these terms means very much to most people or adequately represents the importance and contribution of the organizations they purport to encompass. Peter Drucker called it the human change sector, because its products are changed human beings. I see what he's getting at, but that term seems as incomplete as the others and equally ambiguous, if not more so.

I don't have a valid suggestion of my own. It's no easy task. If any readers would care to venture their idea of a suitable catch-all word or phrase to describe our industry, please let me know.

When I originally wrote the preceding list for the first edition of this book, I thought that a lot of it was just wishful thinking, pie in the sky, and I was right. But I choose to cling to these aspirations, for if these wishes could come true, the future for fundraisers would not just be brilliant and full of promise, it would be guaranteed even greater success. Perhaps changes such as these just take a lot of time.

I ended the first edition with the following observations: *In the future fundraisers will pay increasing attention to the simple fact that is the core of this book: if people know you and like you they are far more likely to want to do business with you. For fundraisers the future will certainly be one of more and more intensified relationships.*

Sadly, my optimism then wasn't all that well founded. When it comes to a donor-oriented approach to the business of raising money, fundraisers have certainly talked the talk, but too few of them have walked the walk to make any deep, lasting impression on the majority of donors and potential donors. In fact in some ways things have gotten worse. That's why I have added a new closing point of view to this book.

Changing Fundraisers' Behavior

In its first decade at least, relationship fundraising hasn't really produced its promised payback. Everyone now claims to be relationship oriented, but our interactions with supporters continue pretty much as before, only more so, because there are more of us now. Response levels continue to fall, cost levels keep on rising. Competition becomes more and more intense, and fundraisers become more and more desperate. And there are ever more signs of donor fatigue and declining respect for our profession. Looking back, at times I have felt like the Buster Keaton character in the 1928 film *Steamboat Bill Junior,* desperately fighting typhoon winds to shut the front door of a house that no longer has a roof or windows.

Change people's attitudes, they say, and changes in their behavior will follow. It isn't true. So far, most fundraisers have just not been prepared, or able, to effect the organizational changes necessary to practice true relationship fundraising. To put it crudely, they have been unwilling or unable to invest the necessary time, money, and people to make relationship fundraising work.

The question is, will we ever, now? One major threat may prevent us, and it's all around us these days. It's in Stephen Lee and Adrian Sargeant's research into public trust, it's in the caution and conservatism that prevails in our organizations, it's in the lack of real innovation and clear new thinking among fundraisers now, it's in the slender hold we have in the public's affections and priorities, it's in the impressions we fundraisers seem to be almost daily drumming into donors and potential donors that we view them simply as marketing fodder, it's in the evidence of declining donation levels and the increasing cost of fundraising, it's in our failure to attract legacies, and it's in the declining prestige and social standing of the fundraising profession. It's in what modern fundraising so often seems like, through the eyes of a donor.

Reflections on Being a Donor in the Twenty-First Century

The few weeks before Christmas are always a good time to get a donor's-eye view of the vitality and vigor of the fundraising business.

I wrote the following paragraphs at the beginning of January 2001, having just survived another festive season with its traditional bonhomie, overconsumption, and family visits, and its surfeit of charitable appeals. Christmas is still a time for giving and so remains the fundraiser's favorite—and presumably most effective—time for asking.

As usual that Christmas I had found myself on the receiving end of many, many fundraising appeals. Most I looked upon favorably, if not necessarily financially. Some, I found rather worrying. And a few, I confess, really scared me.

Some three hundred years ago the philosopher Jean-Jacques Rousseau wrote in *Reveries of a Solitary Walker* about being a donor:

> A purely voluntary deed is certainly something I like doing. But when the recipient uses it as a claim on further favors and rewards me with hate if I refuse, when he insists on my being his perpetual benefactor just because I initially took pleasure in helping him, then charity becomes burdensome and pleasure vanishes.

Today, many donors would still agree with Rousseau. Being a donor can be grim. Remember the story I relayed about my mother and the piles of mail languishing on her hall table in the Scottish Highlands (see Chapter Twelve)? I wonder how many donors would also identify with her.

Rousseau went on to say, "there is a kind of contract, indeed the most sacred of contracts, between the benefactor and the recipient. These are not explicit conditions but they are the natural consequence of the relationship."

Even way back then a fundraiser's actions could leave a donor feeling uncomfortable and abused. I wonder if Rousseau's sacred contract with donors is firmly in place today?

Christmas Is All About . . . Shopping

Like half the English-speaking world, it seemed, I spent many happy hours last Christmas being squeezed, pushed off the sidewalks, and abused in the shops by the crowds of other shoppers that thronged London's picturesque Covent Garden. But amid the bright shop windows and the eager, expectant faces of the shopkeepers there was an additional treat, or abuse, for festive shoppers—the new fashion of the moment in Britain for "face-to-face" fundraising.

Strolling pedestrians now can scarcely walk a hundred yards in many of their favorite shopping malls without being bushwhacked by an anorak-clad, clipboard-wielding youth from Amnesty International or Greenpeace or Cancer Research UK or suchlike, intent on persuading any passer-by prepared to pause long enough to be signed up to monthly committed giving by direct debit. This fundraising technique works well—for now. And I have tried to give a balanced view of its strengths and weaknesses in Chapter Thirteen.

But it worries me that, unless it is carefully controlled, face-to-face fundraising on a large scale might do substantial damage to our public image. Imagine how popular it will be with our publics when hundreds of fundraising organizations have jumped on this latest bandwagon. Pedestrians and shopkeepers in Edinburgh's fashionable Princes Street recently fronted a TV consumer program called *Watchdog* to bemoan their inability to move along their favorite mile without being hassled by fundraisers. Of course, the public can always say no, but perhaps in this case, that just isn't sufficient protection.

I am aware this type of fundraising can be mutually rewarding if it's done properly and it's certainly too valuable a source of donors and income for nonprofits to ignore. Perhaps that is true, and it's certainly difficult for individual organizations to show restraint when there's money to be made and possibly just a short window of opportunity to exploit. But increasingly the public can be seen crossing the road to avoid these fundraisers. Is this really how we want our profession and our organizations to be viewed by the public? Are we not in danger of becoming as popular as tax inspectors, traffic cops, and time-share salespeople?

While I'm being critical of fundraising communication, what about another favorite child of U.K. fundraisers, the door-drop, or household delivery as it is also known? The block of flats where I stay when in London is clearly high on most fundraisers' lists of favorite targets for door-drops—unaddressed and barely targeted mail. I get two or three unaddressed pieces of fundraising mail each week through my door. Often they're accompanied by the gift of a cheap pen and perhaps a phony questionnaire. Otherwise, they're almost indistinguishable one from the other. This is because, like most nonprofit direct mail, they all seem to follow the standard formulas for fundraising communication that have been adopted hook, line, and sinker by the fundraising profession.

This is indiscriminate mass marketing, of course, which is unforgivable in these days of sophisticated database segmentation. But it's cheap. And at even half a percent response, it pays. Doordrops are on a par with those awful loose inserts that fall out of your Sunday newspapers. When they started they were fun, interesting even. Week after week they quickly became intrusive and irritating. And they make a lot of litter.

Then, I hear you say, what of that instrument of misery or joy, the telephone? In the United Kingdom in recent years fundraisers have turned in increasing numbers and with increasing enthusiasm toward the telephone as a medium for reaching large numbers of people effectively. The telephone is an intimate, one-to-one communication device, so it should be ideal for sensitive relationship building. Instead fundraisers have used it as a blunt instrument of mass marketing to bludgeon their donors. Having first fabricated ham-fisted excuses for calling, they have then led their hapless donors through deathly scripts, usually read by unsurprisingly out-of-work actors with about as much enthusiasm as a pig has for a ham sandwich and a lot less commitment—in fact, they've telemarketed at their donors en masse rather than seeing the telephone as a convenient device for getting directly in touch with their friends—you wouldn't telemarket to your friends, would you?

So the junk phone call has entered our vocabulary, and donors dread the ringing phone as much as they fear the mailman's tread. I don't know if there are more nonprofit calls at Christmas, but I do know donors who are sincerely grateful for their answering machine and automatic number recognition.

Even television has been used to sell good causes exactly like they were detergents.

In short we've become very efficient mass marketers. We've swapped sincerity for technique. And our publics can recognize this quite easily. The point of all this—and it came to me fairly strongly last Christmas—is that we fundraisers communicate rather badly, particularly considering the wealth of material we can draw upon to inspire interest. Surely we fundraisers have the best stories in the world to tell—real drama, urgent needs, touching human interest, life and death issues. Is a free plastic pen really the best inspiration we can offer to coax a potential new supporter?

How Others See Us

Two pieces of relatively recent research caught my eye. One (by the Henley Centre, a prestigious Oxford-based social studies group) reported that nonprofits now figure below banks, insurance companies, the Post Office, and the National Health Service when it comes to measures of public trust and respect. According to Henley, the public's trust in nonprofits has been declining steadily over the past decade at least. (We're only just above the media and the Church—it's that bad!) The other research was conducted by several respected groups following the actions of campaigning nonprofits at the World Trade Organization's infamous Seattle meetings in 1999. This survey found that the majority of a cross-section of people aged thirty-four to sixty-four in the United States, France, Germany, the United Kingdom, and other countries believe NGOs (non-governmental organizations) are more credible than commercial organizations, more trustworthy, more likely to take action on the public's behalf, and much more likely to be effective. When we get it right, people really are prepared to believe we can make the world a better place. But as many donors will tell you, we too often get it wrong.

Short-Term Gain, Long-Term Suicide

The trouble with the warm post-Seattle glow is that it will be short-lived. Sustaining an effective public image and identity is difficult for the nonprofit sector, and has been sporadic since BandAid in the mid-1980s.

What we do rely on is the way the public perceives us through our regular communications with them. Unfortunately, unless the communications output of our industry dramatically improves, as soon as Seattle is forgotten we'll revert to the gradual erosion of public trust, respect, and support that is the inevitable outcome of trivial "lowest common denominator" mass marketing.

Why do we do this? Well, as I said in the last chapter, it's because most of our organizations (and responsibility for this must

rest with boards and CEOs) still find it easier and therefore preferable to go for short-term, rapid-payback benefits, rather than to lay
the foundations of meaningful, long-term donor relationships. But
there are alternatives. There's a huge amount we can all do to communicate more welcomely, more meaningfully, and more effectively with all of our donors.

SAVE THE DONOR—An Urgent Appeal

I started Chapter Twelve with Dale Carnegie's quote—"You'll have
more fun and success when you stop trying to get what you want
and start helping other people get what they want"—because it sum-
marizes the spirit of the views that follow and also because it cheers
me up. Fun and success are two of my personal priorities and it was
specially perceptive of Carnegie to list them in that order.

Fun and success are certainly what good fundraising should be
about. But the picture I painted earlier of elderly ladies confused
by piles of bland, lookalike appeal mailings; of floors and tables lit-
tered by unwanted loose inserts; of strolling shoppers ambushed
by posses of scruffy youths evangelizing for that new god, direct
debit, of free plastic pens, phony public surveys masquerading as
genuine research, and of bewildered supporters betrayed by list
swaps and besieged by reciprocal mailings . . . all seem to indicate
that fun is in short supply and success will be short-lived.

I wonder if we fundraisers, unwittingly or otherwise, are not
sowing the seeds of our own destruction. If in our vim and vigor
for the processes of fundraising we have not dislodged our sensitivity for the fundraised. And whether, through our obsession with
techniques, targets, and volumes, we have not somehow lost our
grip on our own sincerity, and our understanding of the need for
credibility and trust among the people we expect to be our donors.
There's research enough on declining public trust in nonprofits,
most of which appears to confirm my disquiet (see Chapter Six).

Despite the advent of sophisticated segmentation tools and the
apparently widespread acceptance of relationship marketing,
fundraisers seem as committed as ever to a version of "lowest common denominator" mass marketing. Where might this lead?

We fundraisers ought to pause, once in a while, from our endless round of appeals, mailings, events, and promotions, and try to

see what our stream of commercialized asking looks like from the point of view of our donors. Instead of galvanizing society into action with our visions of a more just, fairer, better world, have we not descended, in many people's eyes, to the level of commercial hustlers? Perhaps we annoy more people than we inspire. What a terrifying thought.

In employing such tactics, possibly today's fundraisers might be visiting upon future generations of our profession the esteem and respect previously reserved for badger gassers, despoilers of the environment, and suchlike. It's a depressing future scenario. Donors might be becoming an endangered species. So here I want to concentrate on what we could be doing, now, to save the donor.

Tell the Best Stories in the World . . .

There is light at the end of this particular tunnel. A little speck of light, perhaps, struggling feebly to get noticed by today's cost-conscious, target-driven fundraisers as, in their rush and nervous haste, they strive toward their ever-expanding targets. But a light that is shining nonetheless.

This light is, in fact, in us ourselves, in the nonprofit sector, in our organizations and in the inspiring work we do. And it's in the reassuring but perhaps not surprising phenomenon that donors, by and large, are wonderful, caring, patient, and understanding folk. They want to like and respond to us, and will, sometimes in spite of rather than because of the way we communicate with them.

But taking donations is not fundraising. Real fundraising doesn't happen without effective communication. For one individual to inspire another to give to a charitable cause, that inspiration must be communicated. Seems obvious, doesn't it? Ours is the inspiration business. Yet few fundraisers, in my experience, are expert at the art of communication and most show comparatively little interest in learning about it. Most seem to prefer just to follow the tired old formulas of mass marketing. There's so much stuff around these days competing for our donors' limited discretionary attention that fundraisers won't succeed unless they are very good indeed at this thing called "communication."

But there are signs of good things going on. Perhaps it's a minority, but in some areas, fundraisers are already getting quite a bit better at communicating. The opportunities for the far-sighted fundraiser to get "just fifteen minutes ahead" are many. (I've used this phrase frequently in this book, so here's the origin of it. The American comedian Woody Allen once had a vision of our world's eventual overthrow and domination by an alien species that is not, as is conventionally assumed, light-years ahead of us technologically but is just fifteen minutes ahead. But fifteen minutes ahead in *everything*. This small advance gives the superior aliens just enough of an advantage to soundly beat us in every area. As being light-years ahead of the field is so difficult for fundraisers in these competitive times, I concentrate on looking for areas to be just fifteen minutes ahead, because that will give me all the competitive advantage I need. There are lots of them.)

Producing only exceptional communications is one such area. Luckily for us, we don't need the hard sell. More than most other business areas, we fundraisers have a willing, compliant audience. And more than any other business area we have access to stories and images capable of inspiring and motivating people on a massive scale. We have the best of material at our disposal—drama, emotion, high ideals. We deal with life-and-death issues, we are surrounded by the most photogenic material, the most moving examples, and the most inspirational achievements. If we can't present the work we do compellingly, with pace and passion that will inspire action, then really we are doing something terribly wrong.

All we need to do is to write about it brilliantly, to photograph, design, and package it superbly, to be innovative, passionate, creative, and imaginative enough to present it in a way that will captivate, thrill, and inspire.

That's quite a challenge, of course. But I venture to suggest that it's because of this or some similar challenge that most of us became fundraisers in the first place. So we should see this as a thrilling opportunity and grab it with both hands. Or we should make it our business to attract into our profession the kind of energetic, creative, talented, and committed people who will eagerly take on this challenge and translate it into captivating words and pictures that will inspire generations of donors old and new. Committed giving is much more than paying a regular sum by direct debit or standing order. It is based on a sound trust in and belief in the cause, and comes—or should come—from the inspiration spun by the fundraiser.

. . . to the Right People, in the Right Way . . .

Mass marketing never made sense for fundraisers. But now, if we aspire to treat our donors more maturely, more individually, and more honestly, then new technology is on our side. The technology for individual relationship building already exists in databases that are faster, more sophisticated, easier to use, and much cheaper than the databases of even a few years ago. They offer us the potential for true relationship fundraising with thousands of donors at the same time. This new technology is increasingly being deployed by fundraisers to provide their donors with real and meaningful communications on a one-to-one basis. And it gets fantastic results.

In addition, we fundraisers are at last beginning to invest properly in research that will give us the chance to fully understand our audiences, to get a much better idea of what makes donors tick and what they want from us. And despite the past fifteen years of donor abuse and commercial ruthlessness, it's not too late to capitalize on the feel-good factor and the fact that, generally, donors are very forgiving, they like us and want to trust and believe in us.

All we have to do is to start treating our donors a lot better, and move from the current practice of "take, take" toward a more mutually beneficial relationship of "give and take." It's not too late to put donors at the center of our activities and to allow their generosity and commitment to drive our relationship with them.

This is what I call relationship fundraising. It takes vision, courage, and the investment of time, money, and people to become a reality. And, of course, a belief in Dale Carnegie's maxim about fun and success.

So what can you do, in your organization, to avoid being considered as one of the time-share sellers of this new millennium? What can you do now, to save some of your organization's precious seed corn for the future?

Well, first, deal fairly and respectfully with your donors. That means no fluff, no faked sincerity, no obtuse language, no promises you can't keep. Instead, base your communications on what your donors want to receive, not on what you want to send. Give your donors choices. Be consistent and distinctive, so your organization will stand out amid the sea of short-term thinkers. Only write when you have a good reason for writing, not when you have a window of opportunity or a target to meet.

. . . with Care, and Flair . . .

Second, fundraising organizations, now, are among the most inept of businesses at the art of customer service. We have consistently undervalued it and underinvested in it. Our donors are more likely to experience efficient, friendly, and effective service at the hands of their favorite airline, bank, insurance company, or even McDonald's than they are at the hands of their favorite nonprofit. (Harsh, maybe, but true. I know. I have tested service levels of hundreds of fundraising organizations in the United States, Canada, and the United Kingdom.) Yet given the business we are in, surely we should be paragons of excellent, efficient, caring, and committed customer service. We are far from it now.

We can change that. We can set an example to all other business areas by being a real pleasure to deal with and by providing world-class customer service. We can also be a model for the rest of the world in openness and accountability. If public trust is a problem, it's up to us to show we can be trusted. That means *radically* changing the way we communicate.

. . . Sincerely, Honestly . . . and Effectively

It's a huge challenge. In short, if we are to avoid long-term suicide we have to move away from our recently acquired money-driven sales orientation, and move toward a service-driven, customer-centered orientation. I don't think donors will give less if we do. I think they will give more.

But this will require fundamental change from us.

Reading this, of course, may depress you. If so I hope you'll take heart from a piece of twenty-first-century Zen I first heard from Anita Roddick, founder of the international chain The Body Shop, and someone who has frequently pitted herself against the odds. You may think your task as a relationship fundraiser is just too big, that it's hopeless, that your bosses will never listen to you, that you're too small a cog in the wheel, that what you do cannot make a difference. If you feel like that then consider and take courage from this closing thought:

"If you think you're too small to make a difference . . . you've never spent a night alone in a room with a mosquito."

Never give up trying to make a difference. You can.

Action Points

▲ Combat short-term thinking whenever and wherever it occurs in your organization.

▲ Encourage management and colleagues to think long term and to set targets in short, medium, and long terms.

▲ Encourage your board members to get involved; to understand your objectives and your problems. Persuade them to take appropriate training courses.

▲ Organize presentations, training sessions, and visits to projects for your board.

▲ Involve your board by encouraging them to meet donors at your functions or in the donors' own homes.

▲ Buy extra copies of this book to give as presents to your board of management (you may detect a mild tinge of vested interest here).

▲ See what you can do to encourage some of the positive developments that might be just round the corner for fundraising.

▲ Always work to build donor trust and confidence.

▲ Make your communications essential reading for your donors.

▲ Pour all your creativity and resourcefulness into creating a unique experience for your donors that will inspire them and bind them to your organization as friends for life.

▲ Never stop trying to make a difference.

Donor Profile: Mr. and Mrs. Christisen

"Who was it?"

"Oh, nobody," answered Mr. Christisen wearily as he hung up. "Just someone wanting to ask us some questions over the phone. I told them Milady wasn't home."

"Couldn't you just have said we're not interested?" asked Mrs. Christisen irritably. "They'll only ring back."

"I don't think so," replied her husband with a chuckle. "I told him she'd gone up the Irrawaddy to pacify the natives and won't be back until after the big monsoon. He seemed thrown by that and rang off."

Mr. Christisen sat down by the fireside.

"I wish I could take these people seriously, you know. From where I sit there seem to be more problems in the world than ever before. Yet all these people can do is make facile phone calls and send me puerile and phony begging letters."

"What people, dear?" asked Mrs. Christisen patiently. "And where exactly do you sit?"

"Where indeed!" Her husband was becoming just a bit indignant. "It's all these worthy causes. I'm as generous as the next man but they're just not reaching me, not at all. When are they going to get their act together and start convincing me that they *can* make a difference in this mess of a world?"

Mrs. Christisen put down her book and began to put on her cardigan.

"You could always join the Friends of Wetherfield Hospital or sponsor a duck or have your head shaved for charity. It's not them that's short of ideas, you know. It's you." Mrs. Christisen turned as she put on her coat. "You really are an old skinflint, you know. You've got pots of money and you never do anything useful with it."

"I'm not convinced it won't just be frittered away," said Mr. Christisen with some resignation. "When they show me it'll do some good, they'll not find me ungenerous. Where are you going?"

"I've got a Greenpeace meeting tonight," his wife replied, picking up her wet suit in the holdall behind the door. "We're blocking the sewage outlet beside the harbor and hanging a 'stop the dumping' banner across the town hall. I should be back by nine, though."

The phone rang again just as Mrs. Christisen closed the door behind her. "Not again," thought Mr. Christisen, wondering what to tell them this time.

Glossary

A/B split copy: Newspapers printed on more than one press often offer the facility to test different advertisements by printing alternate copies of the paper with either advertisement A or advertisement B. It is a very effective way to test different concepts. The term has now been widened to include any equally accurate test, whether in newspapers or elsewhere and even if more than two approaches are being simultaneously tested.

Baby boomer: Someone born during the baby boom after the Second World War, between 1946 and 1964.

Beneficiaries: People who benefit from a will.

Bequest (legacy): A gift left in a will.

Bulk mail: In the United States, a range of U.S. Postal Service services for large volume mailings, including discounts and terms and conditions for the sorting and delivery of mail.

Codicil: A further document making a change, or adding to, an existing will. It must comply with the same formalities as the will.

Customer relationship management (CRM): A focused strategic approach to developing relationships with customers that puts the needs of the customer ahead of the aspirations of the business.

Data Protection Act: The Data Protection Act 1984 enables the U.K. government to comply with the European Convention on data protection and to meet growing concern about the use of personal data. The act applies to those who automatically process personal data.

Data Protection Registrar: All data users and computer bureaus must register with the Data Protection Registrar, who provides guidance on principles of data protection and administers the terms of the Act, including instigating appropriate legal action if the terms of the Act are breached.

Deduplication program: Running two lists together to identify exact duplicates, one of which can be removed to avoid double mailing.

Direct debit: A facility to make regular payments automatically by direct transfer from your bank account. See also Electronic funds transfer.

Distress space: Unused advertising space in a publication, often available to nonprofits for very low rates just before the publication deadline.

Drip marketing: Collecting information about donors and potential donors via repeated on-line contacts, and using it to refine and personalize future appeals.

Electronic funds transfer (EFT): A facility to make regular payments automatically by direct transfer from your bank account. Also known in North America as pre-authorized checking (PAC). See also Direct debit.

Estate: The total of what is left by a deceased person including all property and money.

Executor: The person appointed to carry out the terms of a will.

Foundation: A specially constituted or endowed institution, usually permanent, into which funds are placed for the purpose of charitable distribution.

Guard book: A permanent record of your promotional results, either loose-leaf or bound. A copy of each promotion should be pasted into the book with all salient details including date, competitive activity, relevant events (such as weather and world headlines), tests, costs, and all results.

Inbound: Communication from a potential donor to a nonprofit.

Intestate: The state of not having made a will. Usually used in the phrase "died intestate," which indicates that there's no will and the estate will be distributed according to the applicable law.

Johnson box: The typed rectangle of punchy copy that appears in direct mail letters usually at the top above the salutation. It acts as an extended headline. Presumably someone called Johnson achieved immortality by inventing it.

Legacy (bequest): A gift left in a will.

Legatee: The recipient of a legacy.

Legator: The person leaving a legacy.

Lift letter: The second letter in a mailing pack, designed to improve the response rate to the main appeal.

Mailing Preference Service: The United Kingdom's register of individuals who have expressed the wish to be excluded from certain mailings.

Mailsort: Mailsort is a trademark of the Royal Mail covering a range of services for large volume mailings, including discounts and terms and conditions for sorting and delivery of different types of mail. The mailsort symbol is a distinctive letter M where the stamps usually are.

Nonprofit: For this edition, the term *nonprofit* covers any organization that might otherwise be described as a charity, voluntary organization, a not-for-profit, or an institution or organization that derives at least part of its income from public donations.

Outbound: Communication from a nonprofit to a potential donor.

Pecuniary bequest: A gift of a fixed amount left in a will.

Proved will: A will that has been through a formal legal probate process and established to be genuine and valid.

Recency, frequency, monetary value (RFM): Any system that measures donors across the three principal components that demonstrate a donor's value to your organization now.

Reciprocal mailings: An agreement whereby one nonprofit mails to another nonprofit's donors and, in turn, allows that nonprofit to mail its material to a similar segment of its own donors.

Residuary bequest: The gift of all or part of the residue of an estate, after all pecuniary bequests have been distributed.

Residue: What is left of an estate after all debts, tax, costs, and specific and pecuniary bequests have been paid.

Reversionary bequest: A bequest to a named person who has access to its value for life, after which the value reverts to another named beneficiary rather than to the heirs of the first one.

Trust: An organization managed by trustees, similar in purpose and function to a foundation. See also Foundation.

Bibliography

AAFRC Trust for Philanthropy. *Giving USA 2001*. New York: AAFRC Trust for Philanthropy, 2001.

Anderson, A. *Ethics for Fundraisers*. Indianapolis: University of Indiana Press, 1996.

Bayley, T. D. *The Fund Raiser's Guide to Successful Campaigns*. New York: McGraw-Hill, 1988.

Bird, D. *Commonsense Direct Marketing*. London: Printed Shop, 1982.

Brakeley, G. A., Jr. *Tested Ways to Successful Fund Raising*. New York: AMACOM, 1980.

Burk, P. *Thanks! A Guide to Donor-Centred Fundraising*. Toronto: Burk and Associates, 2000.

Burnett, K. (ed.). *Advertising by Charities*. London: Directory of Social Change, 1986.

Burnett, K. *Charity Annual Reports: The Complete Guide to Planning and Production*. London: Directory of Social Change, 1987.

Burnett, K. *Friends for Life: Relationship Fundraising in Practice*. London: White Lion Press, 1996.

Burnett, K. *Friends for Life Video Series*. London: White Lion Press, 1996.

Burnett, K., and Weatherup, K. *How to Produce Inspiring Annual Reports*. London: Directory of Social Change, 2000.

Charity Commission. *Report of the Charity Commissioners for England and Wales*. London: The Charity Commission, 1989.

Cialdini, R. *Influence: The Psychology of Persuasion*. New York: Quill, 1993.

Crouch, S. *Marketing Research for Managers*. London: Pan Books/Heinemann, 1984.

Di Sciullo, J. *Marketing et Communication des Associations* [Marketing and communication for nonprofits]. Lyon, France: Editions Juris-Service, 1988.

Drucker, P. F. *Managing the Non-Profit Organization*. Oxford: Butterworth-Heinemann, 1990.

Earle, R. *The Art of Cause Marketing: How to Use Advertising to Change Personal Behavior and Public Policy*. Lincolnwood, Ill.: NTC Business Books, 2000.

Evans, H. *Pictures on a Page*. London: Heinemann, 1982.

Fraser-Robinson, J. *The Secrets of Effective Direct Mail*. New York: McGraw-Hill, 1989.

Fraser-Robinson, J. *Total Quality Marketing*. London: Kogan Page, 1991.

Gendre, G. *Les Stratégies de la Générosité* [Strategies for fundraising]. Paris: Economica, 1996.

Gordon Lewis, H. *How to Write Powerful Fund Raising Letters*. Chicago: Pluribus Press, 1989.

Gray, J. *Men Are from Mars, Women Are from Venus*. New York: HarperCollins, 1992.

Hind, A. *The Governance and Management of Charities*. London: Voluntary Sector Press, 1995.

Holland, T. P., and Blackmon, M. *Measuring Board Effectiveness: A Tool for Strengthening Your Board*. Washington, D.C.: National Center for Nonprofit Boards, 2000.

Johnston, M. *The Fundraiser's Guide to the Internet*. New York: Wiley, 1998.

Johnston, M. (ed.). *Direct Response Fundraising: Mastering New Trends for Results*. New York: Wiley, 2002.

Kobs, J. *Profitable Direct Marketing*. Lincolnwood, Ill.: NTC Business Books, 1988.

Kotler, P., and Andreasen, A. *Strategic Marketing for Nonprofit Organizations*. Upper Saddle River, N.J.: Prentice Hall, 1991.

Leiderman, R. *The Telephone Book*. London: McGraw-Hill, 1990.

Levitt, T. *The Marketing Imagination*. New York: Free Press, 1986.

Lord, J. G. *The Raising of Money*. Cleveland, Ohio: Third Sector Press, 1990.

Makens, J. C. *The Twelve-Day Marketing Plan*. Wellingborough, Northamptonshire: Thorsons, 1989.

McCorkell, G. *Advertising That Pulls Response*. London: McGraw-Hill, 1990.

McDonald, M. *Marketing Plans: How to Prepare Them, How to Use Them*. London: Heinemann, 1984.

McDonald, M., and Leppard, J. *The Marketing Audit: Translating Marketing Theory into Practice*. Oxford: Butterworth-Heinemann, 1991.

McDonald, M., and Morris, P. *The Marketing Plan: A Pictorial Guide for Managers*. Oxford: Heinemann, 1989.

McKinnon, H. *Hidden Gold*. Chicago: Bonus Books, 1999.

McQuillan, J. (ed.). *Charity Trends*. Tonbridge, Kent: Charities Aid Foundation, 1991.

Mullin, R. *The Fundraising Cycle*. London: Redmond Mullin, 1989.

Nash, E. L. *The Direct Marketing Handbook*. New York: McGraw-Hill, 1984.

Nichols, J. E. *By the Numbers: Using Demographics and Psychographics for Business Growth*. Chicago: Bonus Books, 1990.

Nichols, J. E. *Changing Demographics: Fund Raising in the 1990s.* Chicago: Bonus Books, 1990.

Nichols, J. E. *Targeted Fund Raising: Defining and Refining Your Development Strategies for the 1990s.* Chicago: Bonus Books, 1991.

Nichols, J. E. *Growing from Good to Great: Positioning Your Fund Raising for the Big Gains.* Chicago: Bonus Books, 1995.

Nichols, J. E. *Lessons from Abroad: Fresh Fundraising Ideas from Experts in the United Kingdom.* Chicago: Bonus Books, 1997.

Nichols, J. E. *Transforming Fundraising.* San Francisco: Jossey-Bass, 1999.

Nichols, J. E. *Pinpointing Affluence: Increasing Your Share of Major Donor Dollars.* Chicago: Bonus Books, 2001.

Norton, M. *The Worldwide Fundraiser's Handbook.* London: Directory of Social Change and Resource Alliance, 1992.

Ogilvy, D. *Ogilvy on Advertising.* London: Pan Books, 1984.

Ogilvy, D. *Confessions of an Advertising Man.* London: Pan Books, 1987.

Ostroff, J. *Successful Marketing to the 50+ Consumer.* Upper Saddle River, N.J.: Prentice Hall, 1992.

Panas, J. *Born to Raise.* Chicago: Pluribus Press, 1988.

Pointer, D. D., and Orlikoff, J. E. *The High-Performance Board.* San Francisco: Jossey-Bass, 2002.

Rapp, S., and Collins, T. *MaxiMarketing.* New York: McGraw-Hill, 1976.

Russell, C. *100 Predictions for the Baby Boom.* Cambridge, Mass.: Perseus Books, 1987.

Sargeant, A. *Marketing Management for Nonprofit Organizations.* New York: Oxford University Press, 1998.

Sargeant, A. *Improving Public Trust in the Voluntary Sector: An Empirical Analysis.* Henley-on-Thames, England: Henley Management College, 2001.

Sargeant, A. "What Turns Donors On? What Turns Them Off?" In C. Walker and C. Pharoah (eds.), *A Lot of Give.* London: Hodder and Stoughton, 2002.

Sargeant, A., and Kaehler, J. *Benchmarking Charity Costs.* West Malling, England: Charities Aid Foundation, 1998.

Sargeant, A., and Lee, S. "Public Trust and Confidence." Paper presented to the ICFM Conference, Birmingham, England, July 2000.

Sargeant, A., and McKenzie, J. *A Lifetime of Giving: An Analysis of Donor Lifetime Value.* West Malling, England: Charities Aid Foundation, 1998.

Schumacher, F. *Small Is Beautiful.* New York: HarperCollins, 1989.

Seymour, H. J. *Designs for Fund-Raising.* Ambler, Pa.: Fund-Raising Institute, 1988.

Sloggie, N. *Tiny Essentials of Fundraising.* London: White Lion Press, 2002.

Smith, G. *Asking Properly.* London: White Lion Press, 1996.

Taylor, M., and Shaw, S. *Reinventing Fundraising: Realizing the Potential of Women's Philanthropy.* San Francisco: Jossey-Bass, 1995.

Warwick, M. *How to Write Successful Fundraising Letters.* San Francisco: Jossey-Bass, 2001.

Warwick, M. *Ten Steps to Fundraising Success: Choosing the Right Strategy for Your Organization.* San Francisco: Jossey-Bass, 2001.

Warwick, M., Hart, T., and Allen, N. (eds.). *Fundraising on the Internet: The ePhilanthropy Foundation.org's Guide to Success Online.* San Francisco: Jossey-Bass, 2001.

Weatherup, K., and Burnett, K. *How to Produce Inspiring Annual Reports.* London: Directory of Social Change, 2000.

Weber, N. (ed.). *Giving USA.* New York: AAFRC Trust for Philanthropy, 1990.

Wheildon, C. *Type and Layout: How Typography and Design Can Get Your Message Across—or Get in the Way.* Berkeley, Calif.: Strathmoor Press, 1995.

Williams, I. *The Alms Trade: Charities, Past, Present and Future.* London: Unwin Hyman, 1989.

Selected Web Sites

http://www.afpnet.org

http://www.cafonline.com

http://www.charitynet.org

http://www.charityvillage.ca

http://www.contributionsmagazine.com

http://www.fundraising.co.uk

http://www.instituteoffundraising.org.uk

http://www.kenburnett.com

http://www.malwarwick.com

http://www.philanthropy.com

http://www.resource-alliance.org

http://www.whitelionpress.com

Index

A

Acceptability of use of emotion, 112–116

Accountability. *See* Credibility

Acquisition. *See* Recruitment

ActionAid, 39–40, 113–114, 130–131, 138, 139, 156–157, 167, 276, 277, 288

Additional giving options, 200–201

Administration costs, 20–21, 79, 106. *See also* Charity Commissioners for England and Wales

Advantages of relationship fundraising, 41–43

Advertisements: bequest, 256–257; example of classic fundraising, 168; returns on, 166; small ad campaign, 174–175

Advertising: for awareness, 166, 186–188; basics of, 167–168; bequest, 262; disaster, 188–189; expenditures, 187; valid uses of, 187–188

Affinity credit cards, 240

AICDA (attention, interest, conviction, desire, action), 191

AIDA, 191

Allen, N., 171, 172

Allen, W., 328

Amnesty International, 142, 207

Annual income of nonprofits, 16

Annual reports, 99–100, 116–118, 196–198; test results on using, 197

Application Service Provider (ASP), 55

Applications for funds, number of, 146. *See also* Companies and foundations; Grant-making foundations

Association of Fundraising Professionals (AFP), xvii, 173

Attributes of a fundraiser, 31–32

Awareness advertising. *See* Advertising; Television

B

Baby boomers, 75–76

Balzer, S., 297

Banker packs, 163–165

Barnardo's, 280

Barraclough, C., 285, 287

Bayley, T. D., 160

Bequests: and advertisements, 265–266; and advisory sector, 266–267; average amount of, 250; dependency of nonprofits on, 248; and incentives, 160, 264–265; and information booklet, 260, 263–265; and language, 251–252, 261; marketing, 254–260; and media, 262; promotion of, 253, 255–256, 258, 268, 317; public attitude toward, 252–253, 267–268; and research, 259–260, 267; response and follow-up on, 266–268; strategy and objectives regarding, 255–256, 260; types of, 249, 250

Big gift fundraising. *See* Major gift fundraising

Birthday campaign, 149–152

Blackmon, M., 277
Bluefrog, 294
Boards of governors. *See* Governance
Boaz, D., 23
Botton Village, 41
Brand, definition of, 144
Brand image, 142–144, 186, 188, 278
Brann, D., 268
Briers, R., 163, 164
British Telecom, 68–69, 151
Burk, P., 86

C
Call monitoring devices, 300–301
Campaigns, marketing: drinks man-
    ufacturer, 287; Persil, 286–287;
    Tesco, 282–284; Volkswagen,
    285–286
Cancer Research Campaign, 277
Cancer Research UK, 277
Capital appeals, 52. *See also* Major
    gift fundraising
Career opportunities in fundraising,
    13–15, 17–18, 22–23
Carnegie, D., 326, 329
Carrington, D., 147–149
CASE convention, 150
Celebrities, use of, 151, 163, 164,
    262, 265, 266
Central promotion of nonprofits,
    241–242
Central service agency to promote
    fundraising opportunities,
    234–235
Centre for Voluntary Sector Man-
    agement, 83
Charitable donations: amounts of,
    16; comparisons, European
    16–17; destination of, 21; num-
    ber of, 16; percentages of, 16
Charity Annual Reports Awards, 116
Charity Commissioners for England
    and Wales report (1989), 20
Charity Technology Trust, 280. *See*
    also Raffles
Chisholm, J., 291, 292–293

Churchill, W., 101
Clubs for donors, 151, 158, 159,
    178–180, 269
Codes of practice for fundraisers,
    115, 162, 172–173, 190, 205, 267
Cohorts, donor, 53
Cold direct mail, 162–165, 173, 231
Cole, C. J., 118–119
Collection boxes. *See* Street
    collections
Collins, T., 127
Commercial partnerships, 151,
    234–235, 241
Committees, 227–228
Communications: bequest, 266;
    from donors, 253; inspirational,
    327–328; research and, 89, 90, 91
Companies and foundations,
    145–149, 234–235. *See also* Appli-
    cations for funds, number of
Complaints, handling, 40–41, 176,
    209–210, 253–254
Consumer choice, 129–130
Copy, 99–101, 261. *See also* Language
Cornfeld, B., 225
Coronation Street, 215
Corporate fundraising, 234–235. *See*
    also Companies and foundations
Costs: advertising, 187; database,
    54–55; donor understanding of,
    106–107; face-to-face fundraising,
    289–290; of recruitment versus
    reactivation of donors, 157; rela-
    tionship fundraising, 44–45; tele-
    phone, 205, 208; television,
    213–214; video production, 216
Coupons, 161, 201, 266
Credibility with donors, 88, 326
Customer relationship management
    (CRM), 281–284, 288. *See also*
    Campaigns, marketing
Customer service. *See* Donor service

D
Database: bequest, 257, 267; costs
    54–55; development, 130; man-

agement, 54; research information, 205; RFM, 238; setting up and maintaining, 50–51, 135, 211, 231; systems, 53–54; understanding of, 51–52. *See also* Segmentation; Software

Database, relational, management systems (RDBMSs), 52–53

Demographics, 70, 71, 72, 73, 278

Destinations of donations and bequests, 21

Direct dialogue. *See* Face-to-face fundraising

Direct mail: commercial, 123; comparisons of, with press advertising, 173, 262; effective use of, 189–193; frequency of, appeals, 101, 102; growth of, 101–102; lobbying, 207; mistakes, 96–98, 253

Direct Mail Sales and Service Bureau, 234–235

Direct Marketing Awards UK, 6–7

Diversity of fundraising, 21

Donations as percentage of GNP, 16

Donor pyramid, 47–48, 75

Donor service, 107–110, 209, 210–211, 329–331. *See also* Road tests, donor service

Donor trapezoid, 48–49

Donor wedge, 49–50

Donor-based approach, initiatives to develop, xix

donordigital.com, 171

Donors: alienation of, 88; categorizing, 70–77; different definitions of, 111, 155–156; entrepreneurial, 87–88, 278–279; future, 74–77; lapsed, 157, 175, 253; lifetime, 156–157, 159; lists of, 111, 122, 160, 174, 211; older, 73–74; profiles, 98, 145; protection of, 130–131

Door drops, 323–324

Dr. Barnardo's Homes, 163

Drop-outs, 156

Drucker, P., 5

E

EHS Brann, 281

El Salvador, xxvi

E-mail. *See* Internet

Emotion, use of, 112–116

Employees: fundraising by, 235; numbers of, in the voluntary sector, 16–17

Envelopes, 164, 174, 192, 253

Estates in the UK, 248, 249, 250

Ethics, fundraising, 302–305

Events, 149–152, 158–159

Examples: donation amounts, 229; face-to-face fundraising, 294–295; of mailing pack errors, 96–97; publicity campaign, 149–152; relationship fundraising, 39–40

Expense ratio, 19, 106

Experience marketing, 285–288. *See also* Campaigns, marketing

F

Face-to-face fundraising: benefits and shortcomings, 169–170, 323; body language in, 295–296; development of, 288–293; future for, 293–295; as part of integrated communication, 217; potential, 211–213; trend toward, 137. *See also* One-to-one fundraising

Felton, R., 40

Focus groups, 63, 64, 66, 68, 69, 77

Follett, M. P., 132

Formulas, direct mail, 99, 122, 123, 163, 254, 316

Foster Parents Plan, 156

Fox, R., 162, 175, 217

Fundraising, essentials of, 28–29

Fundraising Institute of Australia, xvii

Fundraising Solutions International Pty, 289

Future in fundraising, the, 305–306; 318–321

G

Gender differences, 91
Gift Aid, 139
Gilbert, M., 173
Giving Campaign, The, 242
Golden generation, 73–74
Governance, 8, 275–277, 314–316
Grant-making foundations, 145–149.
　See also Companies and
　foundations
Gray, J. (author), 91
Gray, J. (National Children's Home),
　150
Greenpeace, 139, 174–175, 207, 239,
　289, 290–293, 296, 301–302
Groman, J., 179
Group discussions. *See* Focus groups
Growth: direct mail, 101–102; volun-
　tary sector, 15–17
Guidelines and principles: for be-
　quest solicitation, 267; for non-
　profit advertising, 116. *See also*
　Codes of practice for fundraisers

H

Hailsham, Lord, 261
Hambley, J., 214
Hart, T., 171
Heineken Lager, 69
Help the Aged, 167, 168
Henley Management College, 83,
　84, 85, 325
Hickson, J., 265
Holland, T. P., 277
Hotline: information, 176; members-
　only, 179
House owners, number of, 76
House-to-house collections, 119
Hunt, T., 281–282

I

"Imagine" campaign, 242
Imperial Cancer Research Fund, 277
Incentives for donors, 158–161, 176,
　263–265
India-Pakistan war, 3

Information service, 176
Innovation: lack of, 165; in mailings,
　317; tips for organizational, 133
Inserts, 161, 168–169, 185–186, 262
Institute of Fundraising, xvii, 105,
　162, 173, 267, 268
Integrated communications,
　217–218, 297, 319–320
International brands, 142
International Fund Raising Con-
　gress, xxiv, 95
International Fund Raising Group.
　See Resource Alliance, The
Internet, 55, 170–173, 266, 296–299,
　301–302
Interviews, personal, 63, 64
Involvement, providing, for donors,
　225, 226–227. *See also* Recognition

J

Johnston, M., 171
*Journal of Nonprofit and Voluntary Sec-
　tor Marketing,* 85
Junk fundraising, 102–106, 163, 173,
　324

K

Kerala, India, photographs from, 114
Kerr, I., 213
Key marketing considerations: five
　P's, 138; place, 139–140; price,
　138–139. *See also* Products,
　fundraising
Kinnock, N., 261

L

Labels, address, 200
Language, 121–122, 204, 251–252,
　261. *See also* Copy
Lee, S., xvii, 83, 88, 89, 90, 321
Legacies. *See* Bequests
Legacy Campaign, 251, 268
Legacy Leadership program, 217
Legators, 249, 250
Legislation, 105, 112, 113, 161, 162,
　205

Leiderman, R., 202–203, 204
Leppard, J., 134
Letters: to accompany question-
naires, 65, 66; to companies and
foundations, 146, 149; facsimile,
163–164, 179; to older people,
74; personalization of, 193; pre-
call opt-out, 190–191, 217, 299;
split mailing test, 232. *See also*
Thank you letters
Levitt, T., 132, 318
Lewis, J., 215
Lipman, M., 68
Lists, mailing, 97, 99, 102, 162, 173
Logos, 142–143
Longfoot, T., 294, 295
Long-term development programs.
See Acceptability of use of
emotion
Lord, J. G., 224, 225
Lynn, V., 266

M

Macfarlane, A., 115, 116
Macmillan, H., 116
Magazines, 194–196. *See also*
Newsletters
Major gift fundraising, 52, 53, 203,
212–213, 218, 225–228
Makens, J., 134
Mallabone, G., 87
Management: database, 56; of non-
profits, 18–19;
Marketing: audit, 131–133; benefits
and risks, 120–122; cause-related
147; considerations, 130–133; de-
scription of, 128; new relation-
ship-based, 128; plan, 128–129,
131, 133, 134, 146; social, 147;
strategy, 133–134, 147; ten, ques-
tions to ask, 140–141. *See also* Key
marketing considerations
Mason, T., 282
Mbazimutima, 113, 114
McDonald, M., 134
McKinnon, H., 162, 279

Media, 187, 259, 261–262
Member-get-member schemes,
160–161, 208
Membership schemes, 169, 175–176,
178–180. *See also* Clubs for donors
Mergers and acquisitions, 277–278
Mitchell, A., 71
Monthly giving, 137–138, 230–231,
299
Moreton, A., 290–291, 292, 293
Morris, P., 134
Motivation to give, 40, 67, 145, 160.
See also Additional giving options
Muscular Dystrophy Group of Great
Britain and Northern Ireland,
163–165
Myers, T., 87

N

Names, gathering, 173–175
National Center for Nonprofit
Boards, 277
National Children's Home, 115,
149–152, 158
National Council for Voluntary
Organizations, 16
National Society for the Prevention
of Cruelty to Children (NSPCC),
xx, 115, 137, 158, 232, 266
National Trust, The, 139, 280
Newsletters, 194–196, 239, 267. *See
also* Magazines
Nichols, J., 73, 75
Non-event, the, 223–224
Nonresponse, 110–111

O

Off-the-page advertising. *See* Press
advertising
Ogilvy, D., 150, 227
One-percent club, 269
One-to-one fundraising, 53, 140,
211–213, 217, 267. *See also* Face-
to-face fundraising
On-line fundraising. *See* Internet

Ostroff, J., 74

Oxfam, xxiv, xxv, 5, 118, 142, 166, 167, 194, 206, 280, 267

Oxford Committee for Famine Relief, 166

P

Panas, J., 31

Pareto principle, 75

Payroll giving, 235

Pegram, G., xx

Permissions: for on-line activities, 172; for photographs, 113–115

Philanthropy, venture, 279–280

Philosophy of relationship fundraising, 40–41

Photographs, 113, 114, 115

Pirelli, 142–143

Planned giving, 137, 240–241. *See also* Bequests

Pledge forms, 263–264

Potts, J., 171, 172

Press advertising, 166–168, 173, 174, 186, 188–189, 201, 209, 262

Pre-testing advertisements, 68–69

Pricing and propositions, 228–232. *See also* Marketing

Products, fundraising: creating new, 239–240; design of, 138; investments and insurance, 212; monthly giving, 137–138, 230–231; recognition and reward schemes, 137; sponsorships, 137, 138, 139, 156

Profession: the fundraising, 6–7, 15–18. *See also* Career opportunities in fundraising; Salaries in fundraising

Proximity London Limited, 285

Psychographics, 70–71

Public image of nonprofits, 14–15, 107–110, 323, 325

Public relations, 149–152

Publications, 116–118. *See also* Annual reports

Q

Qualified leads, 173–175

Queen Elizabeth II, 98

Questionnaires: postal, 63, 64, 65; response to, 111; telephone, 67

R

Radio, 215–216, 262

Raffles: on-line, 280; paper-based, 119. *See also* Charity Technology Trust

Rapp, S., 127

Reactivation and renewal of donors, 156–158, 159, 175, 205

Reagan, R., 178

Reasons for giving, 30–31, 89

Recency, frequency, and monetary value (RFM) method of monitoring donors, 237–238

Reciprocal mailings, 136–137, 161–162, 200

Recognition, donor, 15, 137, 158–161, 178–179

Recruitment: of donors, 155, 156, 157, 159, 160, 162, 166–168, 169–172, 175–176, 177–178; of legators, 249

Red Cross, 171, 296

Registered nonprofits, number of, in Britain, 17

Relationship building, keys to, 45–47

Relationship fundraising, definition of, 38

Reliability. *See* Credibility with donors

Research: on annual reports, 197; bequest, 259, 267; confidentiality of, 66; flaws, 67–69; implementation of, findings, 69–70; on indirect response to promotion, 111; methods, 62–65; on percentages of dissatisfied customers who complain, 209–210; skepticism about, 85; storage of, information, 205; on trust and confidence, 88–91, 325; what you need to know from, 62

Research and development, of fundraising products, 239–240
Resource Alliance, The, 27
Responders, first-time, 111, 156
Response: to annual reports, 197–198; to inserts, 185–186; to mailings, 110–111, 190, 232; to newsletters, 194–195; to pre-call opt-out letters, 190–191; to press advertisements, 265–266; to price, 231; to reciprocal mailings, 162; telephone, 205
Road tests, donor service, 107–108. *See also* Public image of nonprofits
Rodd, J., 52, 238
Roddick, A., 330–331
Romney, G., xv
Ross, G., 156
Rousseau, J.-J., 322
Royal National Institute for the Blind (RNIB), 264–265
Royal National Lifeboat Institution (RNLI), 75, 169, 255–256
Royal Society for the Prevention of Cruelty to Animals (RSPCA), 207, 208
Royal Star and Garter Home, 197–198
Ryton Gardens, 137, 165, 229, 230

S

Salaries in fundraising, 22–23. *See also* Profession
Salvation Army, 3
Sargeant, A., 83, 88–89, 90, 321
Schools, fundraising in, 39–40
Schumacher, F., 37
Secombe, H., 266
Segmentation of lists, 65, 122, 135–137, 160, 164, 218, 232
Self-regulation, 313–314
Sense, 294–295
Sloggie, N., 289–290, 293
Smee and Ford Limited, 248
Smith, G., xiv, 95, 96, 98, 99–100
Smith, T., 248

Software, 54–55
Sponsored events, 174
Sponsorship of publications, 232–233
Stevenson, T., 150
Strategy: bequest, 255–256; communication/contact, 217, 266, 282; integrated contact, 282
Street collections, 118–119, 240
Stringer, G., xxiv–xxvii, 24, 206
Stroud, L., 41
Sumption, H., 27, 261
Supporters, meeting with, 63, 64, 66. *See also* One-to-one fundraising
Surat, India, xxv
Surveys, omnibus, 63
Sweatman, P., 280
Sympathetic Hearing Scheme, 215

T

Targeting, 134–135, 169, 232, 249, 259. *See also* Marketing
Taylor, M., 91
Techniques and practices: management, 24, relationship fundraising, 267–268
Technology, 95–99, 122, 130, 136, 329
Telephone: campaigning, 207–208; creative use of, 202–204, 206–207; credit card donations, 175, 298; culture, 69; dealing with, complaints by, 209–210; fundraising, 67, 144–145; inbound calls, 204, 209; interviews, 67; name gathering by, 174–175; power of, 203–204; reactivation/renewal of donors by, 175, 205; relevance of, script, 204; research, 63, 64, 67; scripts, 67, 204; and tie-ins with new technology, 298–299; training, 210
Telethons, 215
Television 104, 112, 175, 187, 213–215, 252
Tesco, 281–284

Testing: annual reports, 197–198; donor lists, 160, 164, 232; envelopes, 192; inserts, 169; Internet, 301–302; media, 113–114, 262; newsletters and magazines, 194–195; pre-call opt-out letters, 190–191; price, 230; use of emotion, 112

Thank you letters, 193–194. *See also* Welcome packs

Three roles (chess player, Robin Hood, double agent), 23

Tonypandy, Lord, 150, 151

Turner, S., 251, 268

U

U.K. Mailing Preference Service, 41

Unique reason to give (URG), 141–142, 264

Unique selling proposition (USP), 141–142

United Way, 235

Upgrading donors, 159, 208, 237–238

Upsall, D., 305–306

V

VALS (values and lifestyles) categories, 71–73, 76

Video, 177–178, 216–217, 260

Visitor relationship management project, 301–302

Visits. *See* One-to-one fundraising

Voluntary sector: donations as percentage of GNP, 16; employment statistics, 16, 17; growth, 16

Volunteers, xxi, 16–17, 140, 159, 177, 203, 226–228, 236–237, 267

W

Walker, P., 163, 164

Warwick, M., 171, 297

Watchdog, 323

Weatherup, K., 196

Web sites, 173, 297, 298, 299

Welcome packs, 53, 118, 193–194, 238–239

WillAid, 264

Will-making clinic, 268–269

Will-making initiative, 262

Wills: information booklet on, 263–265; statistics on, 248–250

World Trade Organization, 325

Wyvern Books, 193

Y

YMCA, 266